TO UNDERSTAND
YOU MUST UNDE
TO UNDERSTAND
YOU MUST UNDERSTAND
WATERGATE.

Now at last a book enables you to understand both the man and the ultimate scandal of his checkered career. It is a story that ranges from Whittier to Key Biscayne, from the Miami Cuban underground to the Los Angeles office of Daniel Ellsberg's psychiatrist, from the "Checkers speech" to more recent Nixon orations. Its cast of characters includes ex-CIA men, cabinet officials, lawyers, advertising men, heads of great corporations, mysterious millionaires, and of course the central figure, Richard Nixon himself. Some of it is not pretty reading. All of it, however, is essential reading for those who care about where our country is and where it is going.

"Both profound and a delight!"   —*Chicago Sun-Times*

"Chilling logic and reams of evidence . . . powerful!"
                                                —*Indianapolis News*

"Frank Mankiewicz knows politics. He's been writing about it, working for candidates, running, and watching Nixon for decades. The body of evidence that he offers against Nixon is much more than appalling. It opens up whole new areas of guilt."   —*Seattle Post-Intelligencer*

PERFECTLY CLEAR

NIXON FROM WHITTIER TO WATERGATE

by Frank Mankiewicz

POPULAR LIBRARY • NEW YORK

*To Holly, who shared it all,
and to my mother,
who always knew her children
would be writers.*

The summer flow'r is to the summer sweet
Though to itself it only live and die,
But if that flow'r with base infection meet,
The basest weed outbraves his dignity:
   For sweetest things turn sourest by their deeds;
   Lilies that fester smell far worse than weeds.

WILLIAM SHAKESPEARE: from Sonnet 94

CONTENTS

CONTENTS

ACKNOWLEDGMENTS

I acknowledge gratefully the assistance of many people in the preparation of this book. James Reston, Jr., abandoned the pleasant surroundings of Chapel Hill to share in my labor, and his ideas and judgments were of great value. In addition, much of his research and draftsmanship is retained in Chapters 4, 6, 7, and 9. His wife, Denise Leary Reston, a Duke University law student, performed copious legal research, including poring over the transcripts of hearings and trials.

For the sections on California, I am indebted to many colleagues of my own political past. I must, of course, first mention delightful and rewarding hours spent with Helen Gahagan Douglas and Jerry Voorhis. Steve Zetterberg was helpful in recalling details and furnishing documents from his 1948 brush with Nixon Politics. Alvin Meyers, who managed the Douglas campaign of 1950, cheerfully recalled many events of that battle which I had forgotten.

I am particularly indebted to Roger Kent, the Democratic chairman in California who successfully fought through both the 1962 campaign and the lawsuit that followed. Kent is a good politician and a good lawyer, and he keeps good records which he was kind enough to make available to me. I am also pleased to acknowledge the assistance of Amelia R. Fry, of the Bancroft Library at the University of California, who was able to direct me to excellent sources of information. And the staff of the library of the Los Angeles *Times,* in Los Angeles as well as in Washington (where the efforts of Lucy Lazarow were particularly appreciated), was most helpful and cooperative.

Special mention must be made as well of the assistance I received from Professor Paul Bullock at U.C.L.A. Dr. Bullock, whose biography of Jerry Voorhis is in preparation, made available to me a chapter, soon to be published in the *Southern California Quarterly,* which contained a great deal of otherwise unobtainable material on the 1946 campaign. For accounts of the 1946 election, as well as that of 1950, I found the relevant chapters in *Nixon, an Unauthorized Biography*, by William Costello (Viking Press, 1960), most useful.

For the material in Chapter 2, "Politics as Usual," I talked with a number of people active in past presidential campaigns, including Clifton White, Lawrence O'Brien, Pierre Salinger, Myer Feldman, Ted Van Dyk, and James Haggerty, and I found their accounts and judgments both wise and of great assistance.

My friends from the McGovern campaign were extremely generous in furnishing information. I am particularly indebted to press secretary Kirby Jones, and to Steve Robbins, Tony Podesta, Ed O'Donnell and Joel Swerdlow.

Marylin Bitner and Pamela Diamond worked hard under great pressure to obtain much of the research that went into the writing, and my thanks are also due to Betty Baker and Rosemary Peterson for help in typing the manuscript.

Myer Feldman and his law partners were generous in providing an office in which to work, and Leonard and Ginetta Sagan gave me shelter during the many days I spent in California.

I would be remiss if I did not acknowledge the work of my colleagues in the Washington press corps, without whose diligence there would have been no Watergate books because no one would have known about Watergate. Foremost, of course, are Bob Woodward and Carl Bernstein of the Washington *Post*, but many of the facts in this book were first uncovered and later developed by Nick Kotz of the *Post*, Bob Walters and James Polk of the Washington *Star-News*, Adam Clymer of the Baltimore *Sun*, Saul Friedman of the Knight newspapers, Jack Nelson of the Los Angeles *Times*, and Seymour Hersh of *The New York Times*. In addition, mention should be made of the steady vision of syndicated columnists Jack Anderson (the nonpareil), Clayton Fritchey, Mary McGrory, Anthony Lewis, and my old friend and comrade, Tom Braden. I particularly admire the work of Daniel Schorr and Dan Rather of CBS News, whose television reporting and commentary on these events has been steadily informed by a larger vision than that which might have been theirs had they yielded to a legitimate desire to strike back. Roberto Fabricio of the Miami *Herald* was especially helpful with respect to the material in Chapter 6.

My family—Holly, Josh, and Ben—has been extremely

loving and supportive throughout this hectic enterprise, for which I am most grateful. Josh's newspaper clipping service was invaluable. My sister, Johanna Davis, was an inspiration at all times.

Herbert Nagourney and Emanuel Geltman of Quadrangle were extremely helpful throughout, contributing encouragement and wise counsel, as did Sydney Gruson, our guru from the parent company.

Finally, I should like to acknowledge my debt to two men who greatly shaped my life and my ideas. I have no deeper regret than that neither is alive to participate in these times. My father, Herman Mankiewicz, taught me the history and relevance of American politics, and from Robert Kennedy I learned that its practice can be both joyous and honorable.

Washington, D.C.
September 1973

1. "High Crimes and Misdemeanors"

This is a book about Watergate. It is therefore a book about conspiracies and burglaries, about plans for kidnapping, prostitution, and blackmail. It is about breaking and entering, wiretapping, and unlawful disclosure of private wire communications. It is also about the attempt to cover up the crimes of Watergate, so it is about perjury and the conspiracy to commit it and to procure it. It is about the obstruction of justice—the destruction of material evidence and the sequestering of material witnesses. It is about the intimidation and bribery of defendants and a conspiracy to obstruct justice by compromising the integrity of government agencies and institutions. It is also about plain lying.

But beyond Watergate—beyond the criminal entry into the Democratic National Committee and its cover-up—"Watergate" has come to mean more. As President Nixon observed on August 15, 1973, Watergate "has come to mean a whole series of acts that either represent or appear to represent an abuse of trust." This book is about those things, too.

It is about another burglary, too, this time publicly to degrade a defendant in a criminal case, and about a forgery to defame the memory of a slain president. It concerns a list of "enemies" and plans to "screw" them by the illegal and improper use of agencies of the government, including the Internal Revenue Service. It includes the use of other agencies to spy on and harass people who were political rivals of the President or who held outspokenly different views.

This book is also about plans to firebomb a building, the frustration of a Senate Committee by spiriting away a witness and of a House Committee by pressuring its members. It is about an attempt to influence a judge in a civil case, and about wiretapping in the private homes of journalists and govern-

13

ment employees, and in the apartment of a woman who had just been killed in an auto accident. It is about a scheme to extort information from women *thought* to be—but who turned out *not* to be—prone to seduction, and then to black-mail.

An "abuse of trust"? Then it must also be about the approval by a President, sworn to faithfully execute the laws, of a proposal to deliberately break several of those laws, including the laws against burglary, wire-tapping, and opening the mail of others, all without even attempting to obtain a warrant. And it is about the deliberate employment of sabotage and espionage in a political campaign, including the use of forgery, fraud, and impersonation to harass Democratic candidates with everything from the false cancellation of their meetings to accusations of sexual misconduct and the father-ing of illegitimate children.

It includes, as well, a White House campaign to make voters believe that the opposition candidate was behind real and fancied acts of violence, that his campaign was financing revo-lutionary activities, and that other activities in his behalf were financed by foreign revolutionary sources, all without a shred of evidence, and with a good deal of evidence to the contrary.

It is also the story of how a successful New York lawyer could—once elected President of the United States—acquire, with a modest cash investment, Florida and California real estate valued in millions of dollars (and tell three different stories as to how it was done), how his Appointments Secre-tary was convicted of perjury, how his chief domestic aide, his under-secretary of transportation, and two important aides were indicted for burglary, and how his government was avail-able for favors to his friends and to the great commercial in-terests in grain, milk, carpeting, insurance, and drugs. It is about the waiver of the antitrust laws to favor the President's friends and secret campaign contributors, and about personal business dealings by his White House aides and key depart-ment officials.

These activities, whether criminal, unconstitutional, or sim-ply improper or deceitful, were all carried out by or in behalf of Richard Nixon, his reelection, and his prosperity. So this is also a book about him and his time. It will trace his political career—he has no other—through the unbroken series of frauds and deceptions that have marked a quarter-century and more of what will now be called "Nixon politics." And that

14

postwar quarter-century of Nixon politics shows a limitless appetite for victory and electoral triumph. No one can point to a Nixon ideology, beyond winning the next election, or to personal boundaries of conscience as to how that might be accomplished.

It was also a quarter-century of unparalleled militarization in America, of the growth of the "garrison state," and of the application to more and more areas of previously civilian life of techniques and ideas once limited to the military and the espionage organizations. It was an age which saw the American Democracy debased to something approaching Empire. This book will show how Richard Nixon took advantage of the time—of a growing obsession with "national security"— to advance his own politics, and how a group of men (all over-achievers), entranced with that militarization of life and language, joined Richard Nixon in a quest to achieve and use a power they thought unlimited by either the Constitution or their own sense of restraint. To Nixon and his men, as Arthur Balfour once said of an opponent, conscience was not a guide, but an accomplice.

So Watergate is not just a "caper," or a "deplorable incident," or something "petty, murky and indecent" in which people who are out to "get Nixon" may wish to "wallow." Nor is it an example of "politics as usual," something both parties do—the difference being that in this case someone got caught. It is not even, like Teapot Dome, a symbol of the time, in that case of an age of mediocrity in government when "the business of America was business."

Finally, Watergate is not what Richard Nixon seems now to hope desperately the American people will come to believe —a sort of "national security as usual." At his August 1973 press conference, he baldly asserted that the kind of burglary associated with Watergate, either at Democratic headquarters or the office of Daniel Ellsberg's psychiatrist, particularly the latter, was nothing new. Nixon said, "I should also like to point out to you that in the three Kennedy years and the three Johnson years through 1966, when burglarizing of this [Ellsberg] type did take place, when it was authorized on a very large scale, there was no talk of impeachment and it was quite well known."

[Nixon was referring to a memorandum from former FBI Assistant Director William Sullivan, which described a special FBI "second-story" unit, which apparently had functioned

15

since the time of Franklin Roosevelt's administration and which had committed a number of burglaries, almost all in foreign (mostly Communist) embassies and offices of the Communist Party.

[But the point of the Sullivan memorandum was that J. Edgar Hoover—precisely because the burglaries were illegal—kept the existence of the unit and its work a tightly held secret within the FBI and never told any attorney general or president of its existence. That is what Nixon was referring to when he told the press and the public about burglaries that were "authorized" and "quite well known." When he said those words he knew the burglaries to be *unauthorized* and *secret* from the very men—all of them dead—he was accusing of knowing about them.]

It is, instead, a still-unfolding chronicle of the most corrupt President and the most corrupt administration in our history. It marks the precise delineation of the principle that though we may have a government of laws, we also have a government of men. Separation of powers, after all, never meant to the Founding Fathers that each branch of government could conceal its crimes from the others.

There was a surreal quality to the debate in July 1973 between John Ehrlichman, speaking for the President before the Ervin Committee, and the listening Senators, over the limits of Presidential power. Particularly the Southerners, Ervin of North Carolina and Talmadge of Georgia, listened with amazement as Ehrlichman put the crime of burglary "well within" the President's power. And this was no ordinary burglary they were discussing, nor was it only technically a "burglary" in the sense that it bore any relation to national security.

This was a burglary, according to memoranda which Ehrlichman acknowledged bore his initials (he called it his "chopmark," in the absurd British secret agent-*cum*-World War II movie pilot-*cum* computer key-punch operator jargon affected by the Nixon men), designed for a purely political purpose, to smear Daniel Ellsberg and perhaps cut him down in the esteem of his colleagues in the peace movement. Ellsberg had delivered the Pentagon Papers to *The New York Times,* an act he freely admitted; he had been arrested and was due to go on trial. The memorandum setting forth plans for the burglary made it clear that if the files of a psychiatrist who had once treated Ellsberg could be stolen, they might yield some embarrassing information, which could then be "leaked" to the press.

16

According to Ehrlichman, the President had power to order this wretched act, and indeed perhaps *had* ordered it. Talmadge and Ervin kept pressing him, wanting to know, in effect, what kind of criminal activity would be marginal if burglary was "well within" the ambit of presidential authority. Bank robbery? Murder? Ehrlichman was belligerently evasive, suggesting that the outer boundaries of permissible presidential power had not yet been firmly fixed. Ehrlichman even seemed to relish the "erosion" of the principle that the humblest citizen in the land could be protected in his cottage against even the King.

The debate itself would once have seemed absurd. Thomas Jefferson would not have understood an argument that, upon his own determination that "national security" was involved, a president—or anyone acting for him—could commit a burglary. Alexander Hamilton, one imagines, would have thought it quite possible that some man elected to the Presidency would try it.

The Constitution resolved the conflict, such as it was. The Bill of Rights, in language strong enough for any strict constructionist, explicitly limits the power of government—all of it, including the president—as against the people. The first amendments bristle with absolute prohibitions: "Congress shall make *no* law." ". . . The right of the people to keep and bear Arms, shall *not* be infringed." "*No* Soldier shall, in time of peace be quartered in *any* house. . . ." "The right of the people to be secure . . . against unreasonable searches and seizures *shall not* be violated. . . ." "*No person* shall be held to answer . . . nor be deprived of life, liberty or property, without due process of law." "In *all* criminal prosecutions . . ." "Excessive bail *shall not* be required."

And in Article II, the president is given wide power and the duty to "take Care that the Laws be faithfully executed." And then, at the end of the article describing the limits of executive power, the framers of the Constitution, mindful that there might one day be elected a president who neither performed the duties of the office nor observed its limits, added a stern warning. The president, they wrote, "shall be removed from Office on Impeachment for, and Conviction of Treason, Bribery, or other high Crimes and Misdemeanors." After one year of Watergate, four years of Richard Nixon's presidency, and twenty-seven years of his politics, that is language which cannot be ignored.

2. Politics as Usual

New Hampshire, even in presidential primary years, still retains some of the more relaxed New England customs. One is the coffee reception given by the governor for each presidential candidate when he officially files his nomination papers at the State House. When Ed Muskie came into the building on January 5, 1972, and made his formal entry into the presidential race, the coffee and cakes were ready in an adjoining reception room for him, his official party, and a large contingent of the national press.

It was quite a moment. For two years, Muskie had been playing the national game of pretending he was not yet a candidate, while raising money, hiring a staff, renting a headquarters, and to be sure, running way ahead of everyone else in the polls. For George McGovern and those of us in his campaign, it was a historic day; no longer would McGovern be known in the media as "the only announced Democratic candidate." We thought we'd liven things up a little.

As the candidate sipped his coffee and engaged in some light banter with the press (Muskie's New Hampshire chairman had said she'd cut her throat if he didn't win with more than 50 percent of the vote but no one thought her throat would even be nicked), the guests began reaching the bottom of their coffee cups. As they did, some amusement spread through the room. Pasted inside each cup, looking up at them as they finished the last drop, was a paper replica of a campaign button, with a smiling face and "McGovern" under it. It was the high point of all the McGovern "dirty tricks" in 1972.

It was also fairly typical of the campaign of 1972—for all the candidates except Richard Nixon. It is worth going into some detail about the other side of the 1972 campaign, as well

18

as earlier ones, since in the spring and summer of 1973 the word was around that "both sides do these things." Gallup reported that 40 percent of Americans think the Watergate revelations are typical of what politicians do.

They are not, of course. Even the phrase "dirty tricks" was unknown in politics, until the Year of Watergate. The phrase has its origin in the CIA and became somewhat current in the mid-1950s when news of what the CIA was doing in places like Guatemala and Iran (overthrowing governments, as it turned out) became public. "Dirty tricks" first saw light in the press—probably the Washington *Post*—where its meaning was faintly ambiguous. You were involved in "dirty tricks" if you were doing something plainly illegal, but it was O.K. since you were working for the United States against bad guys—usually nonwhite bad guys. There was even something faintly admirable about it if you did it successfully.

In domestic politics nobody ever talked about "dirty tricks." For one thing, there weren't enough people with enough of an Ivy League background in politics at the professional level to appreciate the anomaly of a gentleman acting like a second-story man. For another, no campaigns except those of Richard Nixon ever devoted more than a minuscule portion of time or money to anything which could remotely be called "dirty tricks." Thus there was no need to coin a phrase to describe the domestic use of what Dean Rusk had called "back alley" tactics.

As politicians also know, it is not a sense of morality or fair play alone that has traditionally assigned "dirty tricks" to so low a campaign priority, although that is part of it. The major reason is that the results are so minimally useful. Ten full-time spies in the "enemy" headquarters, reporting hourly and intercepting mail, and a bug in the opposing candidate's tic clip would yield two things: a mountain of material to listen to and read and a tiny residue of worthwhile information, almost all of which could be obtained without technical assistance.

Thus it has always struck me, and I told the press people who wandered into McGovern headquarters after the Watergate break-in was disclosed, that John Mitchell must have been its guiding genius. The public Mitchell record, I thought, made it clear he was the only politician in Washington ignorant enough to think there was anything worth listening to at the Democratic National Committee. After all, what would a full tap on Larry O'Brien's phone yield? A conversation with a low-level official of American Airlines, wanting to know when payment would be made on a bill already four years overdue, or a discussion with a hotel manager in Miami Beach from whom O'Brien tried to get the vacation rate if the Democrats took over every room. This is the stuff of a national headquarters before a convention, and the yield from a candidate's headquarters during a campaign is not much more exciting.

You might learn, for instance, that the candidate is having money trouble or that there is a power fight going on between the "issues" people and the speech writers. You might pick up the fact that the candidate is fighting with his schedulers, who have booked him into too many speeches with too little rest. But what do you know when you know all this? To the Mitchells and the Magruders and the Colsons, unable to perceive the difference between politics and war because they have experienced neither, it might seem like heady stuff. According to Magruder, they wanted "intelligence" on O'Brien because he was the most effective Democratic spokesman on the ITT issue.

ITT was much in the news at that time. A memorandum from ITT's Washington lobbyist had appeared in Jack Anderson's column. It described how an offer of $400,000 from the company to help defray GOP convention expenses had yielded from John Mitchell a withdrawal of antitrust threats against a merger with the Hartford Insurance Company. The revelation was shocking at the time and delayed and threatened the confirmation of Richard Kleindienst as Mitchell's successor. (As it turned out, the price was high; Mitchell's favors to businessmen in trouble with the government seem to have been available at half price.)

The Democrats went to work on the ITT issue. Larry O'Brien, as party chairman, was often an effective spokesman. But it would have been clear to anyone with other than the Mitchell-Nixon view of the world that O'Brien's statements, for all their skill and tough language, were utterly predictable and that his sources were the newspapers. Would it really have helped to know a day ahead of time the text of a statement by O'Brien calling the ITT deal a "sellout to wealthy special interests" or that he was discussing a reference to the Nixon administration as "favoring big business at the expense of the wage-earner and the consumer"?

There is, of course, another explanation for this particular "dirty trick." It occurs regularly to those politicians who refuse to credit the Nixon men with the ignorance of politics I have assigned them here. This theory holds that O'Brien was a target, not politically but personally. The White House, so the theory goes, wanted to blackmail O'Brien. There are two flaws in the theory. The first is that two extensive audits by the Internal Revenue Service—a major scandal at any other time, but conceded casually by the President during the week he sought to discredit John Dean—failed to uncover anything that the administration could use against O'Brien. The second is that if O'Brien had been silenced by the threat of exposure (a most unlikely hypothesis, in any event, to anyone who knew O'Brien), the public would hardly have known, since someone else would have issued the statement anyway. Ignorance, hubris, and an unwillingness to accept the American system remain the best reasons to assign to Nixon's reliance on "dirty tricks."

There remains the argument that "everyone does it," and that troublesome 40–50 percent who believe that forgery, burglary, perjury, and a giant conspiracy by the Justice Department to obstruct justice are politics as usual. What *is* politics as usual?

What follows in this chapter is as complete a picture as I have been able to assemble of the extent of espionage, sabotage, or related activities in all non-Nixon political campaigns since 1960, and I will begin with the McGovern campaign of 1972.

Early in the primary season, we made a serious misjudgment about the nature of the opposition. We made other errors in the period prior to the Convention, but this was the only one based on press reports. I had an article of faith—and retain it to this day—that a political journalist's exposure and reputation for political sagacity is almost always in inverse ratio to his understanding of the situation. We went against this rule when it came to John Lindsay's candidacy. Everybody from CBS to *Life* to *The New York Times*—especially *The New York Times*—told us John Lindsay was a major candidate and that he would cut heavily, if not fatally, into McGovern's natural sources of liberal strength. The result was that an inordinate amount of attention was paid to Lindsay's candidacy, particularly in Florida where the Mayor was making his greatest—and, as it turned out, final—effort to emerge as a major candidate.

An aide to Queens Democratic Leader Matthew Troy, Jr., was dispatched to Florida where, largely under Troy's direction, he "worked" groups of transplanted New Yorkers. Troy himself is a product of New York politics, and he lent himself to the anti-Lindsay effort with zest. He was the second Democratic county chairman in the country (and the only one in the East) to announce his support for McGovern. His high ranking with blue-collar voters (he climbed the flagpole at City Hall to raise the flag after Lindsay had ordered it lowered to half-mast after Kent State) made him a special hero to us. When he suggested that Martin Steadman, an ex-newsman and old Democratic hand, was available to go to Florida, we agreed to send him. Marty did some good work. He supplied major Florida dailies with news clips from *The New York Times* and other New York papers that chronicled the astonishing scandals in New York City government, and he reached (in person and by mail) almost all of the retired New York City employees, mostly police and firemen, living in Florida.

In a celebrated two-day stunt Steadman even lent a little laughter to a rather humorless and lifeless campaign. At the height of the Florida campaigning, much attention—media attention, anyway—was given to the beaches. Lindsay had gone scuba diving for the TV cameras one day (his advisers said it was to inspect pollution of the coral reefs), and he had spent a good deal of time striding up and down the boardwalks. Steadman topped him. He hired a small plane to fly down the shore at Miami Beach, towing a banner with a strange message, "Lindsay Means Tsouris." It was spottily reported. The next day the message was repeated, with a companion plane towing the message "Tsouris Means Trouble." It made the evening news.

There were other anti-Lindsay moves in Florida. The Mayor had scheduled a mammoth press conference for his official entry into Florida's primary, and we tried to think of a question that would fluster him. There was no point in asking about corruption in his government—surely he would have a good answer. So we tried to think of a question on a subject which even the Lindsay brain trust could not have anticipated. We came up with it, and we got lucky. The McGovern plant was front and center at Lindsay's press conference, and he was the first reporter recognized. "Mayor Lindsay," he asked, as three network and five local cameras zeroed in, "if you are elected President, how would you change U.S. policy toward Mexico?" The puzzled look on Linsday's face made it all worthwhile.

After that it was all downhill. One of Lindsay's commissioners, Robert Rickles, paid his own way to Miami and spent several days talking about the Mayor's failures in the field of environmental protection. City Councilman Robert Postel led a contingent of elected New York City officials around the state to "tell the Lindsay story."

It rattled the Lindsay camp somewhat, particularly since the McGovern spokesmen constantly reminded the Florida Democrats that it was Lindsay who had nominated Spiro Agnew for Vice-President at the Republican convention in 1968. Matt Troy said it best: When Lindsay denounced him with Agnevian alliteration as a "petty piranha of politics," Matty observed, "First he nominated Agnew; now he's starting to talk like him."

The McGovern forces did only one other thing to Lindsay which could remotely be called a "dirty trick" or which involved any espionage. Yancey Martin of our organization, who had formerly headed up the minorities operation at the Democratic National Committee, began hearing stories from one local black politician after another, up and down Florida, about the amounts of money the Lindsay campaign was paying them, ostensibly for "organization work." When he had a few of the stories nailed down from within the Lindsay camp, we made the story public. It annoyed the black leaders who had not been paid—or who had not been paid enough—and couldn't have helped very much with those Floridians who weren't yet sure that blacks should even vote, let alone be organized.

During the rest of the preconvention period, we did very little else that could fall in the "dirty trick" category. Senator Muskie most unadvisedly had told an audience of black officials in California in 1971 that he would not take a black vice-presidential candidate on the ticket because it would cause him to lose. There was more talk, all of it quite honest, about the cultural lag in our politics, that Muskie deplored the situation, and so on. In the end Muskie may even have come out slightly ahead on points, largely because he had

23

the courage to say publicly—or at least semipublicly—what other candidates believed but would not say.

But the issue hurt among blacks and other minority groups. Throughout Florida, McGovern students were ready to keep the issue alive at Muskie question-and-answer sessions. If he would not take a black, they would ask, how about a Catholic? A Jew? A Mexican? Or (hisses and whistles) a woman?

On Labor Day, Muskie was scheduled to address an AFL-CIO picnic in Alameda County, California, and we nearly pulled off what would have been the great political stunt of the campaign. William Lockyer was simultaneously the Democratic County Chairman in Alameda County, a friend of the AFL-CIO officials sponsoring the picnic, and the McGovern coordinator for northern California. In his capacity as County Chairman, Lockyer was asked to handle the logistics for Muskie's arrival and travel to the picnic grounds. Lockyer hired a long black limousine with maximum ostentation and arranged for the services of a black chauffeur, in full livery, who was prepared to bow as he opened the door for the candidate. I added the suggestion that he be prevailed upon to tug once or twice at his forelock as the news cameras zeroed in. Muskie sized up the situation as he came down the steps of the airplane and quickly arranged to be whisked away by a waiting advance man in a modest late-model Ford.

The only other anti-Muskie jab we were able to get in came through Ted Van Dyk, once Hubert Humphrey's chief domestic aide, who had gone from Washington to oversee the Florida campaign for McGovern. We were trying hard to arrange a debate among the Democratic candidates, and Van Dyk went to a meeting of candidates' representatives and TV officials to try to work out an acceptable format. Muskie's representative, a young staffer named Chris Hart, had instructions from Muskie's managers not to agree to any format, but to make his refusal seem plausible. Muskie, whose image and reality are those of a thoughtful man, not given to quick definitive answers, comes off badly in a format where short questions are asked about rather complicated issues. Unfortunately, young Hart showed too much candor and a little confusion. He informed the group that he would not approve any debate format, since "We don't want to put Ed Muskie in any situation where he has to think quickly." Van Dyk promptly reported the gaffe to a few local newsmen and it made a box on page one.

Van Dyk's professional shrewdness showed up in other ways. He knew that it was possible to fool not only other candidates, but also the press. He ran the Pennsylvania primary for McGovern largely as a holding-and-salvage operation, with the understanding that McGovern would limit his major efforts to Massachusetts (the primaries were held the same day), that Joel Swerdlow, the state coordinator, could spend only what he could raise, and that national headquarters would send only $25,000 for everything else. Van Dyk put all the money into radio and TV and confined the TV to markets between Philadelphia and Pittsburgh, on the theory that the press would thus confirm our poor-mouth stance since none of the national reporters would watch television in Allentown or Harrisburg. Meanwhile, he went heavy on radio in Philadelphia and Pittsburgh, confident that no national press writer ever listens to the radio, anywhere.

Hubert Humphrey was never a target for any McGovern tricks, although the Humphrey people in California didn't believe it until the Nixon sabotage activities became public. During the California primary campaign there was a barrage of anti-Humphrey and anti-McGovern material circulated, calculated (by the Nixon strategists, as it turned out) to make the two men and their camps not just opponents, but enemies. There were vile distortions of McGovern's record and remarks about Israel distributed in Jewish neighborhoods (an activity—distribution but not composition—to which TV actor Lorne Greene lent himself enthusiastically and whose effects lingered into the fall campaign). A "California Labor Committee" covered the state with anonymous leaflets citing antilabor votes that McGovern never cast. Other "committees" reported hostile positions on civil rights that McGovern had never held.

On the other side, savage leaflets circulated by fake "peace" committees showed Humphrey as the original architect of U.S. policy in Vietnam. Some of these had a picture of a large, particularly unpleasant-looking fish, with Humphrey's face superimposed, and the message, "There's Something Fishy About Hubert Humphrey."

The result was what the Nixon men might have anticipated. By primary day, the possibility of reconciliation between Humphrey and McGovern was far more remote than it would have been had they merely been opponents in a free election. But as we shall see, Richard Nixon has rarely participated in

25

a free election by his own choice, and in 1972 he even sought to prevent one from being held to select his opponent.

We did receive one piece of political intelligence from within the Humphrey camp, but it turned out to be worthless. A few weeks before the primary election, someone purporting to be a Humphrey "insider" told us that a private plane at the Burbank airport was at the disposal of the candidate and that he would fly in it to Las Vegas to pick up a substantial cash contribution to his campaign. The informant even gave us the plane's registration number. There *was* a plane at Burbank with this number, and there it stayed throughout the campaign. It may still be there.

It is important to recount McGovern activity that could conceivably fall in the "dirty trick" category. There has been a low-level White House campaign ever since Watergate came to public consciousness to make people believe that "everybody does it" and that the only difference between the Nixon and McGovern campaigns is that the Nixon people got caught.

For a while, the White House story that the McGovern campaign was up to "dirty tricks" had at least the courage of conviction; some White House people, including Mr. Nixon himself, believed it to be true. We learn from the Watergate testimony that the President—and therefore everyone else, from Haldeman down to poor Bob Odle, the office manager at the Committee to Re-Elect the President (CREP)—actually believed for some time that McGovern money was behind the antiwar demonstrations, particularly those of the Vietnam Veterans Against the War. There was also a belief, which died harder, that "foreign" money was behind other antiwar demonstrations, but surely Mao and Brezhnev disabused the President of these notions.

John Dean made it clear that extensive investigation by the FBI, and even by the freehanded investigators at the White House, could find "not a scintilla" of evidence that any of the demonstrations were funded or otherwise sponsored by either the McGovern campaign or a foreign power. The knowledge thus conveyed by Dean and other investigators, however, did not deter Nixon from repeating the lie in his famous statement of May 22, nor did it stop Haldeman from repeating the slander when he testified in July.

Sticking with a good story even after it has been proven false is a habit with Nixon. He told every White House staffer who would listen, apparently, that he had been wiretapped by

Lyndon Johnson in 1968, a story he ascribed to J. Edgar Hoover. But Johnson had never caused Nixon's phone to be tapped. Theodore S. White and others had reported that Nixon had been *overheard* advising Anna Chennault, an old China (and Nixon) hand, to encourage President Thieu of South Vietnam not to go to the conference table before the 1968 election, but to wait for a better deal with Nixon. The tap was placed on *Chennault's* phone, and as James McCord was to learn, it's almost as good to be overheard on someone else's tap as it is to be tapped yourself. But McCord's Law applies only if you're a defendant in a criminal case, and not if you're a president of the United States trying to discount criminal activity on the grounds that somebody else did it too.

The tap on Chennault's phone may have been illegal, since it is not clear whether the attorney general (Ramsey Clark at that time) ever signed an approval for it. But if *any* national security wiretapping is legal, that one was. After all, the lady was advising a foreign government to go back on the solemn agreement it had reached with her government. If that isn't a matter of national security, then what is?

Nixon persisted with the notion that his phone had been wiretapped, and he kept badgering the FBI for confirmation. It was not forthcoming because no confirmation existed. When the matter became acute in the spring of 1973, and some LBJ wiretapping (or JFK wiretapping, or HST wiretapping, or FDR wiretapping, or wiretapping by *somebody*, except possibly Ike) became a White House evidentiary necessity, Haldeman played his trump card, and it turned out to be, as is so often the case in Nixon's career, Pepsi-Cola.

The relationship between Nixon and Pepsi-Cola, through the company president, Donald Kendall, has been a long and mutually profitable one. The men first met in the 50's, when Nixon was Vice-President. At the American exhibit at the Moscow Fair in 1959, Nixon was accompanied by Kendall at the celebrated "kitchen debate" with Nikita Khrushchev, and indeed Khrushchev, Nixon and Kendall stopped for a Pepsi (and pictures which included the product) at the company's exhibit just adjacent to the modern home whose kitchen was the site of the impromptu discussion.

Kendall had an opportunity to help Nixon in 1963, and he seized it. After his defeat in the California gubernatorial race, Nixon had, literally, no job and no place to go. Kendall and another Nixon friend, Elmer Bobst, the president of Warner-

Lambert, went to the New York law firm of Mudge, Stern, Baldwin and Todd. In exchange for making Richard Nixon a senior partner, with a generous salary and travel expenses, they offered the firm the reward of the legal business of their companies. The deal was made, and the firm became Nixon, Mudge, Rose, Guthrie, and Alexander (and later absorbed a prosperous municipal bond firm headed by John Mitchell).

Kendall received one highly tangible reward at the Moscow summit in 1972, although for tactical reasons it was not announced until January 1973 when the election was safely over. While most of us had believed that the fruit of the Moscow summit was an arms control and limitation agreement (which, it turned out, would only add $3 billion or $4 billion to our arms budget), the *real* accomplishment was that Pepsi-Cola would become the only American soft drink sold in the Soviet Union. It was, although the President unaccountably failed to announce it as such, another historic Nixon "first"—the first time in our history that a president used his foreign policy power to bestow great financial benefit upon a friend to whom he was indebted.

It came, consequently, as no great surprise that, at the height of the President's Watergate troubles in the winter of 1973–74, it was Kendall who came forward as the "non-partisan" leader and financier of one of those short-lived Committees for the Defense of the Presidency. Kendall promoted signatures from former Nixon cabinet officers by promising that other "big names" had already signed on. But unlike earlier successful Nixon front organizations, this one didn't get off the ground because those approached were smart enough to check with those alleged to be already on board. But Kendall gave it a big try.

Thus Haldeman turned to the Pepsi connection when he needed corroboration that Nixon had been wiretapped by Johnson in 1968. Kendall had hired as vice-president of Pepsi, Cartha (Deke) DeLoach, a longtime FBI executive and confidant of J. Edgar Hoover. DeLoach would know about the wiretapping, and if he didn't, perhaps he would tell the right story anyway.

DeLoach had maintained for four years, whenever asked, that Johnson had not tapped Nixon's phone—and DeLoach would know, since he was the FBI liaison with the White House in Johnson's time. Watergate in 1973, the White House reasoning went, was one of those crises when the truth was not enough. By February 1973, Watergate pressure was growing. Haldeman sent a memo to Dean. In it he referred to the 1968 wiretap story and told Dean to "get the fullest possible information" about it from DeLoach.

In a memo dated February 9, 1973, Haldeman got specific about the remedy. Dean was to get in touch with John Mitchell and instruct him to get in touch with his old client Kendall. Mitchell was to have Kendall "call DeLoach in and say that if this project turns up anything that DeLoach hasn't covered with us, he will, of course, have to fire him." Pepsi-Cola, it seems, was one government agency where Civil Service protection had not yet been extended to the employees.

That approach apparently yielded nothing. On March 1, according to Dean, Nixon himself said he was convinced he had been wiretapped in 1968, "and since DeLoach had not been forthcoming, DeLoach was probably lying." The President, said Dean, "told me I should call Don Kendall, DeLoach's employer, and tell him that DeLoach had better start telling the truth because 'the boys are coming out of the woodwork.' He said this ploy may smoke DeLoach out."

DeLoach apparently thought all the boys who could get out of the woodwork had already come out because he never confirmed the 1968 story. The White House, naturally enough, has never withdrawn the charge, just as it has never withdrawn the story that the antiwar demonstrations were financed by McGovern funds.

An interesting possibility exists that at least some of the antiwar demonstrations were financed by *Nixon* campaign funds. Herbert L. Porter, who was entrusted with some recruitment responsibilities in the area of "dirty tricks," testified that Charles Colson once hired an antiwar picket to make a spectacle of himself, complete with hippie garb and large McGovern buttons, in front of the White House, and there have been other reports that some hippies, "gays," and generally raunchy types who frequented McGovern rallies were actors, hired for the occasion by the Committee to Re-Elect the President.

Indeed, the combination of Porter's testimony about the lone picket from the Colson Drama School in front of the White House, and Dean's testimony about a lone picket one day in 1971 gives rise to the notion that perhaps they were one and the same.

At the beginning of his testimony, in order to set the White

House mood, Dean told of one morning when the President saw a single picket across from the White House in Lafayette Park. Nixon told Haldeman, and Haldeman told Higby, and Higby told Dean, that the picket must go. When Dean told Dwight Chapin, the dapper appointments secretary, since convicted of two counts of perjury, about the problem, Chapin said not to worry, he would call a "few thugs" and have the man taken care of. Dean handled it nonviolently, as it turned out.

Suppose the picket who so offended the President had been posted there by Colson to offend everyone else? One imagines a strange scene—the limits of manpower for this kind of activity being what they were—in which Chapin calls one of his reliable thugs to ask him to get rid of the picket, and Mrs. Thug answers the phone and says, "I'm sorry Dwight, but he's working for Mr. Colson today, picketing the White House. I'll have him call when he gets back."

The fiction, then, was that the McGovern "dirty tricks" were legion and included violence and incitement to violence at Nixon rallies. The nominal head of CREP, ex-Congressman Clark MacGregor, joined in the charge one day in California and echoed the White House allegation that the McGovern campaign had taken part in encouraging some violence at the Century Plaza, where Nixon was making a campaign nonappearance in October. At the time I thought critically about MacGregor, usually a decent man and not a disciple of the Chotiner-Colson to-hell-with-the-facts school of political attack. But since then Dean has testified that along with Ron Ziegler, MacGregor was kept entirely in the dark about the campaign he was running. MacGregor was not lying at all; he just didn't know what he was talking about.

What the McGovern campaign *was* doing in the fall of 1972 was a good deal more prosaic and much closer to the "politics as usual" of presidential campaigns. Under the direction of Ted Van Dyk, a research group set to work monitoring the Nixon campaign. Since the candidate rarely appeared in public and gave set speeches when he did, the task was easier than for campaigns in previous years. The research group tried, wherever possible, to listen to the "surrogates" as well—by getting the advance schedule from the Republican National Committee publications and then having a volunteer in the particular city go listen. It was tedious work, but occasionally, as when *all* the surrogates were sounding the same theme, it could be helpful because we'd know what to stress and what to be prepared to answer.

The Van Dyk group was able to track down some of the more brazen Nixon corruption stories during the campaign. With information from some staff members of the Senate Agriculture Committee and some research into grain prices and Agriculture Department records, Sandy Berger of our staff was able to break the Great Grain Scandal of 1972. Berger discovered, and put the facts together for a McGovern speech, that the USDA—armed with information about a disastrous Russian wheat harvest which it kept secret from its clients, the American grain farmers—helped negotiate a secret grain sale to the Soviet Union. The sale enormously benefited a few big grain traders whom the department's top officials had thoughtfully tipped off ahead of time.

A little more checking into public records yielded the information that a resourceful assistant secretary of agriculture, Clarence Palmby, had made, in advance of his trip to Moscow to negotiate the deal, employment arrangements with the grain company that was to benefit most from the deal. When the Russian deal was struck, Palmby moved to a New York apartment he had agreed to buy before he left ("just speculation," he said with a straight face) and took on a high-paying job with the corporation he had served so well while on the federal payroll. To take his place, a grain corporation executive moved over to the Department of Agriculture to handle foreign grain sales, thus preserving the balance.

Berger's revelations were airtight but involved nothing that could remotely be called "espionage." That was really the beauty of doing research on the Nixon administration—it was all out in the open. Secretary of Agriculture Earl Butz called it a "bald-faced lie" after McGovern's charges began to be picked up in the press, but the facts were just as McGovern described them. The deal was a classic piece of government corruption—inducing growers of early wheat to sell their crop at a low price by concealing the fact of the Russian shortage, and then adding to the favored insiders' profits with a rigged subsidy price. It was the kind of scandal Americans understand. In the Western movie it is the slick agent for the corporation (usually Richard Widmark) who fraudulently induces the young widow to sell her land, knowing (but not telling her) that there's oil under it or that the railroad needs it.

The research team also picked up, without a single electronic device, the details of other scandals. From research by the staff of the Senate Commerce Committee came the story that representatives of the carpet manufacturing industry had met with Maurice Stans and arranged a delay of tougher flammability standards for their product, for a campaign contribution of $94,000. Since Stans, as Secretary of Commerce, had been responsible for setting and enforcing the standard, the carpet men knew the deal would stick.

We also monitored the announcements and decisions of the Price Commission, matching them up, where relevant, with the names and corporate affiliations of Nixon campaign contributors. We could have used some espionage here to get the names of the contributors, which were concealed until April 7. Stans (a member of the Accountants Hall of Fame, as he was later to tell the Ervin Committee proudly), did release the *total* amount of contributions, which gave us some guide. He reported the total secret contributions at $10 million. It was really $20 million.

In the course of the routine, our "spies"—volunteers working out of Van Dyk's office—came up with some real nuggets. They discovered, for instance, that Clement Stone, a Chicago insurance executive who had contributed $1 million to the Nixon campaign in 1968 (by his own account) and who planned to double that amount for 1972, had received an *unlimited* price increase from the Price Commission just seven days after he had dined at the White House late in 1971.

They also turned up the information that Ray Kroc of McDonald's, who dropped $250,000 into the Nixon campaign (Stans's figure, and therefore subject to upward revision as the facts become known), was lobbying in behalf of an exemption from the increase in the minimum wage for his teenage employees.

Operating legally, it is possible to learn all you need to know about the other side. We knew from reading the newspapers, for example, that in 1971 then Attorney General Mitchell had overruled his own assistant in charge of the Anti-Trust Division at the Justice Department, and had brushed aside objections from the staff of the Federal Trade Commission, to approve a merger between Warner-Lambert and Parke-Davis, two giant drug companies whose combined power created the second largest factor in the market.

The interesting thing about this merger—which the press went into only sketchily, if at all—was that the chairman of

Warner-Lambert, the dominant survivor in the merger, was Elmer Bobst. Bobst was one of Richard Nixon's oldest friends, often referred to as his "honorary father."

The "honorary father" had played an almost godfatherly role in Nixon's dark days after the California gubernatorial election of 1962. It was Bobst, together with Don Kendall of Pepsi-Cola, who had gone to the New York law firm and made the deal for Nixon to become a senior partner in return for the legal accounts of the two companies.

What I wanted to know was how much Bobst's personal stock holdings in Warner-Lambert had increased as a result of Mitchell's intervention in the merger. Through his contacts on Wall Street, where he had previously worked in one of the larger investment banking houses, my assistant Bill Cobbs was able to come up with the answer: Bobst, the "honorary father," had made a cool $18 million.

(The "honorary father's" job carried perquisites as well as financial reward, it turned out. In 1973, Bobst conceded that the Nixon administration had asked him to screen candidates for the job of director of the Food and Drug Administration— a task he willingly took on.)

Finally, in the 1972 campaign, there was Watergate. We relied mainly on the reports of the Washington *Post*'s investigators Bob Woodward and Carl Bernstein. As can be seen from Senator McGovern's speech in the Appendix, Woodward and Bernstein knew a great deal, and every word has turned out to be true. Through the long campaign, McGovern and his people hoped this news would strike some spark in the country. When in the past had a president's campaign funds been used by present and past Cabinet members and White House aides to pay burglars?

In August, the McGovern campaign hired Walter Sheridan as its only pure investigator. Walter was awaiting the publication of his book *The Fall and Rise of Jimmy Hoffa*. In large part (the Fall, at least) it is an account of facts about Hoffa that Sheridan had uncovered while he was an investigator on the staff of Attorney General Robert F. Kennedy. He and I had become friends during my time as press secretary to Senator Kennedy and during Kennedy's presidential campaign in 1968. We remained friends during the time he worked as an investigative reporter for NBC and while he was writing the Hoffa book. I knew him as a careful man with a wide acquaintance among the newsmen we both respected, so I gave him as his main assignment the job of keeping Senator McGovern informed of the latest Watergate developments. He brought us up to date every few days with the latest stories from the *Post* and the latest upcoming stories he had gleaned from his friends in the press.

Sheridan also undertook one other assignment, at which he did very well, but which hardly saw the light of day. John Connally had "organized" a group of Democrats for Nixon. Their bills were paid by the CREP, but they took a number of advertisements in leading newspapers to make it appear as though the committee really was composed of Democrats who had spontaneously come together. In fact, the list contained some "Democrats" who had never supported a Democrat in recent memory, and some others in immediate or prospective trouble with the government. Sheridan took on the job of finding out, through public records at the Justice Department and elsewhere, just which ones were in real or prospective trouble.

The only trouble was that we couldn't find any newspaper or television people willing to use Walter's information. The result was that "Democrats for Nixon" continued to function through the campaign, giving the impression that it was something other than a fully financed arm of the CREP.

Only two other bits of 1972 McGovern "espionage" remain to be listed. Through the summer and early fall, much was made of the impracticality and high cost of the McGovern "$1,000 for Everybody" welfare plan. In reality, it was a version of a negative income tax plan proposed at various times by a number of able economists, conservatives as well as liberals. It was hard to explain, since it involved a declining level of receipt to the citizen and a rising level of tax on the $1,000 as income rose from $4,000 to $12,000. McGovern maintained that the plan was difficult to cost, given varying projections of income, budget levels, and employment from year to year, but that it was, in any event, less costly than President Nixon's Family Assistance Plan and that it would not substantially increase the taxes of anyone below the level of a $20,000 annual income.

It was heavy going. We lacked the computer capability to make the determinations we needed and, in any event, the idea of a presidential candidate presenting a major reform whose cost he was unable to fix was not a reassuring one. In addition, Nixon was backing away from his Family Assistance

Plan of a minimum of $2,400 per year for a family of four, and finally adopted a more modest FAP which consisted only of Bebe Rebozo's buying a $150,000 home in Washington for David and Julie Eisenhower.

In July, an economist at the Office of Management and Budget sought me out with a fascinating story. He had been asked, as a part of a team at OMB, to prepare an analysis of the "McGovern Welfare Plan" for the use of the Committee to Re-Elect the President. He had done so and had passed along the analysis to the CREP. It was not well received, he told me, because the analysis showed, using several different methods of calculation, that the McGovern proposal would cost the taxpayers less than the Nixon plan and that there would be no significant impact on any taxpayer earning less than $20,000 per year.

He was then disgraced at OMB, and the CREP asked for a new analysis—this time to be prepared by a team at Treasury —and there were strong suggestions that my informant was some sort of McGovern spy in the Executive Branch. Imagine his pleasure when he heard that the Treasury analysis had come out the same way—the McGovern "crackpot" scheme would cost less than FAP and would not raise taxes for 70 percent of all taxpayers.

The result was that all copies of his analysis were ordered to be destroyed. He had thoughtfully retained one, which he gave me one night at my home. Unfortunately, we were unable to use the story at the time because any release of it would have made things too tough for the informant since the story would probably be traced directly to him. I asked him to let me know when things were sufficiently blurred in his agency so that we could set some reporter loose on the story. Although he was willing to take the risk by late September, I thought it would be a mistake. His job would certainly be jeopardized, and by that time McGovern himself had retreated on the welfare issue and the matter was largely moot.

The other bit of "espionage" was strictly a job for the "Plumbers," if only we had been so inclined. At least four or five times during the campaign, I was told by guarded telephone callers that the Shah of Iran had made a secret contribution of $1 million to the Nixon campaign on the occasion of the presidential visit to Teheran in May, 1972. The story seemed superficially plausible—it was in character for both men. We were never able to produce even a trace of supporting evidence, so nothing was done with it. Now if the Nixon operation were really "politics as usual," we would have fitted out our own Howard Hunt with a red wig and sent him to Iran to blow the Shah's safe. Or we could have considered the advisability of sending an ex-policeman to the Iranian Embassy to firebomb the place and recover any evidence of the contribution in the confusion. We didn't do any of these things. We never considered any of these things because the McGovern campaign of 1972, just as any other non-Nixon presidential campaign, *was* pursuing "politics as usual." That does not include, as Senator Weicker put it so well on June 29, 1973, acts that are "unconstitutional, illegal, or gross."

Ethics and honesty—though a large part of it—are not the only reasons for shunning this kind of activity in a campaign. The uses of "intelligence" are limited, and the value of "espionage" therefore is extremely low, particularly in proportion to the risk. I asked Larry O'Brien what he would have done in any campaign (he had a major role in the last five national Democratic efforts) if he had been guaranteed the fruits of a phone tap and bug, recording everything that went on in the other headquarters and everything said by the major figures on the other side. His reply was that he would reject it. O'Brien's reasons, shared by all non-Nixon politicians with whom I have talked, including the 1972 chairman of the Republican National Committee, Senator Robert Dole, are that apart from the moral reasons, the effort is time-consuming and unrewarding.

In the first place, somebody has to listen to the tapes and probably somebody else has to transcribe them. Then someone in authority must read the endless chitchat of politics. According to O'Brien, "If you have any brains, you already know 90 percent of what the other side is saying. They're saying the same things you are, about money, scheduling, printing, and television, and the other 10 percent isn't worth listening to."

This attitude toward espionage and "intelligence-gathering" is apparent from interviews with campaign officials and observation of other Presidential campaigns. Clifton White, manager of the Goldwater campaign in 1964, echoes O'Brien when it comes to "secret" inside information. White calls the Nixon-type espionage of Watergate "a waste of time" and points out that whatever information may be obtained, people who can be put to better use must spend extraordinary amounts of time listening to and transcribing tapes. "Hell," White says, "conversation in campaigns are all the same. You don't need to listen to the other guy's conversations; you can make them up."

White fondly remembers two "dirty tricks" from the 1964 campaign, and they rank with the McGovern coffee cup stickers. Once during the campaign an employee of the General Services Administration gave White the story that Lyndon Johnson was having an immense office built for himself—with governments funds—in Austin. The dimensions, recalled the GSA man, included a fireplace capable of burning 14-foot logs. White put out a short press release, calling the LBJ office complex a "Taj Mahal." (White's public relations instincts are traditional; every opulent building put up with public funds is a "Taj Mahal." It goes along with Cadillacs and color televisions as gross luxuries whose attainment by welfare clients is regularly exposed.) He even mentioned the 14-foot logs. What made it a telling shot was the mistake LBJ then made. When reporters showed up to look at the Texas Taj Mahal, the Johnson forces denied them access, and for the next few days people were distracted (quite properly, from White's viewpoint) from Goldwater's views on TVA and Social Security while they tried to imagine a fireplace large enough to burn 14-foot logs.

White is also proud of having placed a Goldwater billboard ("In Your Heart You Know He's Right") near the entrance to the Democrats' 1964 convention hall at Atlantic City. TV cameras would have to pan over it whenever they showed anyone entering or leaving the hall. That is some distance from forging a cable so as to implicate a dead President in murder, or even from hiring people to pose as homosexuals at your opponent's rallies.

"Competition is what makes politics," White concludes. "And the more spirited and fair it is, the more likely people are to reach the right verdict. If you believe in your candidate, you ought to encourage as much real competition as possible." Keeping with the metaphor, he points out that football coaches now exchange films of their games with opposing coaches.

White would probably rather not remember one genuine 1972-type event that took place in 1964, one for which he had no responsibility at all. After the Goldwater nomination, the professionals with White opened a Goldwater headquarters, and the zealots who had helped earn the nomination were turned loose on the Republication National Committee. This split between professionals and idealogues was duplicated in 1972, but in reverse. The Nixon people, who had never been in any campaign except a Nixon campaign (that is to say, who had never participated in a free election), manned the Committee to Re-Elect the President, with direction from the White House; the professionals, headed by Senator Robert Dole of Kansas, were left at the National Committee.

In 1964 the hot-eyed amateur zealots, led by Dean Burch, were at the Republican National Committee, and with not too much to do. No one was more hot-eyed than John Grenier of Alabama, who had lined up southern delegates for Goldwater with a straight racist pitch and who had been rewarded with a job as executive director of the committee.

According to a four-page affidavit prepared by Louis Flax and read to the press on October 13, 1964, Flax had been recruited by the Republican National Committee to collect information on the Democrats and pass it along. Flax was uniquely equipped to do the job, since he was the nightshift teletype operator for the Democratic National Committee. The allegation was particularly ugly, since the approach to Flax, through an unidentified caller, was to threaten him with exposure if he didn't go along. Flax had recently served time at a Maryland House of Correction on a bad check charge and was trying to earn some money to make restitution.

Flax went to Wayne Phillips, the Democratic National Committee news service chief, and told him of the approach. Flax and Phillips worked out a trap. Flax made regular deliveries to John Grenier at the Republican National Committee (Grenier had told him he especially wanted a full LBJ schedule for the rest of the campaign). Phillips provided the information for Flax to deliver. After Flax had made the deliveries to Grenier, a third (unidentified) man whom Grenier had introduced to Flax would follow Flax out of the building and give him varying amounts of cash, sometimes as much as $1,000.

On October 13, Phillips sprung the trap. He summoned reporters, had them listen to Flax's story, and then had Flax make a delivery to Grenier while reporters followed for the payoff. Perhaps scared off by the presence of so many reporters, the payoff man never appeared, but the reporters went to Grenier's office and found the envelope Flax had delivered. Grenier refused to comment, but the Republican National

Committee, true to the genre, put out a statement charging the Johnson administration with covering up corruption in the cases of Bobby Baker and Billy Sol Estes.

Except for the Flax incident and one or two others, the 1964 campaign made its own contest on the issues and the personalities of Johnson and Goldwater. In late August, Drew Pearson (a longtime LBJ partisan) called Johnson and suggested that the President form a unit to meet the Goldwater charges and to anticipate and develop what Pearson called "non-issue issues."

Johnson asked Myer Feldman, a JFK holdover serving as counsel to the President, to organize such a group. The result was the 5 O'Clock Group, so-called because of the time it met each afternoon. Feldman's group used volunteers to get advance copies of Goldwater's speeches whenever they were distributed and did a rather effective job of sending surrogates to the same cities—either just before or just after—to reply.

In addition, depending on the "hot" Goldwater issue—whether it was selling the TVA or "lobbing an atom bomb into the men's room at the Kremlin"—Feldman's group would notify the advance men to arrange for embarrassing placards and, occasionally, LBJ partisans at Goldwater's rallies.

As to the "non-issue issues," very few developed and few were used. Considering the bitterness of the campaign, it is surprising that so little appeared that related personally to either candidate. Perhaps it was believed that anything of that nature would "backfire." Feldman says his group once developed a story that Senator Goldwater's mother was a nonworking employee of the family-owned department store in Phoenix, but the decision was instantly made not to use the story.

A few other 1964 incidents approach the "dirty tricks" levels, but remain far short of the Nixon standard of 1972. The Goldwater campaign produced and was prepared to use on television and in movie theaters a short film called "Choice." The film tried to contrast the clean-living, old-fashioned Americanism of the Goldwater candidacy with the filth and permissiveness of the opposition. It intercut patriotic and war scenes with shots of pornography displays, lewd movies, and even one memorable shot of a beer can sailing out of a speeding limousine. The beer can was supposed to put people in mind of a story about Johnson driving his Cadillac around the LBJ ranch. On one such occasion a columnist reported that Johnson threw beer cans out the window while discoursing about the joys of the bucolic life.

Dick Tuck, the grand old man of dirty tricks, obtained a copy of "Choice" before it had been distributed, and the Democrats called a press conference to show the film and to release a transcript of it. Tuck even persuaded Walter Lippmann to write a column about it (the column ended, "I shall now go to wash my hands"), and the resultant uproar caused the Republicans to announce they had decided not to use it, anyway. In that simpler time, it was thought somehow reprehensible to exploit crime (there were a number of shots in "Choice" of muggings, robberies, and worse) as a partisan issue.

Tuck's other coup in 1964 was to plant a lovely girl named Moura O'Connor on the Goldwater train to distribute a daily news bulletin to every reporter. The news bulletin, bearing Tuck's name and clearly a Democratic effort, was placed under the door of every reporter's compartment in the morning. It embarrassed the Goldwater people, but it was all taken in the spirit of fun. When O'Connor was discovered—a feat made somewhat less difficult by the fact that she had no credentials and was known as a friend of Tuck's—she was, in the words of Goldwater's press secretary, Vic Gold, "detrained" at Petersburg, West Virginia. Charles Mohr of *The New York Times,* playing off a bestselling novel of the time, referred to her as "The Spy Who Was Thrown Out in the Cold," and thereafter the story grew that Tuck had put a "spy" on the Goldwater train.

There was no spy on the Goldwater train, just somebody whose job—soon discovered and with no concealment—was to distribute a gibing newsletter. But in 1972, it turns out, there were two real spies on the McGovern campaign plane. The late Murray Chotiner, who had been with Nixon in every campaign since Nixon Politics began in 1946, put two people on the McGovern press planes, and outfitted them with press credentials so they could pass.

The two, Seymour Freidin and Lucille Cummings Goldberg, were each paid $1,000 per week to provide the Nixon campaign with information—size of crowds, morale of the candidate, gossip about strategy—which might be useful. Goldberg was reported to have told the Washington *Star-News* she was also supposed to report on the "juicy stuff," such as drugs and sexual misconduct, but later denied she had so described her duties.

The significant thing here is that the identities of the Nixon agents were concealed, they lied about their roles in order to be certified as "correspondents," and Chotiner defended it all as "good practice" in a campaign. He clearly went ahead with the scheme (just where he got the money to pay the spies has not yet been made clear) on his own, knowing that Nixon would approve.

But can anyone imagine Chotiner doing such a thing on his own, counting on the approval of the candidate, if the candidate were Eisenhower, or Goldwater, or for that matter Kennedy, Humphrey, Johnson, or McGovern? Indeed, can anyone imagine that any of those non-Nixon candidates would ever have Chotiner involved in a campaign at all?

Tuck deserves special mention. He is most offended that when Jeb Magruder first recruited Herbert Porter as the Nixon Committee's "dirty tricks" man, he told Porter it would be in the nature of "Dick Tuck-type" activity, but Porter didn't know who he was talking about. Tuck is right to be offended; anyone who was prepared to assume a major role in a campaign in 1972 should have heard of him.

A Californian, Tuck had worked in a number of state and local campaigns by 1960. In that year, he joined the Kennedy campaign, largely through his friendship with Frederick Dutton, a strategist for then-Governor Edmund G. "Pat" Brown of California. Dutton worked in the Kennedy campaign, and Tuck became a national figure for the first time.

Tuck's major attribute is unquestionably his sense of humor. He makes people feel good, and when he is on the campaign plane or train, the reporters know they have a friend, one who will liven up the day and even, perhaps, their stories. When a team of researchers was sent to Florida in 1968 by the Humphrey camp to look into some real estate deals of Nixon's friend Charles "Bebe" Rebozo, Tuck offered to take some reporters on a sight-seeing tour of the Rebozo land, "on a glass-bottomed boat." It could hardly have been said better.

In 1960, Tuck's job was to needle Richard Nixon, and he evidently succeeded. After the first Nixon-Kennedy debate, in which Nixon may well have squandered whatever lead he had, Tuck arranged for a sweet little old lady to meet the Nixon plane at the first stop to shake hands. "Don't worry,

Richard," she said pleasantly, in full vision and hearing of reporters clustered around, "you'll do better next time."

Tuck is given credit (he denies it, somewhat hollowly) for putting on an engineer's hat and waving the Nixon train along in 1960, somewhat enraging the candidate who had just begun a rear platform speech. He is also alleged to have rapped sharply on the glass of the driver's compartment in the Nixon campaign bus one day in Iowa, ordering the driver to start up. He did. The only problem was that Mrs. Nixon was still in town, a fact that was not discovered until the caravan was several miles down the road.

Tuck is most fondly remembered for the "fortune cookie caper," surely one of the high moments of any political campaign. Toward Election Day 1960, Nixon was coming under some fire because of the circumstances of a loan to his family from Howard Hughes. Then, as now, Hughes was a reclusive billionaire with no known interest in politics. Thus it came as somewhat of a surprise to learn that Hughes had loaned Nixon's brother (the one who was found twelve years later to be involved with financier Robert Vesco) more than $200,000.

As always, the Nixon explanation left a number of un-answered questions. (No one asked them very hard—Nixon's reputation for deviousness where his own finances were concerned was yet to be fully earned.) They included, for instance, why the security for the loan (a piece of property owned by Nixon's mother) had never been valued at more than $60,000, or for that matter, why a man with countless business interests that might be affected by federal governmental action would make a secret loan to a vice-president, even to help the vice-president's brother?

In any event, Nixon wasn't talking about the loan, and in the last week of the campaign he went to San Francisco for a traditional Republican affair—a luncheon and rally in China-town. In those days, the Chinese community was solidly Republican. At the preluncheon rally, Nixon appeared before a large banner, in Chinese characters, and the picture was duti-fully sent around the country by the news services. It was only the next day that the story appeared that the Chinese charac-ters—written at the bidding of Dick Tuck and a Chinese-American friend—read "What About the Hughes Loan?"

To nail the point down, Tuck proceeded to his great coup. At the luncheon, with the Chinese community leaders and the national political press in attendance, Nixon started to speak while the dessert and the fortune cookies were being served. Laughter, led mainly by the press, interrupted the speech as it was discovered that every diner's fortune cookie contained an identical message, "Ask him about the Hughes loan." Tuck became immortal in American politics.

[In 1972, when it appeared that Hugh Sloan, the treasurer of the CREP, had knowledge of the money paid in cash to Gordon Liddy and others to burglarize the Watergate, Tuck swore to newsmen that he was devising a new fortune cookie message with a typographical change: "Ask him about Hugh Sloan."]

There is more of Tuck in the campaigns of 1960, 1964, and 1968 (when, in addition to keeping everybody happy with his wit, he functioned with great competence as wagon master of the Kennedy campaign plane during the primaries), but this is a fair sample. Anyone who suggests that "Dick Tuck-type" tricks were the inevitable precursor of Watergate—or that "everybody does it; what about Dick Tuck?"—simply doesn't know what he's talking about. More likely, he does know what he's talking about, and hopes *you* don't. Loaded fortune cookies with a campaign message on a current issue is not the same as an obstruction of justice, and jokes are not burglaries.

Late in the day, the Nixon men have come up with some new accusations. According to a group of conflicting affidavits, the Nixon campaign either was or was not subject to wire-tapping and bugging in 1960. The key affidavit, by a man who died shortly after signing it, alleges that Robert Kennedy arranged for the surveillance and that Carmine Bellino coordinated the activity. Bellino was a Kennedy campaign aide.

The affidavit has a lot going for it, by Nixon standards. First of all, it goes beyond the forged cable and implicates two dead men in a crime. Second, it assigns a key role to a man with an Italian name who is presently a chief investigator for the Ervin Committee. Under the circumstances, it is not surprising that Senator Hugh Scott—who has come over the years to the point where he will say *anything*—could round up 21 Republican Senators to propose that Bellino be fired until the allegations could be proved or disproved.

But the charge was found to be false, and anyone who knows Carmine Bellino knew that Scott & Co. have picked the wrong man to try to pin it on. Bellino is an accountant, and since his days on the McClellan Committee staff investigating labor racketeering, he has been the scourge of wrongdoers who think they can mask their acts by cooking the books. But wiretapping? Never. An affidavit from a dead man is better than an admittedly forged one, but not much better.

The pattern that emerges is that there *is* a "politics as usual" in national campaigns, whether practiced by Eisenhower, Stevenson, Kennedy, Humphrey, Johnson, Goldwater, or McGovern. It gets its "intelligence" from the newspapers and the opponent's published material; it assigns a low priority to "espionage" and inside information, particularly that of a personal nature; and it operates within boundaries (or "parameters," as the Nixon men would say) which assume that politics is a contest, or even a business, but never a war. The opposition is just that—the opposition or the opponent—not the enemy. Hard as it must be for the Nixons, the Haldemans, and the Mitchells to realize, political professionals operate under the presumption that there are worse things than losing an election.

On the other hand, there is a *Nixon* "politics as usual." It has its list of "enemies" and treats them as though they are enemies. It includes deception, espionage, sabotage, and crime. It has always included willful distortion of the issues, and assignment of a conspiratorial intent to the enemy, thus justifying a permanent conspiracy as a defense. And it has led straight and true to the national shame which will forever be known as Watergate.

3. The California Proving Ground

Richard Nixon was elected to Congress from the 12th District of California in 1946 and was reelected in 1948. He was elected to the Senate in 1950. He was defeated as a candidate for the presidency in 1960 and for governor of California in 1962. He was elected president in 1968 and reelected in 1972. A survey of these contests clearly demonstrates the proposition that, with the possible exception of 1968, he has never won a free election.

A free election, for these purposes, is one untainted by major fraud. In 1972, of course, the fraud was immense. Not only was espionage widely used (apart from Watergate itself), but the activity of almost every major figure in the campaign was devoted in whole or in part, after June 17, to a vast cover-up of the original crime. The actual perjury of men like Jeb Magruder and Herbert Porter was no more contributory to the fraud than the merely false statements of Ronald Ziegler, John Mitchell, and Clark MacGregor—and, for that matter, Richard Nixon. When one adds to this the forging of a cable, the extraction of secret (and illegal) campaign contributions under circumstances which may amount to extortion, the use of paid saboteurs and deliberate slander of the opposition, "fraud" becomes almost an inadequate description.

It is in the earlier campaigns—three victories and one defeat in California—that the pattern begins to come perfectly clear. Fraud, as Richard Nixon learned in law school, classically consists of five elements: There must be falsehood; it must be known to be false when made; it must be made with intent to deceive someone; it must deceive him; and it must be to his detriment.

These elements were present in Nixon's California campaigns, where the Nixon team began to assemble—Chotiner,

Ehrlichman, Haldeman, Ziegler, Chapin, Kalmbach. As they assembled and deployed, they made California a political laboratory—as the Germans had made Spain—for the testing of methods and techniques. The blitzkrieg would come later.

During the 1930s and through the war years, the political face of California was changing perhaps more rapidly than that of any other state. In 1930 the Republican heirs of Senator Hiram Johnson (who would remain a senator until 1945) dominated the state, but Johnson's Progressivism no longer dominated the GOP ideologically. Of 100 members of the State Legislature in 1930, only 13 were Democrats, and some of them shared their Republican colleagues' hard-shelled conservatism.

The Depression, the New Deal, and the migration from the Dust Bowl changed all that. It changed radically and swiftly. In 1934 a utopian socialist novelist, Upton Sinclair, won the Democratic nomination for governor on a platform of "End Poverty in California" (EPIC), and carried with him into the Democratic Party every radical, reformer, and crank in the state, along with millions of discontented and disillusioned migrants (mostly from the normally Democratic states of Oklahoma and Arkansas), small farmers, and rural families (many of them transplanted to the big cities in a vain search for employment).

Out of this vast, inchoate coalition of Roosevelt liberals, Single Taxers, socialists, communists, syndicalists, vegetarians, old-age pensioners, Wobblies, populists, "goldbugs," and calendar reformers was forged a political force stronger than a party, although it bore the name of Democrat. Sinclair went down after a bitter contest, but many of the men who ran with him became California's leaders. Culbert Olsen, who always called himself a Social Democrat and openly proclaimed his atheism, was elected governor in 1938 and freed Tom Mooney (a left-wing and labor martyr) from San Quentin as his first official act. Some radicals of the 1930s, men like Sheridan Downey (elected to the U.S. Senate in 1938) and Sam Yorty (assemblyman, congressman, Senate candidate, and later mayor of Los Angeles), turned steadily more conservative as they enjoyed the fruits of office. Others, like State Senator Robert Kenny (later to run for governor against Earl Warren and today a Los Angeles judge), kept the liberal faith. One of the latter was Jerry Voorhis.

46

Voorhis, like Sinclair an early Socialist, became a Democrat and ran for the legislature in 1934. He lost, but came back in 1936 to win a congressional seat in the FDR landslide. His district was conservative by today's demographic standards; it consisted mainly of farmers, ranchers, and small home owners in the predominantly residential areas lying immediately east of Los Angeles.

Voorhis was reelected four times, with consistent majorities, and only partly because he spoke for his constituents in Washington. The rest of the reason undoubtedly involved the great respect in which he was held, even by his opponents. Voorhis was regularly voted at or near the top of any poll or rating of congressmen by Washington correspondents or even by other congressmen.

He was a most independent legislator. Thus he was the only member of the California delegation who opposed state ownership of the vast oil reserves off the coast (the so-called Tidelands oil); he opposed the split-income provisions of the income tax law which because of the state's community property law uniquely favored California's married citizens; and he was alone in the delegation in opposing the internment of Japanese-Americans during World War II.

This independence got Jerry Voorhis into trouble within his own party by 1946. In 1940 he had sponsored and steered to passage the Foreign Agents Registration Act, aimed in that year of the Stalin-Hitler Pact at both Nazi and Communist agents. In addition, he had spoken out as frequently against what he saw as the Russian threat to Europe as he had against Nazi Germany. It was a natural position for an ex-Socialist who had abandoned the label but not the principles, and it earned him the hostility, not only of the Communist Party but of its allies among the Democrats.

By 1946, Communists had begun to exercise a power somewhat beyond their numbers and their means in the Democratic Party of California. They controlled the statewide council of the CIO, and their operation in Hollywood, though never a fraction of what various legislative committees claimed it to be, was sufficient to guarantee a good flow of money to favored causes and candidates.

As we have seen, one of those favored candidates was *not* Jerry Voorhis. He served on the Un-American Activities Committee, where he tried hard to be a force for sanity before he resigned in protest; he had been a supporter of the Baruch plan submitted by the United States for international control of atomic energy; and he was plainly a supporter of President Truman in the emerging Cold War debate with Henry Wallace over how to respond to Soviet postwar moves in Europe. Any one of those stances would have been enough to earn Voorhis the enmity of the state CIO and a large portion of the left wing of the California Democratic Party.

Voorhis had other weaknesses in the 12th District (actually, his anti-Communist stance didn't hurt him much *in* the district; it was in the larger, urban world of contributions and endorsements that such things mattered). His largely small town, small farm constituency, which had always respected him for his independence, was beginning to wonder about some of the fruits of that independence. In addition to the banks, the insurance companies, and the large real estate interests, whom he had regularly offended by his more or less orthodox New Deal record, there were new dissatisfactions emerging.

Voorhis, for example, had voted against some of the tougher restrictions on labor organizing imposed by a preview of Taft-Hartley which had come up a year earlier. It was a thoroughly principled vote, since the union strength in his district was negligible, but it put him on the side of "big unions" beginning to seek large postwar wage settlements, and threatening some major strikes in the process.

In addition, two typically Voorhis proposals had earned him some opposition in the district. During a wartime grain shortage, he had proposed the suspension of the use of grain for the manufacture of alcoholic beverages. It was as though he had proposed in 1973 to call off the Indianapolis 500 until the oil shortage eased. In the 12th District as elsewhere, patriotism often stops short at the edge of the cash drawer, and Voorhis estimates he was opposed by every tavern owner in the district. And tavern owners, unlike bank directors, spend a lot of time talking to voters.

Moreover, in a legislative initiative reminiscent of the EPIC days of Sinclair, Voorhis had proposed an amendment to the Internal Revenue Code which would have forbidden corporations to deduct advertising expenses beyond a fixed percentage of their annual profit. Since the code otherwise encouraged keeping profits low at the expense of high costs, this was not only a double blow at corporations (and tax accountants), but was seen by the newspapers in the district as an arrow pointed directly at their hearts. The result was that the always substantial anti-Voorhis sentiment of community newspapers in the district hardened into near unanimity—31 of 32, to be precise.

(By Election Day, an echo of the Voorhis proposal to cut down advertising deductions was observed in the district. Huge billboards, whose use had previously been unknown in Congressional races, appeared with the message "A Vote for Nixon is a Vote for Change." Most of the billboard space had been donated to Nixon by companies who used them the rest of the year for commercial messages, and in this way an "excessive" advertising expense—and therefore, a tax deduction —contributed to Voorhis' defeat.)

By late 1945 the Republican leaders in the district were casting about for a candidate, sensing that 1946 might be the year to knock off Voorhis. A "Committee of 100" was formed but failed to come up with anybody who looked good enough, until the head of the Bank of America in Whittier, Herman L. Perry, thought of Richard Nixon. Perry had known Nixon's grandfather (on the Milhous side) when they had served together as Whittier College trustees, and he knew Nixon to be a safe Republican. Perry called Nixon in Baltimore, where he was finishing his Navy duty by doing contract termination work, and asked him if he were interested. He was. He came to Whittier for the interview, and the Committee of 100 voted unanimously to make him the nominee.

Nixon's appearance before the committee, according to the Whittier *News* of October 3, took only ten minutes, but his remarks, as reported then, are a remarkable foreshadowing of his style. The instinct for the banal cliché did not, evidently, have to be acquired.

Nixon spoke of two different ideas about the American system. The one "advocated by the New Deal," he said, "is government control in regulating our lives. The other calls for individual freedoms and all that initiative can produce. I hold with the latter viewpoint. I believe the returning veterans—and I have talked to many of them in the foxholes—will not be satisfied with a dole or a government handout."

It should be noted that in this, his first political speech, there is also present a Nixon trait which was to grow stronger through the years, the tendency to untruth, palatably stated. There is no record of Nixon's ever having been near a foxhole during his Navy service in the rear echelons of the Pacific, nor is it likely that anyone in a foxhole would want to talk about conflicting economic philosophies.

49

By early January 1946, Nixon was campaigning; with the support of the Committee of 100 and *their* influence on the news media in the district, a victory in the Republican primary in June was assured. But there was work to be done because of California's curious primary election law.

A relic of the muscular progressivism of the early years of the century when Hiram Johnson was the reform governor, the California primary law—as with almost everything else relating to elections—was designed to minimize the influence of political parties. (The law was repealed in the early 1950s.) Each party held a primary to determine a nominee for the fall campaign. Only voters registered in a particular party could participate in that party's primary. So far, so good. But there was no such stricture against candidates, who could run in every party's primary at once, and without any indication on the ballot of which party they really belonged to.

Thus an incumbent congressman or legislator (or governor or senator) could run for his own party's nomination and for the other party's, too, and no one voting, for example, in the Democratic Party primary could tell that the candidate labeled "Congressman" was in fact a *Republican* congressman. It was a boon for incumbents, particularly Republican incumbents, since they had the overwhelming press advantage. Realistically speaking, there was not a major newspaper in the state that did not regularly endorse the Republican candidates, and they could be counted on to tell Republicans how to distinguish the candidates in the primary. In addition, the name of the incumbent, without party designation, always had the coveted top line on the ballot in *both* primaries.

So Nixon, with an easy ride to the nomination, nevertheless wanted to make a good showing in *both* primaries, and he largely succeeded. In 1944, Voorhis, running in both Republican and Democratic primaries, had picked up 60 percent of the vote; in 1946 he received only 53.5 percent, a total margin of only 7,000 votes over his largely unknown challenger.

It was a figure that did not escape Nixon's attention, and he commented on it in a letter to the GOP chairman. "All we need," he said, "is a win complex and we'll take him in November." He also urged party workers to use the line that "we were opposed by a PAC-backed candidate." It was the first use in the campaign of the PAC (Political Action Committee of the CIO) issue, and its careful placement in the letter, along with a reference to the fact that the Nixon campaign was "holding back some stuff" for the fall campaign, suggests that the PAC avalanche which was about to engulf Jerry Voorhis was not loosed accidentally.

There is another indication that the PAC issue was a carefully planned strategy, and that is the presence in the Nixon campaign of Murray Chotiner. A Los Angeles lawyer, Chotiner was mainly engaged in the campaign of Senator William Knowland for reelection in 1946, but for $500, paid by the chairman of the Committee of 100, he agreed to serve as publicity adviser and consultant to Nixon. It was a political association which lasted until Chotiner's death in 1973, and there was not a Nixon campaign in which Chotiner did not have a public or private hand.

Chotiner was then just beginning his career as a campaign strategist, but became a celebrated one. In 1955 he set out his ideas in a series of lectures at Republican meetings, and the transcripts have been circulating ever since. The gist of Chotiner's message—as it was to young candidate Nixon in 1946—was "attack." In discussion with those who say they do not want to run a negative campaign, Chotiner was withering: "They say we want to run a constructive campaign and point out the merits of our own candidate. I say to you in all sincerity that if you do not deflate the opposition candidate before your own candidate gets started, the odds are that you are going to be doomed to defeat."

Chotiner was also precise in the 1955 speech about what to do if attacked, and he took as his primer the advice he urged on Nixon in 1952, when reports of a "secret fund" nearly drove the vice-presidential nominee from the Eisenhower ticket. When your candidate is under attack, runs the Chotinerian gospel, keep quiet until all the charges are made and chewed over; you may find public interest has died down. "But if you find the attack has reached such proportion that it can no longer be avoided in any way, when you answer it, do so with an attack of your own against the opposition for having launched it in the first place." And Chotiner concluded this section, with its eerie precognition of Watergate, with a triumphant reference to the Checkers speech of 1952, in which he had played the central role. "May I suggest to you that I think the classic that will live in all political history came on September 23, 1952, from Los Angeles, California, when the candidate for Vice-President answered, if you please, with an attack on those who made one on him!"

51

Chotiner's presence in the campaign in the 12th District in 1946 may have been overkill. There is evidence enough that the young Nixon, who was later to tell an interviewer that he "had to win. That's the thing you don't understand. The important thing is to win," had enough Chotiner in him to win without the master.

Two more glancing blows at the truth began the campaign. During the primary campaign, Nixon frequently told his service club luncheon audiences about his wartime experiences and the troubles his buddies were having with the federal bureaucracy. It was a nice touch. He described the group he had commanded as a "typical melting-pot crew. There was a man from the slums of New York; one from a well-educated and socially prominent family; one from the plains of Texas; one was the son of a railroad engineer; one was a Mexican; one an Indian."

And once again, as the campaign began, the war record became enlarged, this time with a sly attack on Voorhis's manhood. Nixon, according to his campaign leaflets, was "the clean, forthright young American who fought in defense of his country in the stinking mud and jungles of the Solomons." Voorhis, on the other hand, "stayed safely behind the front in Washington." Nixon's Navy duty in the Pacific, as a full lieutenant, was in command of a group whose job was to set up landing and other supply facilities behind the combat lines. There was danger and the mud probably stank, but the rest of the description seems extreme.

The major distortion of the campaign—one which is generally credited with turning the tide in Nixon's direction—had to do with the relationship between Jerry Voorhis and the PAC. It was straight exploitation of the Communist issue, in this case rendered somewhat more loathsome by the fact that his opponent had a better anti-Communist record than he, and by the fact that the central charge ("Voorhis has been endorsed by the PAC") was not only false but, in the classic definition of fraud, known by Nixon to be false.

"Communism was not the issue at any time in the 1946 campaign," Nixon was later quoted as saying. "Few people knew about Communism then, and even fewer cared." It is hard to find a bigger and bolder lie in the entire Nixon canon. A correct statement would be—at least so far as the 12th District of California is concerned—that almost everyone knew about Communism then, and Nixon made most of them care.

It is hard, from 27 years' distance, to understand how the

political action group of a national labor organization could have had such an impact on a largely nonunionized district, but it must be remembered that the 12th District, although largely rural and small town in 1946, was still a suburb of Los Angeles, and was within the circulation area of the Los Angeles *Times,* which had by far the largest circulation within the district, despite the 32 community newspapers.

And it is safe to say that in 1946, and for at least 34 years before that, the *Times* had been the most antilabor newspaper in America. In 1912 the *Times* was bombed in the course of a labor dispute and 20 employees were killed. After that (and, for that matter, for some time before) the *Times* was ready to link organized labor with Communism with very little evidence, and from time to time with no evidence at all. "True Industrial Freedom," read the banner on the *Times* masthead, which translated very simply into "Open Shop," and Los Angeles, until some time after 1946, was a notorious open shop city.

In the case of the PAC, however, the *Times* did not have to impute Communist ties with very little evidence—there was ample evidence at every hand. The Political Action Committee (very quickly shortened to its initials) had been set up by the CIO to mobilize union support for the reelection of Roosevelt in 1944, and remained the national arm of the CIO for the election of congressmen, senators, and governors with CIO-approved records, almost all Democrats.

In Washington the Communist influence in the CIO had reached into the PAC, and in California it was dominant. The test for support and endorsement by the CIO-PAC in California had to do almost exclusively with foreign policy issues. If a candidate opposed "the continuation of wartime unity," or if he supported in any way the stiffening of U.S. policy toward Soviet expansion in Europe, he would be denied endorsement by CIO-PAC even if his labor and civil rights record was blameless.

Thus there was never any question of a Voorhis endorsement, and the Communist newspaper, *The People's World* (frequently quoted by Nixon through the campaign), went out of its way not only to attack Voorhis but to stress that, almost alone among Democratic congressmen running for reelection, he had been denied the CIO-PAC endorsement.

There was *another* PAC, and the action of a committee of one of its affiliates gave Nixon the scintilla of evidence he needed. In 1944, recognizing that the idea of a political action committee to cross ideologies and support Roosevelt was a good one and ought not be confined to labor alone, the FDR strategists caused to be created a National Citizens PAC, originally under the chairmanship of Sidney Hillman, also head of the CIO-PAC.

The NCPAC, as it quickly came to be called, was largely a letterhead group, but its endorsement was good for something, either contributions or at least a recognition factor among politically aware liberals. It had its share of Communist influence, but in Los Angeles an anti-Communist caucus within the NCPAC chapter succeeded, one evening, in getting a narrow majority for a Voorhis endorsement out of one committee, which recommendation was sent on to the national headquarters. Since the recommendation didn't even represent a majority of the local chapter, and for many of the same unworthy reasons which animated the CIO-PAC, the NCPAC didn't endorse Voorhis either.

But the tentative local committee recommendation was enough for Nixon and Chotiner, and by the end of the campaign they had parlayed it into not only a CIO-PAC endorsement, but a vote of confidence from the Politburo itself. Here is the record:

☐ After carefully explaining that "I have no personal criticism of my opponent as a man, and I do not believe that personalities should be inserted into the campaign," Nixon began his campaign on July 26 charging that Voorhis "was endorsed by the PAC and allied with the left-wing group which has taken over the Democratic Party in California."

☐ On April 24, Nixon's campaign manager said, "Now that the Political Action Committee has publicly endorsed the candidacy of Jerry Voorhis . . . American citizens who resent the efforts of a minority group to control the people's representatives have the opportunity to rally to the support of Richard Nixon." The Nixonian quality in this statement is that both Political Action Committees had formally *refused* to endorse Voorhis earlier that month, and the statement also has a nice touch of bigotry. It wasn't clear in 1946 whether "minority group" meant blacks or Jews, but in the 12th District, either would do.

☐ In early September a community newspaper ad listing the address of Nixon headquarters proclaimed, "A vote for

Nixon is a vote against the Communist-dominated PAC with its gigantic slush fund."

☐ The local newspapers picked up the line early. Barely a month after the CIO-PAC and the NCPAC had officially (and, in the *People's World*, publicly) refused to endorse Voorhis, the Alhambra *Post-Advocate* was editorializing about "radical PAC endorsements," conspicuously including Voorhis among the endorsees. (The news editor of the *Post-Advocate* was Herbert Klein, who admired Nixon in that 1946 campaign and later joined the team, remaining at his side until driven out of the inner circle by Haldeman in 1969 and, finally, out of the White House in 1973.)

☐ One week later, the South Pasadena *Review* took up the theme "Voorhis is endorsed by CIO-PAC" and went on to describe his "radical" positions. In connection with the virtual unanimity with which the community press, in practically identical language, echoed the Nixon-Chotiner theme, it might be worth noting what Chotiner, in his 1955 summation of the wisdom he had acquired in ten years in politics, had to say about the local press generally. In order to insure favorable publicity, he said, the candidate should write to every newspaper as the campaign begins, asking for their advertising rates. "It tells them we are thinking of putting an ad in the newspaper," he said (Chotiner was never one for letting an audience think things through for itself), "and it may help on some of our stories." There were a lot of ads in 1946, and it did help on the stories.

☐ In a Labor Day address in Whittier, Nixon played the PAC theme and the "I-will-not-stand-idly-by" theme. "It is a satisfaction and a privilege to accept the challenge of the PAC," he began. "I will not in the course of this campaign remain silent concerning the radical doctrines fostered by this and other extreme left-wing elements that are seeking to eliminate representation of all the people from the American form of government. I will not stand idly by in the face of the attempt being made by high-powered pressure groups to seize the people's government from the majority of the people." Later he would perfect this style only slightly, adding that "many people" had urged him to stand idly by as the "easy, popular course," but even by 1946, the gnarled prose and the claim to great political courage—which would delight a generation of satirists—were already highly developed.

☐ On September 11, Voorhis replied. He was by then aware of the extent of the effort to link him with the PAC, but true to the political habits of a lifetime, he assumed that truth would dispel the charges. It was "politics as usual," but it was up against what would soon emerge as "Nixon Politics," and truth would be an early victim. Voorhis's response, in a newspaper ad and a press release, was denial of the PAC endorsement charge. He cited an editorial attack on him in the *People's World* to the effect that "Voorhis is against unity with Communists on any issue under any circumstances." He pointed out that the CIO leadership in California was under left-wing, if not Communist, influence. And he adopted the line which was later to become a standard on the non-Communist left—that the most effective enemy of Communism is the progressive liberal who can prove by reform and social advances that the democratic system can create solutions to grave problems.

☐ In the same issue of the newspapers which carried the Voorhis ad or the press release (in obvious collusion—the papers had shown the Voorhis material to the Nixon camp) came the answer. Nixon's campaign manager was quoted as saying that "we are prepared to offer proof of [Voorhis's] endorsement by the PAC," and that the proof would be offered "at the proper time."

☐ The "proper time" turned out to be two days later, but the "proof" never did appear. On September 13, the first (and, for all practical purposes, the last) in a series of debates between Voorhis and Nixon took place at a junior high school auditorium. Voorhis spoke first and stuck to "politics as usual." He spoke of his work on the Congressional Postwar Planning Committee, he discoursed on the relationships between the legislative and executive branches, full employment bills, and foreign affairs. It was, in short, the kind of earnest political speech people had come to expect from Voorhis, who was always more professor than politician.

Nixon was in good form. He attacked rationing and "the mess in Washington," and with a bow to the *Times*, he attacked big labor leaders, particularly Harry Bridges, the longshoremen's leader whose deportation on Communist charges the *Times* had long sought and Voorhis had opposed.

Then came the event which, in hindsight, made Nixon's election a certainty. Voorhis (who knew the PAC had not only refused to endorse him but had attacked him in the *People's*

56

World as a "phony liberal") demanded that Nixon produce the "proof" of which his manager had spoken.

Nixon promptly produced a document. It was a mimeographed memorandum, for internal circulation within the local chapter, of the action by the political committee of the Los Angeles chapter of NCPAC, recommending Voorhis's endorsement by the national headquarters (a recommendation which had been rejected). Walking up to Voorhis, Nixon waved it dramatically and proclaimed it his proof.

Voorhis, who had never been told about the abortive move by his anti-Communist supporters within the local branch of NCPAC to get an endorsement, was flustered and showed it. The best he could come up with in reply, from reading the bulletin, was that it seemed to be from a different organization. He could have said, but he did not (it appears he was totally unbriefed on the event), that it was an unsuccessful attempt by an anti-Communist caucus, that he had never sought the endorsement, that he had told PAC representatives that he would refuse the endorsement if it were proffered, and that he was regularly attacked by both groups—all of which were true. But he let Nixon have the initiative and the debate victory.

Nixon seized his advantage. He read from lists of the national officers of CIO-PAC and NCPAC, selecting only those CIO officials who were on the board of both, ignoring the majority who were not, in an effort to lump them all together, including the local chapter.

☐ Within a short time the advantage of the debate was exploited, but in a typically Nixonian way. "The Truth Comes Out. Voorhis Admits PAC Endorsement," began an ad put out by the Nixon headquarters one week later. It went on to claim Voorhis's admission that he had been endorsed by the "National Political Action Committee" and that he had not repudiated it. The ad even quoted an article in the *People's World* as proof of Voorhis's endorsement, although anyone who read the article in full would see that opposite Voorhis's name, on a list of candidates endorsed by a number of organizations, were the magic words, "No CIO Endorsement." The ad wound up with a tentative entry into the "numbers game" Joe McCarthy was to dominate a few years later: "Forty bills backed by the PAC have been considered by Congress during the past four years. Voorhis voted against the PAC only four times!"

That ad, under any analysis, offers the quintessential Nixon,

57

although it would not be apparent for some years. It combines flat lies (the PAC endorsement), half-truths (Voorhis was *mentioned* in the *People's World* article), and what might be called half-lies (facts that require some research to disprove; in this case the "forty" votes turned out to be twenty-seven).

☐ Within a week, by mid-September, Nixon was back on the attack. In a speech in Pomona, he warmed up with a discussion of "those walking in high official places who would destroy our constitutional principles through socialization of American free institutions," and moved on to those "who would lead us into a disastrous foreign policy whereby we would be guilty of collusion with other nations in depriving people of smaller nations of the very freedoms guaranteed ourselves by our Constitution." Then he got to the point: "The American people are faced witth the choice between two philosophies of government. One of these, supported by the radical PAC and its adherents, would deprive the people of liberty through regimentation; the other would return the government to the people under constitutional guarantees, and needless to say, that is the philosophy for which I will fight in Congress."

☐ By October the attack on "radicals" had been stepped up. On October 11, Nixon told campaign workers in a pep rally that "the Communist-dominated Political Action Committee has opened campaign offices right here in our district [the CIO had opened a small organizing office in the one semi-industrialized community in the 12th District]. As you all know, this organization has endorsed my opponent. While I welcome the opposition of this radical group, I have to warn you that they have a huge slush fund to spend freely." Campaign spending requirements in 1946 were lax, as were reporting laws, but no one doubts that Nixon outspent Voorhis —not counting time and space "donated" by business allies— at least three or four to one.

☐ Voorhis's response was ill-advised. A few days after the first debate, he sent a telegram to the national headquarters of the NCPAC—which had never endorsed him, anyway—and asked them not to do so, even though the Los Angeles chapter's political committee had recommended it. He gave as his reason, which was certainly true, that the NCPAC supported a foreign policy he opposed. He sent copies of the telegram to the newspapers, which treated the telegram as an attempt to get out of an endorsement already made and accused Voorhis of trimming for reasons of expediency.

☐ At the next debate, on October 23, Voorhis, still under the impression that the contest was one concerning issues, one in which the truth might be decisive, challenged Nixon for the evidence to support the charge that he had opposed the PAC on only four out of forty votes. The issue had become acute, since five days before all the community papers had carried a Nixon ad which alleged that Voorhis had opposed PAC on only three of forty-six votes.

Nixon cited both the CIO *Labor Herald*, the union's house organ, and a voters' supplement prepared by the *New Republic* magazine. Typically, Voorhis stayed up all night checking the documents. He learned a lesson in how Richard Nixon campaigns, but it was too late. First of all, there was no PAC list of votes at all—it had no list of issues by which it judged congressmen (the reason probably being that the current attitude toward the Soviet Union was the real litmus). The Nixon list had been compiled by the *New Republic* staff and the Union for Democratic Action, a strongly anti-Communist liberal group whose leadership later was to provide the nucleus of Americans for Democratic Action. In addition, the Nixon people had overlapped the votes, using duplicates from the lists to reach the total of forty (or forty-six). There were, in fact, only twenty-seven separate votes.

Furthermore, the list of "PAC votes" included, for example, reciprocal trade agreements, a loan to Britain (opposed strongly by PAC), unemployment insurance for federal employees, civilian control of atomic energy, repeal of the poll tax, and the school lunch program. None of these could be called part of a plot for a Communist take-over of America, and Nixon favored all of them anyway.

Finally, the citation of the CIO *Labor Herald* was pure Nixon. The paper carried the *New Republic* summary in the issue Nixon had cited. It also listed the Congressional districts and boldly stated, "12th District—Jerry Voorhis—No Endorsement."

☐ Voorhis's answer to this was too little, too dignified, and too late. With a week to go in the campaign, he put out a long press release, a handbill, and a newspaper ad, analyzing the votes and describing his legislative record in some detail. As a news story, it got buried, and without the volunteer help the

CIO-PAC provided its *endorsed* candidates, the handbill did not get wide distribution.

☐ Nixon went on to tell an audience in October that it was "too late for Voorhis to repudiate his PAC endorsement," and that he had earned it by consistently voting the PAC line. "I do not question the motives of my opponent in voting the PAC line in Congress," he said, as he would later generously concede the right of antiwar protestors to demonstrate, even as he was ordering their removal. "As for me, I welcome the opposition of the PAC."

☐ Some measure of the "news" treatment accorded the campaign can be seen in an October article in the Monrovia *News-Post.* "Pro-Russian Votes Alleged," read the headline. The news story began: "Campaign statements that Jerry Voorhis is not pro-Russian were placed in serious doubt today by a check of the official Congressional Record [as opposed, one imagines, to the *unofficial* Congressional Record] by the Republican National Committee. Sympathy for Russia and for left-wing programs in the United States is revealed in six votes by Voorhis, the record showed."

☐ The Copley newspapers ran strong anti-Voorhis editorials, many of which later appeared in other newspapers in the district as news items. On October 8, long after it had been established that Voorhis did not have the CIO endorsement, the Alhambra and Monrovia papers carried the editorial question: "Why Does CIO Back Voorhis?" This was followed in the week before Election Day by an editorial entitled "How Jerry and Vito Voted." It compared Voorhis's votes with those of Representative Vito Marcantonio, the only member of the American Labor Party in Congress. Marcantonio regularly voted with the Democrats, except on foreign policy issues affecting the Soviet Union, when he did in fact follow the Communist line. The comparison was not very apt because "Vito and Jerry" differed on almost all foreign policy issues, but it is important as the first use of a technique that was to destroy Helen Gahagan Douglas four years later. Chotiner later claimed credit for the idea, although there were no serious contenders for the claim.

☐ The final press release was right on target. The newspapers carried their closing Nixon campaign news a few days before the election. This time it was an endorsement by Buron Fitts, a recent district attorney in Los Angeles County (which included all the 12th District), who attacked Voorhis for "consistently voting the Moscow-PAC-Henry Wallace line in Congress." Fitts also commented scornfully on the "insolence of Moscow in telling the American voter to elect PAC candidates, such as Mr. Voorhis."

In the final few days, Democratic voters throughout the district received anonymous phone calls. The caller would ask only, "Did you know Jerry Voorhis was a Communist?" The calls were widespread, and there is no doubt that they were made. The only question is whether they were the work of the Nixon organization. Nixon's managers flatly deny it. A Voorhis supporter, Mrs. Zita Remley, recalls that her niece responed to an advertisement for paid workers and went to the Republican headquarters to work (the job paid $9 per day). She reports that her niece went to work on a phone bank where her job was to call a number and ask the question, "Did you know Jerry Voorhis was a Communist?" Unfortunately, Mrs. Remley's niece has since died and thus direct evidence is once-removed. Earl Mazo, a sympathetic Nixon biographer to say the least, suggests in a sort of precursor of the Watergate defense that perhaps the calls were made in order to make Nixon seem guilty of vicious tactics.

Nixon won with better than 56 percent of the vote, giving rise to the possibility that he might have won without fraud. After all, 1946 saw the election of a Republican Congress, and in California four Democrats went down with Voorhis. A free election, at least, would have been closer.

The 1948 election is not often given much attention in histories of Richard Nixon's political career, but in restrospect, it appears to be the hinge. After the 1946 election, in which the national trends made it seem as though Nixon would have defeated Jerry Voorhis in a free and fair contest, the problem became reelection. Nixon had his eye on the Democratic Senate seat of ailing Senator Sheridan Downey in 1950. All that remained was reelection to Congress in 1948.

Even for a California congressman that was not easy. Cross-filing gave an incumbent an enormous advantage, as we have seen. It permitted him to seek the other party's nomination as well as his own, while concealing his true party affiliation. It entitled him to do so under the label of "congressman" at the top of the ballot. Proof of the incumbent's edge lay in the fact that of all California's congressmen in 1946, more than one-half had won both major party nominations in the primaries. Earl Warren won both the Republican and Democratic nominations for governor.

The problem for Nixon in 1948 was not the general election, which he wanted to avoid, but the Democratic primary race. So Richard Nixon became nonpartisan for two years. His press releases during his first term in Congress never once identified him as a Republican, and he attended the GOP convention in 1948, not as a delegate, but as a spectator in the gallery.

The newspapers in the 12th District were only too willing to cooperate. For those two years, they carried extensive news stories about the Congressman, but never identified him as a Republican. And Nixon's big break came when Jerry Voorhis, who had moved to Chicago as the executive director of the Cooperative League, declined—after much urging from the Democrats in the 12th District—to return to run again for the seat.

After a vain search for a "name" candidate to oppose Nixon and perhaps capture enough name recognition to win the Democratic primary, the Democrats at the last minute turned to Stephen Zetterberg, an attorney who had been the chairman of the "search" committee.

Zetterberg had little financial support, and this time, ironically, the CIO-PAC elements which so strongly opposed Jerry Voorhis had formed their own party. The Independent Progressive Party had qualified for the ballot as a vehicle for the national candidacy of Henry Wallace, and in California it was squarely in the control of those who wished to punish any Democrat who had supported the Truman foreign policy.

The result was that Zetterberg lost votes in the Democratic primary to Nixon on his right and to the IPP candidate on his left. It was to prove fatal, but not without a struggle. Nixon conducted a district-wide mailing to registered Democrats, with a postcard addressed to "Fellow Democrats." The salutation appeared directly next to a large picture of Nixon, captioned "Congressman Richard M. Nixon. He Gets Things Done!"

Nowhere on the postcard—and nowhere on the Democratic primary ballot—was it indicated that the congressman "Who Gets Things Done" was a Republican. The card had some reassuring words about able and progressive representation, and down at the bottom, in small type, was the message, "Democrats for Nixon, J. R. Blue, chairman."

On Election Day, Nixon won the Democratic primary with

slightly over 50 percent of the vote. The IPP candidate sliced off nearly 4,000 votes which would otherwise have gone to Zetterberg. The postcard clearly made the difference.

Had Zetterberg won that primary and forced Nixon into a straight Republican-Democratic contest in November, it is likely Nixon's career would have ended then. The election statistics show that this was the likely result. Harry Truman gained strength through the fall campaign and defeated Thomas E. Dewey in California (despite 250,000 votes for Henry Wallace on the Independent Progressive line). In California as in the rest of the country, the Democrats gained in the House of Representatives, and a sizable number of Republicans elected in the GOP sweep of 1946 became one-term congressmen.

In January 1957, according to the able and accurate *New Republic* reporter Richard Stout (known professionally in the magazine as TRB), Vice-President Richard Nixon gave an interview to visiting British publisher David Astor and his Washington correspondent. The interview went well (it was a time for the emergence of one of the New Nixon images), and Astor finally asked the Vice-President how he could have carried on the smear campaign which elected him to the Senate in 1950 against Helen Gahagan Douglas? Nixon cast down his eyes, apologized for the episode, and said, "I want you to understand I was a very young man."

The Voorhis and Zetterberg campaigns behind him, Nixon was a "very young man" of 37 when he began in 1950 to campaign for the California Senate seat. It was a race he had had in mind since his 1948 reelection. Nixon was shrewd enough to know that he was not cut out for the House road to power —seniority and noncontroversy—and if he did not run for the Senate in 1950, he might have to wait a long time. The seat was Democratic, but marginal, and the other senator was Republican William F. Knowland, a healthy man who enjoyed the Senate.

The sitting senator was Sheridan Downey, a former populist who, like Jerry Voorhis, had come into elective politics with Upton Sinclair, but unlike Voorhis, had rapidly moved to the right. Elected to the Senate when Culbert Olsen was elected governor in 1938 and reelected in 1944, with the help of FDR, Downey had become by 1950 a reliable spokesman for the large oil and agribusiness interests in his state. But his health was failing, and he had never enjoyed the Senate. When liberal Congresswoman Helen Gahagan Douglas announced in 1949 her intention to challenge Downey in the Democratic primary, the senior senator hesitated briefly and then announced his retirement. He stayed in the Senate through 1950, directly and indirectly announcing his opposition to Douglas. After Nixon's election in November, Downey resigned in order to give his successor an edge in seniority and to get an early start on his new vocation as a lobbyist for the oil industry.

By 1949, Congressman Nixon was moving onto a wider stage than that offered by the 12th District. As a member of the House Committee on Un-American Activities (now the Internal Security Committee), Nixon had played the leading role in arranging the confrontation between Alger Hiss and Whittaker Chambers. It resulted in Hiss's conviction for perjury for denying he had given secret documents to Chambers for transmittal to the Soviet Union, and the case gave Nixon nationwide publicity and a reputation in his party as a leading anti-Communist.

In July 1949, after Hiss had been freed at his first trial by a hopelessly hung jury, Nixon suggested that the trial judge, Samuel Kauffman, be investigated. Nixon based his grounds on "fitness," but the implications were obvious. No investigation resulted. Two statements Nixon made during that period are interesting in light of his new-found constitutional principles now that Watergate is lapping at his shoes.

☐ On January 19, 1949, Nixon attacked Attorney General Tom C. Clark for Clark's proposal to legalize wiretapping to combat espionage. It was, Nixon told a Dartmouth College audience, "far too drastic." Twenty years later he attacked Clark's son, Attorney General Ramsey Clark, for opposing wiretapping in domestic security cases as "permissive" and "soft-headed." It would then be asserted in Nixon's name, without his objection, that the President had the right to wiretap anyone and even, for that matter, to order a burglary.

☐ On March 29, 1950, brushing aside President Truman's claims of "executive privilege," Nixon strongly attacked Truman's refusal to turn over State Department files to a Senate committee, files which Nixon alleged might have demonstrated the extent of subversive penetration of the department.

The contest between Nixon and Douglas was widely advertised in early 1950 as a classic confrontation between two representatives with sharply divergent voting records. Douglas, an

64

actress and operatic singer who had come into politics as a protégée of Eleanor Roosevelt, had served three terms in Congress and was no amateur in Democratic politics. She had served in important policy positions and had wide backing among Democrats, particularly in the congressional delegation and in the party's predominantly liberal wing.

Helen Douglas had made up her mind to challenge Sheridan Downey more than a year before the senator gave up the race. She held the belief, and kept it to the end, that an election campaign should be, at least in large part, an educational experience, and she was strongly opposed to Downey's positions on two issues of importance to California. She was right on both issues, but her concentration on them, in a real sense, cost her the election.

Nixon, in keeping with national Republican policy, concentrated on only one issue—was his opponent a Red? Douglas was not a Red, just as Jerry Voorhis had not been endorsed by the PAC, but the result was the same. A close contest through the primary—with Douglas running against Nixon and Nixon running against Hiss—turned into an uneven struggle with the start of the Korean War in June and into a rout when the Chinese entered Korea in force in September.

Helen Douglas's issues were crucial, but were never debated. In the first place, Nixon did not want to debate them; in the second place, nobody in California really cared about them. The first issue was difficult to explain at best; it involved the conflicting claims of California and the federal government to oil rights in the so-called Tidelands off the Pacific Coast (always called the "oil-rich" Tidelands, an adjective they have now yielded to Kuwait).

The issue with respect to the Tidelands had been made "perfectly clear" for a decade. The press without exception, the business community, the professional spokesmen, and every politician of both parties, except Douglas and Voorhis, put the matter on a basis of state patriotism—the oil is in California, it should remain in California. The real issue, of course, was much more complex. Boiled down, it was whether the private oil companies would be dealing with state and local governments to obtain drilling licenses, or whether they would be dealing with the feds. The feds, for a quarter of a century, had meant FDR's secretary of the interior, Harold Ickes, so the oil companies opted for states' rights—and so did their clients throughout the state's Establishment.

So in 1950 the people of California would have voted overwhelmingly for state control, and although Downey shirked the race, it is not at all clear that Douglas could have prevailed, at least on the Tidelands issue.

The other issue was even more abstruse. It involved Douglas's defense of, and Senator Downey's attack on, an old law which limited to 160 acres the amount of land any one person could own and still be entitled to water generated by federal reclamation projects. Downey, and later Nixon, were out-and-out spokesmen for the large landowners—mainly corporations —who needed federal water and who owned not hundreds of acres, but hundreds of thousand of acres.

On this issue also Douglas stood alone among California politicians. It was a good populist issue, one which had turned the state progressive in the time of Hiram Johnson, but industrial development and rising expectations had made Douglas's side of the issue unpopular. Even among small landowners, for whom the reclamation water was intended and for whom the acreage limitation would have guaranteed a supply, there was no great support for the Douglas position. The reason undoubtedly was that most of them had in mind the day when *they* would have thousands of acres and would want them irrigated.

(This reaction found an echo in the McGovern campaign of 1972. The Democratic candidate, in the best populist tradition, had attacked the inadequacy of estate taxation and had deplored the piling up of great fortunes by the accident of inheritance. He proposed a limit on inheritance of $500,000 per child and ran into a buzzsaw of opposition. Not from the wealthy alone, although their reaction was predictably shrill, but from ordinary working folk who saw, or thought they saw, the day when they too would have estates valued at more than half a million dollars per child.)

Finally, Douglas's two issues roused little excitement in the cities, where the votes were. In Los Angeles, San Francisco, and Alameda Counties lived fully three-quarters of the state's voters, and in none of them was the acreage limitation even faintly an issue, and in all of them state control of Tidelands was as much a part of Californianism as orange juice, real estate, and the private automobile.

The result was that Douglas, although *intellectually* aware of Nixon's penchant for red-baiting and having a full knowledge of the Voorhis campaign, was totally unprepared *polit-*

ically for the fury of the assault on her patriotism which began once the primary was past and Nixon and his politics were her only opponents.

The primary campaign was not without incident. Downey had withdrawn, but not until he and his supporters among the conservative Democrats had appointed a candidate to oppose Douglas. He was Manchester Boddy, a Los Angeles publisher, whose *Daily News* had been the only occasionally Democratic major city newspaper in the entire state. Boddy was a curious candidate. He had no previous political experience of any kind. A vain, pompous man, his platform manner was diffident when it was not absurd. He affected a Colonel Blimp-type mustache and, indeed, an English manner generally. Even the first three letters of his first name were a self-Anglicizing effort, he having been born plain Chester Boddy.

Boddy carried the anti-Douglas colors in the Democratic primary, and when he was not droning his own incomprehensible philosophy of politics as history, he denounced Douglas as the candidate of the "red-hots" in the Democratic Party. His integrity in this effort, as well as his stout defense of California's right to the oil-rich Tidelands, came under question three years later. It was revealed that the Hearst Corporation, which published a rival newspaper in Los Angeles, paid Boddy $250,000 per year for an option to buy his *Daily News*. It was also revealed that Boddy was indebted for $2 million to various private oil interests. But, to paraphrase Christopher Marlowe, "that was in another country and, besides the wench was [at least politically] dead."

Douglas beat Boddy handily in the Democratic primary and polled nearly as many votes in both primaries as Nixon. In two other memorable results that Primary Day in 1950, James Roosevelt (then as now inflexibly described as "the eldest son of the late President") barely won the Democratic gubernatorial primary race against Governor Earl Warren, who entered both primaries, and I squeaked by a Republican incumbent to win the Democratic nomination in my state legislative district. I was ready to campaign with Helen Douglas on all the issues, but the only one that mattered turned out to be Murray Chotiner's old friend, Vito Marcantonio.

If Vito Marcantonio had not existed in the late 1940s and early 1950s, Richard Nixon (or, more properly, Murray Chotiner) would have had to invent him. A fiery speaker who seemed to share the common concerns of the largely working-class citizens of his East Harlem district (once represented by Fiorello LaGuardia), Marcantonio came to Congress as a Republican, later ran as a member of the American Labor Party, and once captured the GOP, Democratic, and ALP nominations.

If not a Communist (and no one ever seriously denied it), he was, as the saying goes, "cheating the Party out of its dues." In his time in the House, he followed every twist and turn of the Party line, with the result that in the postwar years he voted fairly consistently with the Democrats on domestic issues (price control, public housing, civil rights, health insurance) and with the Republicans on foreign policy issues (British loan, Marshall Plan, aid to Korea, NATO). The dominant Republican line at that time was still largely "isolationist" and therefore against foreign alliances or aid, even if they were explicitly anti-Communist.

Since domestic issues far outnumbered foreign issues, and since on some of the foreign issues the dominant administration view coincided with the Soviet line (support for the U.N., refugee relief, etc.), Marcantonio more often agreed with the Democrats than the Republicans. Futhermore (and worse, for Helen Douglas), he took the civil libertarian line with respect, for example, to witnesses cited for contempt before various un-American Activities panels—at least when the witnesses were accused of pro-Communist activities, which was most of the time. (Marcantonio had very little time for civil liberties for Klansmen or alleged neo-Nazis, but then, neither did the Un-American Activities Committee.)

The result was that Marcantonio—a "liberal" at home but an "isolationist" abroad—found himself far more often on Douglas's side of a House vote than on Richard Nixon's. By the time the campaign was over, California voters had an image—cultivated almost daily by Nixon and his aides—of Marcantonio and Douglas as a sort of two-member axis in the House, determined to flood the nation with Soviet spies while depriving it of the ability to defend itself against an expected Russian strike.

I have deliberately cast the Nixon argument in the extreme, absurd form in which it was presented. The tragedy was not only that no one laughed at the ludicrousness of the charges Nixon was to raise, but that few were offended at their crudity and vulgarity. As the election results demonstrated, not enough of the people saw the baseness and falsehoods upon which the Nixon campaign was wholly based. Here is the record:

☐ Ten days before the "official kickoff" of the Nixon campaign, a reliable Hearst political columnist, George Rothwell Brown, tipped the Nixon strategy. "Helen Gahagan Douglas," he wrote, "has generally been found voting in the House of Representatives with Vito Marcantonio." The "found voting" is a nice touch; obviously, it is more sinister to be "found voting" than merely to have voted.

☐ On August 30, Nixon's southern California chairman, Bernard Brennan, sounded the charge in the first campaign press release from Nixon headquarters. Brennan cited Douglas's "soft attitude toward Communism" and brought up for the first time in the campaign a tentative magic number—353. "On 353 times," said the statement, "the actress-candidate voted exactly the same as Vito Marcantonio, the notorious Communist party-line congressman from New York."

Brennan purported to be concerned that Douglas "has been cast by her supporters in a new role of foe of Communism." (She had stressed her leadership in fighting for the Marshall Plan and mutual aid treaties with, among others, Korea.) Brennan called Douglas "the pink lady" and described her and Marcantonio as "heroes" of the Communist movement.

(Brennan's concern was not self-motivated. Disturbed by Douglas's emphasis on her role in making foreign policy as a member of the Foreign Affairs Committee—in which she played a leading role in what were essentially anti-Soviet legislative initiatives—Chotiner had sent a memo to all campaign chairmen, including Brennan: "Helen Douglas is trying to portray a new role as a foe of Communism. Do not let her get away with it! It is a phony act.")

☐ Chotiner's role in all this is interesting. In the memo quoted above and in many others, he clearly laid down the line of the campaign: Helen Douglas was the "pink lady." A "pink sheet" explaining her "Communist" connections was distributed to thousands of voters. Richard Nixon developed this theme in virtually every speech. And in those speeches, Nixon began in that now-familiar "look-how-lonely-and-courageous-I-am" litany, "I have been advised not to talk about Communism, but I am going to tell the people of California the truth." No one ever asked him just who it was who was advising him to lay off Communism and eschew "the truth." Not Chotiner, that's for sure.

Nixon, whatever the advice, talked about nothing but Communism throughout the campaign. He received the enthusiastic support of every major newspaper in the state (all traditionally Republican) and 90 percent of the minor papers. He got the coverage he wanted.

☐ On September 9, in San Diego, Nixon stated that "if she [Douglas] had her way, the Communist conspiracy would never have been exposed, and Alger Hiss would still be influencing the foreign policy of the United States." Douglas, of course, had nothing to do with the Hiss case, and Hiss, who never influenced foreign policy anyway, had left the government long before Nixon ever heard of him.

☐ On September 19 he made it clear there would be "no name-calling in this campaign." Having made that perfectly clear, Nixon went on, "It just so happens that my opponent is a member of a group which joins the notorious party-liner, Vito Marcantonio of New York, in voting time after time against measures that are for the security of this country."

☐ On September 20, Nixon asked of Douglas, "Why has she followed the Communist line so many times?"

☐ On November 1, Nixon repeated an earlier charge, credited to Senator Downey, that Douglas "gave comfort to Soviet tyranny." Once again, he went off on the "what if she had her way?" theme, and this time came up with the thought that there would be no draft, Greece and Turkey would have "gone Communist," there would be no Committee on Un-American Activities, no "exposure of traitorous conduct" (none was ever exposed, as it turned out), and no Communist registration. This last was a reference to the remains of what once had been called the Mundt–Nixon Bill, Nixon's only legislative initiative. The parts of this bill that required registration of Communists and Communist groups survived as a section of the McCarran Act. The Nixon portion was patently unconstitutional, as Douglas had pointed out when she voted against it; the Supreme Court agreed, and no one ever registered.

The argument on Greece and Turkey represented a clear conflict between the two candidates, but Nixon never debated it in those terms. Douglas had opposed Truman's proposal for military aid to Greece and Turkey, to replace the retiring British, because she wanted more safeguards for the people against their governments and because she wanted economic aid included. She had been roundly denounced by U.S. Communists for supporting any aid at all.

70

☐ On October 2, Nixon, back on the Marcantonio theme, put the coincidence of the Douglas–Marcantonio vote axis at the level of 354, explaining "we stopped when the total reached 354." What he meant was that only by including every single vote on every noncontroversial domestic issue in the House could Chotiner's researchers get to 354.

☐ On October 7, Nixon demanded that Douglas state her "position on American foreign policy without pussyfooting, double-talk, or evasiveness." (What ever happened to "fear or favor"?) Then he went on to identify his opponent with Yalta and "our State Department's policy in the Far East." After a routine statement that "recognition of Communist China and her admission to the United Nations would be a tragic betrayal of the men who have fought and died in Korea," Nixon asked Douglas to state "without equivocation whether she stands with Owen Lattimore and Dean Acheson or with General Douglas MacArthur."

☐ I cite so many of these attacks if for no other reason than to show the intensity of the rhetoric. Throughout the campaign, the juxtaposition of Helen Douglas and Communism came almost daily—and more than once daily in cities with both morning and afternoon newspapers, such as Los Angeles and San Francisco. "Mrs. Douglas has a record that Communists applaud." "Mrs. Douglas has voted with Marcantonio, the Communist-line Congressman, and against the leadership of the Democratic Party on measures involving the national security." "On no occasion has Nixon ever cast a vote that would give aid and comfort to the Communists." "Helen Douglas votes with a small clique which has regularly voted with the Communist party-liner Vito Marcantonio." These and more rolled out from various surrogates, and were reported in full and echoed in editorials in the newspapers.

☐ The position of the press in this campaign must also be mentioned. The *Los Angeles Times*, on October 30, carried a straight news story that the Nixon campaign needed volunteers. Under the headline, "Flying Squadron Needs Help," the paper reported that the chairwoman of a group of volunteer women for Nixon needed workers to help get out the vote on Election Day. "This is the group," the *news story* ran, "that did such a good job in the primary and they want to repeat it and keep left-wing Helen Gahagan Douglas out of the Senate." The article went on to give the address and

71

phone numbers of thirteen regional branch headquarters where those interested might report.

☐ On October 16, the *Times* reported a paid Republican campaign radio program as a straight news story, calling a discussion of how Nixon would make a great senator, and of the 354 times Douglas had voted with Vito Marcantonio, a "review of the issues." The participants were all Republican party officials. The news article wound up with a listing of the main address and phone number of the Nixon headquarters, and the name of the person taking volunteer applications.

☐ A lead story in an April issue of the *Times* reported that civic leaders had endorsed Nixon as the "only savior of the Tidelands." The foremost "civic leader" the *Times* could find was Jack Drown, a well-known neighbor and close friend of Nixon from the early days in Whittier. It was an arrogant move by the *Times*; there was no dearth of real civic leaders in California who were available to endorse Nixon on the Tidelands issue. The use of Jack Drown as a "civic leader" in this case resembles the CREP's sloppy work in 1972 when a fake "citizen's committee" was formed by the Nixon campaign to support—in a *New York Times* ad—the mining of Haiphong harbor. The best Charles Colson could do for a chairman was the wife of one of the admen who wrote the copy.

☐ A cartoon in the San Francisco *Examiner* (a Hearst paper; the identical cartoon probably appeared as well in the Los Angeles *Examiner*) on November 3 is not an excessive example. The cartoon, entitled "Rough on Rats," shows Nixon resolutely standing guard with a shotgun in front of a walled farm. His sleeves are rolled up, and in addition to the shotgun, he carries a net labeled "Communist Control." Uncle Sam is farming contentedly behind the wall, while rats (labeled variously "Appeaser," "Professional Pacifist," "Conspirator," "Spy," "Soviet Sympathizer," and "Propagandist") run about. Hearst cartoons and editorials in those days left very little to the imagination. The editorial under this cartoon, for example, accuses Douglas of favoring "reckless government spending" and "giving away atomic bomb secrets" and of opposing military assistance programs, Selective Service, the Communist Control Act (truth, for a moment, intruded), and "weeding out poor security risks."

It is hard to calculate now the effect in 1950 of accusations that a candidate for the Senate—at the time a congresswoman —favored giving away atom bomb secrets, because it is doubtful that even Nixon would countenance such an attack in today's climate. But "at that point in time" it was devastating, and it must be remembered that this drumfire of accusations of near-treason was a daily fact to newspaper readers throughout the state.

There was a pro-Douglas press, but it was small and inconsequential and included no big-city daily. One of the Democratic newspapers, a weekly law journal called the *Independent Review*, coined a phrase in 1950 and it stuck. In an editorial on September 29, the *Review* charged a conspiracy against Helen Douglas "by falsely accusing her through infamous insinuations and whispered innuendo of being a Communist." The insinuations and innuendos, the paper said, are being spread by "representatives of her senatorial opponent, Tricky Dick Nixon."

Douglas was never able to regain the offensive. The "pink sheet" broke into the news regularly, and the facts about the "Douglas–Marcantonio axis" could never be properly explained in the heat of a campaign. The niceties of politics in the House of Representatives are hard enough to master when one's livelihood depends upon it. To expect voters to understand them in a 3-minute campaign speech reference is too much.

In vain did Douglas and her surrogates—I was proud to be among them—memorize and explain the statistics. Nixon himself had voted with Marcantonio 112 times in the four years he served in the House. That ratio of 112 Nixon votes to 354 Douglas votes was roughly the ratio of foreign policy votes to domestic policy votes, and Republicans, being generally more "isolationist," often voted with Marcantonio against foreign aid, military assistance and, mutual security, but for different reasons. It never got across to the voters.

When Douglas's advisers went on the attack, it was worse than useless—it was counterproductive. "YOU pick the Congressman the Kremlin loves!" began a Douglas leaflet, pointing out (correctly, but uselessly) that it was *Nixon* who had voted with Marcantonio on key military and foreign aid issues, including opposition to military support for South Korea. Nixon called it "a smear," and so did his surrogates, but they didn't have to say anything. If there was anything the voters of California were conditioned to disbelieve in 1950, it was that Richard Nixon had ever done anything which could possibly have helped Communists or made them feel good.

Chotiner saw at once the disaster for Douglas in attacking Nixon as "soft on the Soviet Union." "She made the fatal mistake," he said later, "of attacking our strength instead of sticking to attacking our weaknesses."

Douglas brought top Truman administration officials into the state—Averell Harriman, to talk about her help in programs to strengthen European resistance to Soviet expansion, and Attorney General J. Howard McGrath, to scoff at Nixon's record in exposing domestic saboteurs—but they got scant coverage.

Nixon brought Joe McCarthy into California for one appearance, and McCarthy fit right into the campaign. He gave a speech in Los Angeles, over regional radio, about the "blunders and traitorous acts of the crowd whom the Democrat candidates have pledged to protect if they are elected." "The chips are down," said McCarthy in Nixon's support, "between the American people and the Administration Commicrat Party of betrayal."

Nixon was never able to win the support of his running mate, Republican Governor Earl Warren. Warren had always run more or less of a lone wolf campaign, and he had let it be known that this applied particularly strongly where Richard Nixon was involved. He steadfastly refused to be drawn into expressing a preference in the Senate race.

Chotiner was determined to get Warren on the record for Nixon. Consequently, he sent squads of hecklers to Douglas's meetings, to ask her in the question period if *she* supported James Roosevelt (Warren's opponent) for governor. Douglas, somewhat of a lone wolf herself and mindful that win or lose, she would run ahead of Roosevelt, always replied only that she was a Democrat and running on the Democratic ticket.

On the last weekend before the election the hecklers became too much, and she snapped back that indeed she was supporting Roosevelt. That was enough for Chotiner, who arranged for the reply to get to Warren immediately. The governor went further than he ever had, and noted that Roosevelt was Douglas's candidate. "I'm sure," said Warren, "the voters of California will know who my candidate is for the Senate." Chotiner took it and ran, treating it as a Warren endorsement of Nixon. It seemed to be, but my own hunch—and that of many other Californians—has always been that Earl Warren voted for Helen Douglas. For what it may be worth, I voted for Warren.

Nixon had other help, some solicited and some rejected. He publicly rejected (after considerable prompting) the gutter campaign of professional anti-Semites Gerald L. K. Smith and Wesley Swift. Both were going full steam in Los Angeles ("Help Richard Nixon get rid of the Jew-Communists"), but a substantial telephone campaign (similar to the one against Jerry Voorhis four years earlier) went on for the final weeks of the campaign, stressing that Douglas's husband Melvyn, the noted actor, had begun life with the name Hesselberg.

Meanwhile, the Archbishop of Los Angeles, J. Francis A. McIntyre, was leaving nothing to chance. Aware that 75 percent of the Catholic population of voting age in California was registered in the Democratic Party, McIntyre ordered, in an official letter to all parish priests, that the four Sunday sermons in October be devoted to the evils of Communism. The Archbishop also instructed that special attention be paid to the fact that "Communists have infiltrated into high government positions."

Priests were instructed to mention no names from the altar, but they were given a list of candidates the Archbishop desired defeated in the election. Many priests stayed barely within the letter of these instructions by including in their sermon about Communism the statement that the woman running for high office should be defeated.

Catholic laymen, led by local lawyer Richard Rogan, formed a Catholic committee for Douglas and distributed leaflets to churchgoers with the records of the candidates on issues of Catholic interest. In the weeks after the election, Rogan wrote to a church official, deploring the virtual official endorsement efforts of the Archbishop. "I favor keeping the Church out of politics," Rogan wrote. "California is not France and Archbishop McIntyre is not Richelieu." Twenty years later he might have drawn a more apt parallel between Richard Nixon and Louis XIV.

In the final days of the campaign, the Los Angeles *Times* laid it on the line in an editorial. California, said the paper, "was the only state where Communism becomes a main issue." And then it went on to describe Representative Douglas as "a glamorous actress who, though not a Communist, voted the Communist Party line in Congress innumerable times," and wound up calling her "the darling of the Hollywood parlor pinks and Reds."

When the votes were counted, Nixon had won with 56 percent, running behind Earl Warren but ahead of the Republican Congressional slate. It was a substantial victory, but it was the last time Nixon would rely solely on a fraudulent description of his opponent's record. The use of secret campaign funds and the manipulation of the electoral process itself became from then on the major elements of the fully formed Nixon Politics.

In 1952, Richard Nixon was nominated by the Republicans to run for Vice-President with Dwight Eisenhower, and the ticket was elected by a substantial margin. There are two aspects of Nixon's participation in that campaign—one dealing with his road to the nomination, the other with a disclosure of a secret "Nixon fund" during the campaign—that require close examination if we are to trace fully the road to Watergate.

The contest in 1952 for the Republican nomination is remembered now as a battle between General Eisenhower and Senator Robert A. Taft of Ohio. But before the convention, some people felt there was a third alternative. To Earl Warren at least, halfway through his third term as governor of California, the possibility of a Taft–Eisenhower deadlock and his own nomination seemed a very real possibility. To that end, Warren formed a California delegation pledged to him and won the primary against a strong challenge from a right-wing group nominally pledged to conservative Congressman Thomas Werdel.

The Warren delegation, which would cast 70 votes at the convention, contained every leader of the party throughout the state, including the two Republican Senators, William Knowland and Richard Nixon. Nixon had been approached by the anti-Warren forces that later coalesced around Werdel, but he turned them down and accepted a place on the governor's delegation.

The decision turned out to be a wise one. Nixon was able— by ignoring his pledge to Warren—to manipulate the California situation in such a way as virtually to guarantee Eisenhower's nomination—and his own. Those who have studied the events leading up to the convention can adduce evidence that Nixon had been offered—and had accepted—the nomination to run with Eisenhower two months before the convention convened. The story has it that Thomas E. Dewey made the offer, with Eisenhower's authority. A more likely story is that Nixon knew he was under strong consideration for the second spot and that his selection might well depend upon not only the general's nomination but his own contribution to that nomination.

In any event, Nixon, having first extracted from the Warren forces the right to name some of the delegates in return for his own participation, proceeded from the day of the primary to demonstrate his preference for Eisenhower and his faithlessness to the candidate to whom he was pledged. If a historian wonders a few generations from now why Earl Warren—a lifelong Republican, a GOP candidate for vice-president in 1948, and, as Nixon said once in an almost forgotten gaucherie, "a great Republican Chief Justice"—has never had a good word to say about Richard Nixon, he need look no further for his answer than to the weeks prior to the Republican convention of 1952.

In the days just before the June primary—in which the Warren slate, headed by Nixon and Knowland, defeated the Werdel slate by a 2 to 1 margin—Nixon started ducking out on his commitment. In a radio broadcast he set forth the Warren strategy of a Taft–Eisenhower deadlock, and then pointed out that if the convention did *not* turn to Warren, the California delegation would be in a position to deal with the stronger of the other two. It was hardly the speech of a Warren loyalist, nor was it intended to be.

After the primary Nixon went even further, and in doing so he enraged the Warren forces. Using his Senate franking privilege, he mailed a "poll" to the former Nixon chairman in each of the state's 23,000 voting precincts. The letter made no reference to support for another candidate if Warren were not the choice, but merely asked each recipient to name the "strongest" candidate the party could nominate. Later interviews with the Warren leaders made it clear that they regarded this as virtual treachery, particularly when word began to come back from Nixon's office in Washington that Eisenhower was running well ahead. The Warren people were able to head off any public release of the "poll," but the professionals who were to do the nominating knew all about it—which was the purpose of the exercise in the first place.

McIntyre Faries, then GOP national committeeman and a

key Warren figure on the delegation, hints strongly that the people Nixon put on the delegation in return for his presence were disloyal to Warren from the beginning. Bernard Brennan, who had been Nixon's chairman against Helen Douglas in 1950 (and who had been the first to sound the Marcantonio theme), had been installed as secretary of the delegation. What was worse from the Warren position, Murray Chotiner had been appointed as a sort of "tour director" for the delegation's trip to Chicago, in charge of room assignments on the special train and other such key decisions. It is interesting to note that Warren—a remarkably easygoing politician who believed, according to Faries, that even the outspoken Nixon people would "keep their word"—had given express orders that Chotiner be kept off the train and away from the delegation.

Nixon had gone to Chicago early to serve as a member of the Resolutions Committee and went back to Denver to join the Warren train. From the time he boarded, his compartment became the focal point of intrigue, as delegates were brought to see Nixon and to listen to the argument that there would be no deadlock in Chicago, that Eisenhower was a sure winner, and that only by breaking for the general could California have any influence—including, to be sure, the naming of its junior senator as the vice-presidential nominee.

When the train arrived at Chicago and the delegates went in a special bus to the hotel (there are those who say Chotiner had arranged for an Eisenhower banner to be carried on the side of the bus, but the story cannot be confirmed), the Warren people were astonished to find that Brennan had talked the hotel into giving a cocktail reception for Senator Nixon. But Faries and others convinced Nixon of the impropriety of this, and the event was turned into a California reception to which all delegates were invited.

The final makeup of the delegation came as a surprise to many of those Californians who had thought the 70 delegates were solidly committed to their governor. At the last minute, because of the withdrawal of some of the elected delegates, there were 10 or 12 substitutions. Faries says they were all Nixon–Eisenhower people, added without any clearance from Warren by Bernard Brennan, who apparently took his responsibilities as secretary of the delegation less seriously than his sentiments for Nixon.

At the convention itself, it quickly became apparent that the

Eisenhower–Taft struggle would not be decided on the first ballot, but before that in the voting on credentials. The credentials committee, heavily stacked by the National Committee with Taft men, had come in with a majority report seating contested Taft delegates from Texas and Georgia.

The Eisenhower forces, sensing just the kind of moral issue they needed to sharpen the differences between the aloof "nonpolitical" general and the "old politics" senator, promptly challenged the credentials committee with a minority report. The minority report, advanced by pro-Eisenhower Governor Arthur Langlie of Washington, was promptly called the "Fair Play" resolution, and the issue was joined.

Amid all the talk about the "Texas steal," it became clear that the nomination would be decided by the convention's vote on the credentials issue. If the Taft delegates were confirmed, it would show that he had the lock on the delegates his followers were claiming, because the credentials issue would require a straight yes-or-no vote. There are no favorite sons or dark horses on a procedural vote. Since Taft was thought to be the front-runner, a defeat for his people on the credentials report would slow or stop whatever momentum he had.

The California vote was critical. Neither a Taft nor an Eisenhower state, its votes could not be reasonably guessed in advance, although Faries had told Taft that he had no more than 18 of the 70 votes if Warren were to withdraw. The strategy of the Warren forces thus became clear—preserve the deadlock.

Knowland remained loyal to Warren under precisely the same pressures that made it easy for Nixon to defect; the Taft forces had practically guaranteed Knowland the vice-presidential nomination if he would turn the California delegates in that direction. For that matter, the Eisenhower people also made some passes at Knowland, but he was a true conservative who believed in keeping his word. Knowland remained loyal to Warren (who had appointed him to the Senate), and his loyalty prompted him to propose that on the credentials vote, California's 70 votes be split evenly, 35–35. That would preserve, insofar as California could, the deadlock which alone could win the nomination for Warren.

But when the California delegation caucused before the crucial credentials vote, Nixon took the floor and pleaded the moral issue. If California split its vote, he warned, it would be seen as a cynical act, one which would ultimately hurt the delegation and its candidate. He also played on the merits of the credentials issue itself, on which Eisenhower not only had the advantage but clearly had the country with him. Nixon pointed out, with some merit, that if the Republican Party wanted to raise the issue of corruption in the fall, it could hardly maximize the issue if its candidate had secured the nomination with "stolen" delegates.

It was no contest. Knowland held his ground for loyalty and political realism; Nixon argued for a "free vote" on moral grounds, and Nixon knew he had the votes. In the end, the delegation went 57 to 8 for the "fair play" resolution, the Eisenhower delegates were seated, and two days later the nomination was certified by a first-ballot vote.

The nomination of Eisenhower, with Nixon's support in spite of his pledge to Warren, furnished one more contrast on the convention floor. After the first roll call, some Eisenhower strength, held back for just such a contingency, began to be voted by states that sought permission to "switch." As one state after another switched to Eisenhower, it was clear that he had passed a majority. The Nixon men in the California delegation pressed Knowland—who was delegation chairman and had the authority—to drop the 70 votes for Warren and join the Eisenhower bandwagon. Knowland, loyal to his pledge to the end, could not find Warren to get authorization from him to change the vote, and he refused to do so. The California vote went into the books for Warren, and Nixon went on the Eisenhower ticket later the same day.

Without question, the high dramatic moment of the 1952 campaign came on September 23. On that night, Senator Richard Nixon, under strong pressure to resign from the Republican ticket and threatened by a requirement from General Eisenhower that he be "clean as a hound's tooth," delivered the famous "Checkers" speech and saved his political career. He didn't emerge "clean as a hound's tooth," but he did emerge as a skillful political craftsman with enormous support, particularly from rank-and-file Republicans, and that turned out to be enough for Eisenhower. Both the hound and his tooth were quickly forgotten.

The "Checkers" speech is remembered, however, for its style, and not its content. The style has since become famous. It was the first of a long series of Nixon speeches that defy parody. It was all there—Checkers the cocker spaniel, Pat's Republican cloth coat, the emphasis that the Nixons are not quitters, even the Navy service under falling bombs.

What has been forgotten is the reason that the speech had to be given at all. It was, quite simply, that a secret fund had been discovered. Contributions to the fund were paid regularly to Nixon by a group of 76 men—executives of Southern California oil, real estate, and manufacturing interests. The money was for his personal use, to augment his Senate salary of $12,500, his $2,500 tax-free expense allowance, and his $70,000 for the expense of running a Senate office.

The fund, by the time it was discovered, had paid out no extraordinary sum. Not quite $900 per month had been disbursed to the senator—a total of $18,168.87. But the story, and its explanation by Nixon, deserves some retelling, particularly in light of the fact that since 1969, Richard Nixon seems, through the use of his governmental power, to have enriched himself and his friends more than any president in history. And it is no accident that when a group of businessmen set out to collect $250,000 in order to give Nixon a golf course on his San Clemente property (and maintain it with additional annual funds, presumably in perpetuity), they decided to limit the number of contributors to 76, in honor of the donors to the Checkers fund.

The donors to the 1952 fund, according to an audited statement finally released after the *New York Post* and columnist Peter Edson broke the story, made up a roll call of Southern California's business establishment. They included Nixon's old friend Jack Drown, the "civic leader" of 1950; Bernard Brennan; and W. Herbert Allen, then the president of the company which holds the nominal legal title to the Nixon home at San Clemente. The list also included the father of H. R. Haldeman and Henry Kerns, then a San Gabriel auto dealer and now the president of the Export-Import Bank.

The money was raised by a Nixon friend, Dana C. Smith, and it was he who told reporters about it when the story broke. He said the contributors felt Nixon would be a fine salesman for free enterprise, and they realized his salary and expense authorization were too small to do the selling job. He said Nixon had told them he needed extra money for long-distance phone calls, for 10,000 Christmas cards, for postage on letters that could not be sent under the Senate frank, and for travel to California beyond the official allotment.

When the story broke, Nixon's first reaction was to attack and blame the "smear" on the "Communists and crooks in this Administration" he had exposed. He conceded—to a whistle-stop crowd where hecklers were asking about the money—that he indeed had received the fund, but he said it had some-how saved the taxpayers money. "The expenses of my office were in excess of the amounts allowed under the law. Rather than using the taxpayers' money for these expenses, what did I do?"

The statement is almost incredible, but it went down. Obvi-ously, he wasn't saving anyone a nickel, except himself. He had already used, and continued to use, every dollar of tax money he was authorized to use, and the extra funds simply replaced money he would otherwise have to spend himself. In fact, he told Peter Edson, the contributions from the secret fund had enabled him to make a down payment on a Washing-ton house he could not otherwise afford. In the Checkers speech the same claim was made: "Not one cent of that money went for my personal use." In fact, every penny had gone to his personal use, but by the time this could be figured out, the pea was under another shell.

The Sacramento *Bee* put the issue more sternly. In an edi-torial appearing as the story broke, it declared, "The man who the people of the sovereign state of California believed was actually representing them is the pet and protégé of a special interest group of rich Southern Californians. To put it more bluntly, Nixon is their subsidized front man, if not, indeed, their lobbyist."

That was a bit *too* stern. There is no indication that Nixon ever voted for oil, real estate, or the other interests repre-sented because these men were financing him. On the contrary there is every indication that he would have voted the same way had the fund never existed. But it looked bad; if all he wanted was a political fund with which to carry out his po-litical duties on a broader scale, why not a public fund to which any like-minded businessman could contribute? The secrecy and the deception of the explanation raised questions about Nixon's honor. They should have raised questions about his sensitivity and awareness, or his lack of them, that these limits of propriety that lay well within the limits of legality.

The Checkers speech was a great success. Nixon ended it

with a request for listeners to write to the Republican National Committee if they thought he should leave or stay on the Eisenhower ticket. The response was nearly unanimous in his favor. It only remained for General Eisenhower to greet him two days later with a tearful embrace and a "You're my boy," and the ugly suspicions raised by the fund were behind him.

California's cross-filing law, whereby candidates could run in both primary elections without revealing their own party identity, wasn't the only special contribution Hiram Johnson and his Progressives made to California's election laws. Like other reformers, they added the initiative and the referendum. As California's population grew, this reform became—like everything else in the state—big business.

The initiative and the referendum were devices to get around a reluctant, unresponsive legislature and to get laws passed by direct action of the people. A sufficient number of signatures could put measures on the ballot—substantive legislative matters, like old-age pensions, a confiscatory tax on chain grocery stores, or the legalization of night harness racing. There has not been a general election in California in 50 years which has not had, in addition to the races for office, one or two hotly contested ballot issues.

The difference between California and other states, at least until recently, was that putting a proposition on the ballot had become, for most issues, so specialized a task as to require the service of an expert. The expert collected the necessary signatures (hundreds of thousands of them) for a fee, and he didn't care what the proposition was, so long as he got his fee. Advocates, for example, of the Single Tax or dog racing or the abolition of capital punishment lacked the skills and the manpower to collect hundreds of thousands of valid signatures in the time required by law.

But the expert knew how. He had thousands of canvassers on call, mostly housewives and pensioners anxious to pick up the extra few cents per name the job paid. The expert in California was a man named Joseph Robinson, a legendary figure until his death in 1970. Robinson boasted that, for the right fee, he would qualify *anything* for the ballot, from Communism to compulsory prayer. He was always successful in obtaining enough signatures.

One year he qualified an old-age pension scheme that was

83

so comprehensive it named a friend of the promoter as the new welfare director, the whole thing to be written into the state Constitution. To Robinson's surprise, along with that of most other political observers, the pension scheme was adopted by the voters. Robinson, this time for a fee from the antipension people, promptly qualified a repeal provision for the ballot in a special election. It also carried, and thus the people of the state had no new pension law. Robinson was richer by two fees.

Robinson branched out over the years. He was a student of election returns and a collector of lists. By matching the returns against the registration lists, he was able to amass a considerable knowledge of where Republicans ran strongly in Democratic areas, and vice versa. He knew each party's strong and weak areas, and he had the mailing lists available for candidates who needed to use his information. Thus Robinson had readily available a list of nearly 1 million likely conservative Democrats—that is, Democrats whose districts reflected returns which indicated, over the years, that they voted often, if not always, for Republican candidates. Thus, a congressional or state legislative district, or even a precinct, which regularly voted for Republican candidates despite a heavy edge in Democratic registration was, by Robinson's figuring, an area of conservative Democrats. Since, in California, no Republican candidate could win statewide without a sizable number of Democratic votes, this information was invaluable, and so were Robinson's services in sending out mail to the voters on his lists.

It was Robinson's list that figured most strongly in a bold fraud attempted—nearly successfully—in 1962 by Richard Nixon, then a candidate for governor after his 1960 defeat for the presidency, and by his campaign manager, a Los Angeles advertising executive named H. R. "Bob" Haldeman.

Before the fraud could be undertaken, two more elements had to fall into place. In the fall of 1962, with Nixon running even in the polls against Democratic Governor Edmund G. "Pat" Brown, they were easily found.

First, an issue was needed, and Haldeman and Nixon found it in the California Democratic Council, a sort of 1962 version of Nixon's old running-mate, the CIO Political Action Committee. Unfortunately, however, the Council, known naturally enough as the CDC, could hardly be made into a Communist organization whose endorsement of an opponent would be enough for a full-scale campaign.

CDC was an unofficial party organization in California, made up of local clubs which were open to any Democrat and which were originally formed to get around the cross-filing law. The CDC, it was thought, could endorse Democrats before the primary elections and thus help break the hold of Republican incumbents who were winning Democratic primaries as well as their own. With cross-filing finally abolished by the mid-1950s, CDC became the basic arm of the liberal wing of the party. By the time the Democrats came back to power in 1958 with Brown as Governor, it had become almost an official body. In any event, in 1962 there was nothing controversial about CDC's endorsements—it had routinely supported the renomination and reelection of all the Democrats holding statewide office, with Brown at the head of the ticket.

The CDC had positions on issues, too. It was in those issue positions that Nixon and Haldeman thought they saw an opening. The positions were advanced for 1962. The CDC called for the admission of "Red China" to the United Nations, the abolition of test or "loyalty" oaths for employment or for permits to speak on college campuses, and for the moratorium on nuclear testing which Adlai Stevenson had first advocated and which President Kennedy was even then preparing to effect as part of the Test Ban Treaty.

The second element—expertise—was provided by Leone Baxter, a skilled veteran of California's political battles. Baxter was the widow of Clem Whittaker, with whom she had operated for many years the public relations firm of Whittaker & Baxter. Whittaker & Baxter was the public relations firm behind most statewide Republican candidates in the forties and fifties and behind the conservative side of most of the ballot issues Joseph Robinson had put on the ballot. There were even some observers unkind enough to suggest—facetiously, to be sure—that Robinson sometimes would get a liberal proposition on the ballot just so Whittaker & Baxter could collect a substantial fee to defeat it.

Whittaker & Baxter had gone national too, and with success. In the late 1940s they had undertaken a campaign against President Truman's proposal for national health insurance, and by the time they were finished with their chores for the

American Medical Association, "socialized medicine" was done for—for at least a generation. Clem Whittaker was proud of his work on the socialized medicine campaign, but shrewd enough to realize that the public relations techniques that had brought success could as easily have been used on the other side. "For a million dollar fee," he said, "I could make tuberculosis popular."

It was Baxter who devised the formula that combined the CDC with Robinson's lists of conservative Democrats. She first described the proposal to Nixon, while the candidate was in San Francisco, and then, armed with his interest, convinced other campaign officials and, finally, Haldeman to go ahead.

The proposal was to create a "Committee for the Preservation of the Democratic Party in California." The Committee, of course, would be headed by nominal Democrats, but at all times it would be fully financed and under the control of the Nixon campaign. It was a technique to be followed faithfully ten years later with the Democrats for Nixon in 1972, a group headed by John Connally, Nixon's ex-secretary of the treasury (the greatest secretary since David Kennedy, some said). Like the Committee to Preserve the Democratic Party in California in 1962, Democrats for Nixon in 1972 was fully financed by Nixon campaign funds.

Unlike the Connally front, the 1962 Committee had no distinguished letterhead of "prominent Democrats," just some duly registered Democrats that Baxter had recruited to lend an air of verisimilitude to the project. (One reason for the lack of "big names" in 1962 was unquestionably the fact that unlike 1972, Nixon lacked a governmental base from which to reward—or withhold punishment from—the "Democrats" who lent him public support.)

The scheme was a simple one, once Baxter, Haldeman, and Nixon focused on it. The fake "Committee" would send to Robinson's list of conservative Democrats (as many as the Nixon campaign could afford, a number finally set at 900,000) a statement about the CDC, and at the same time request answers to a "poll" asking the recipients if they shared various CDC positions.

Baxter found some registered Democrats, one of whom went over some past and present CDC issue positions and drafted preliminary copy. Robinson prepared a large two-part postcard, one part with the "Dear Fellow Democrat" message, and the other a self-mailer with the "poll" questions. Then

Haldeman and Nixon went over the copy, and at a final meeting at Nixon's house, Haldeman, Baxter, and the candidate approved the final form.

There is no question of Nixon's participation in this particular fraud. A subsequent court action resulted in a judgment which clearly identified him as an active participant in formulating and executing the scheme, and Baxter testified under oath to a "one hour or so" Nixon-Haldeman-Baxter meeting to approve the final copy.

The postcard began, "This is not a plea for any candidate." According to Baxter in a later deposition, this was language Nixon insisted on. Considering that the entire operation was conceived, executed, and paid for by the Nixon campaign, perhaps the world "plea" was the operative one in his mind. Then it went on to describe the "capture" of the Democratic Party and wondered, "As a Democrat, what do you feel we can do to throw off the shackles of this left-wing minority, now so powerful it can dictate the course of our party?"

Then the Nixon message got down to basics. "We can break the power of the CDC by refusing to elect their candidates." The beauty of this, of course, was that the *CDC* candidates were precisely *all* the Democratic candidates running for reelection. "Or we can take acceptable Republicans —if we can find any," it suggested shyly. Finally, "whatever we do, in the name of the Democratic Party—Let's Not Deliver California to the CDC!"

The 1962 campaign, back on the California proving ground, represented a quantum leap in Nixon Politics. Instead of merely making false charges about Communism and the Communist affiliations of his opponents, in hopes the general voting public would believe him, Nixon shifted for the first time to a conscious manipulation of the election process itself. Now the fraud consisted, not in claiming that Voorhis was a CIO–PAC tool, or that Helen Douglas was somehow part of a Marcantonio axis, but in trying to make Democrats believe that Democrats were supporting him and his campaign, when in fact they were his paid employees, speaking his words in a mailing designed, approved, and secretly paid for by him. The fake phone calls, the forged letters, and the hiring of people to pose as hippies and homosexuals might have seemed —ten years later—a giant step for mankind, but it was just a short step for one man.

By October 20, Robinson—for his fee, which had so far

run to $70,000, masked in the campaign reports as "advertising and publicity"—had mailed out 500,000 copies of the postcard poll. Baxter called it a "directed poll," which is to say that it called—indeed, cried out—for a particular set of answers.

It asked whether recipients agreed or disagreed with, for example, "allowing subversives the freedom of college campuses"; "foreign aid to countries with Communist governments"; and "complete national disarmament as an ultimate goal." Then it inquired, "Can California afford to have a Governor indebted to the CDC—who has stated he will veto any legislation damaging to the CDC—who calls it 'my strong right arm'—who declares, 'I am proud of my membership in the CDC'?" Answer, to be sure, "Yes" or "No."

It is important to bear in mind that this "poll" was sent only to Robinson's scientifically selected list of *conservative* Democrats—those whose voting habits had marked them over the years as most likely to vote for a Republican candidate. The Nixon people proposed to use the poll, and indeed got out some early press releases to that effect, as a cross-section of *all* Democrats. If it had worked, if the plan had been carried out, the state's newspapers would have given it quite a ride, and the influence on Democratic voters might have been considerable.

But it didn't work, largely as a result of an accidental discovery—just as the second Watergate burglary was foiled by the chance discovery of a piece of tape holding back the catches of the fire doors. In a sort of balance of nature, Nixon Politics, at its most unethical and illegal, is likely to be conceptually sound but methodologically weak, as though planned by the Rockettes but executed by Keystone Cops.

On the afternoon of Saturday, October 20, as the Nixon mailings were in their final phase, a Nixon volunteer worker called the headquarters of the Democratic Party in San Francisco. The volunteer was filling in that day for her mother, and she had finished addressing a batch of several hundred of the Robinson postcards. She lacked instructions as to what to do next, and since the postcard referred to a "Committee for the Preservation of the Democratic Party," she assumed the Democratic Party would know what to do with them.

Joyce Farber, secretary to Democratic state chairman Roger Kent, listened to the volunteer's request and decided the Democratic Party would know just what to do. "Bring them right down to headquarters," she said, and within a few minutes Roger Kent was getting his first look at the fraud.

Within hours, Kent was conferring with Gerald O'Gara, the Democrats' attorney, and when court opened Monday morning, Kent and O'Gara were ready with a complaint and a request for a preliminary injunction. The Nixon mailing was against the state elections law, they argued, for three reasons: the address of the printer did not appear, no names of the allegedly sponsoring committee appeared, and the attached letter appeared to solicit money in the name of the Democratic Party without the authorization of any of the requisite party officers. Kent didn't know the facts yet, he had no idea until much later that this was an operation in which Nixon was personally involved, and he had no knowledge of the vastness of the enterprise. But the legal work he and O'Gara had put together over the weekend was enough to persuade Judge Byron Arnold of the Superior Court to issue a temporary restraining order immediately and, a few days later, a preliminary injunction. The judge's orders effectively restrained the Nixon camp from proceeding with further mailing of the postcard and the "directed poll," and, more important from Kent's point of view, stopped any public dissemination of the results on the ground they had been illegally and fraudulently procured. Like Judge John Sirica ten years later, Judge Arnold was a Republican appointee, but also like Judge Sirica, he knew a fraud when he saw one.

The injunction, of course, was only preliminary, pending a trial of the action, in which Kent was seeking $500,000 in damages to his party and a permanent injunction as well. But everyone—everyone but Kent, that is—assumed that when the preliminary injunction went into effect ten days before the election, that would be the end of it. No further damage could result until Election Day, and there would be no point in finishing the mailing and announcing the results of the "directed poll" thereafter.

Pressure on Kent to drop the suit became even stronger when Governor Brown and his ticket were reelected. Brown's victory over Nixon was by a 200,000 vote margin, comfortable for California. And political lawsuits, after all, are brought for political purposes. After an election, political lawsuits brought during a campaign—charges of fraud, libel, and unfair practices—are almost always dropped once the votes are counted.

When a postelection conference of counsel for both sides

was held in Judge Arnold's chambers, the issues were thought only to be how to dismiss the suit and to release some annoying attachments Kent had secured on the bank accounts of the fake "Preservation Committee."

But Kent, who still had no idea of the dimension of the scheme he would uncover, refused to cooperate. Fraud, he said, wasn't funny, and the Democrats weren't willing to pass the whole thing off as "just one more thing" that happens in elections. Kent, whose father and grandfather had been active in California politics, had some principles to vindicate. He had watched Richard Nixon—and opposed him—in two state-wide campaigns and three national campaigns, as well as the 1946 race against Jerry Voorhis, and he wanted a permanent record.

In addition, Kent thought a final judgment, spelling out the fraud and its illegality, might discourage further fake "Democrats For . . ." organizations, always a feature of California campaigns, although never this blatant. He refused to settle the suit, announced his intention to press for a final judgment after trial, and laid plans for discovery proceedings (the sworn depositions of the defendants and their agents).

The case dragged on through 1963 and into early 1964. By this time the Democrats had spent nearly $10,000 in legal fees and costs, but they had hit some pay dirt as well. In the course of discovery, they learned the dimensions of the scheme—the 900,000 planned postcards—and the extent of the fraud. They learned, for instance, of the payments to Robinson and his treatment of the "Democratic" committee as part of the Nixon campaign. They learned, from Baxter's deposition, of Nixon's direct participation in preparing and approving the material to be mailed out. And, perhaps more important for future analysts of Nixon Politics, they caught Bob Haldeman in false testimony under oath.

Haldeman's deposition was taken on September 5, 1963, less than one year after the events involved. He went into as little detail as he could about the origin of the postcard and the poll. He had cleared it, he said, with GOP state chairman Caspar Weinberger, who knew all about the plan to circulate the poll among conservative Democrats using campaign money to pay for it.

(Weinberger, who was later to serve the Nixon Administration as director of the Office of Management and Budget and as secretary of Health, Education and Welfare, denies that

Haldeman "cleared" the postcard and the poll with him, or even that Haldeman discussed it with him. Weinberger points to the proclivity of many Watergate commentators to disbelieve Haldeman on key points, but to believe him on this matter of the California deposition, and he has a good point. There is thus a clear conflict as to whether one should believe Haldeman or Weinberger, who denied at the time any knowledge "that the Nixon campaign organization had helped with the cards." In behalf of Weinberger, it must be said that his reputation for truth and veracity—even among those who oppose his policies—is high, and that he has never even been *indicted* for perjury.)

Haldeman's deposition also provided testimony that the whole Robinson project—the "Preservation Committee" and the postcard "poll"—were also known to two other key Nixon operatives in 1962, Herb Klein and, naturally enough, Murray Chotiner. Chotiner, according to Haledman, also saw the copy.

Haldeman also testified that among other key Nixon people who were informed of the project and the expenditure were finance chairman Maurice Stans and southern California chairman Herbert Kalmbach.

When it came to Mr. Nixon's own involvement in the postcard poll, Haldeman was evasive and, finally, deceitful:

Q: Did you review this Exhibit E, the postcard poll, with Mr. Nixon?

A: [Haldeman] No, I don't think so. I think again I posted him on the fact that we were going into this project on the same basis that I did with Weinberger and [GOP National Committeeman] Martin, which would have been my practice again in this kind of thing.

Q: Did you tell him the contents of Exhibit E, the postcard poll?

A: Perhaps in general terms, not on any specific basis. I don't know.

Q: Did you show him the draft?

A: I don't think so.

Q: How many conversations did you have with him?

A: I am sure only one. [From the transcript of the Haldeman deposition, p. 56.]

But Leone Baxter, in her sworn testimony, by deposition, had another story to tell:

Q: . . . when was your next meeting with Mr. Nixon concerning the campaign?

A: [Baxter] I don't think I had another meeting with him *until I went over the copy with him and Mr. Haldeman.*

Q: About what date was that?

A: All of this seems to have transpired along about in the same timing, very concentrated in late August–early September [1962], as I recall, all of these meetings and conversations.

Q: Where did the meeting take place?

A: Now, which meeting?

Q: The one with you and Mr. Nixon and Mr. Haldeman, *to go over the copy.*

A: *At Mr. Nixon's home.*

Q: That is Bel Air, it—was at that time?

A: Bel Air, that's right.

Q: *Who was present besides you and Mr. Haldeman?*

A: *That's all.*

Q: How long did the meeting last?

A: An hour, probably.

Q: Did you have with you, or did Mr. Nixon and Mr. Haldeman have, proofs of this Exhibit [the postcard poll] or something similar to it?

A: *Yes, they had them.*

Q: *Did you and they discuss the proofs?*

A: *Yes.*

Q: What was the substance of the discussion?

A: Substance of the discussion was what is contained in the card, whether it was valid, legal, and proper, *whether it would be effective.*

Q: Was this in proof form or typed copy, or what?

A: *They had had the proof earlier,* some days earlier, directly from the printer. They had the card as well a few days before. They had the two things, the proof and the—the proof and the copy as it went to the printer from Mr. Robinson, and the proof when it came back. [Emphasis added. From the transcript of the Baxter deposition, pp. 39ff.]

Unfortunately, as it turned out, the matter ended soon thereafter, without a full trial and what would undoubtedly have been at least serious consideration of referring the conflict to the district attorney for a consideration of whether perjury had been committed. But Kent now felt vindicated. With discovery completed he had the whole picture, and the other side was anxious to negotiate.

The alternatives for Kent were either to negotiate a settlement or to spend thousands of dollars more on a shaky damage claim (it's hard to show damage when you won the election), and there were other factors, as well. Under the threat of a deposition of Nixon himself, the Republicans in California were more than anxious to settle, and they were willing to run up the costs in the face of what they knew to be the Democrats' lack of money to continue the suit.

Besides, Kent reasoned—and he would regret it over the next ten years—if ever there was a politician who was "finished," it was Richard Nixon. He had fled California in electoral disgrace and had begun a law practice in New York. And his final press conference had torn away whatever shreds of dignity might have remained after the California campaign.

So Kent settled. He had to forego what would have been the great pleasure of taking Nixon's deposition and going on to trial, but the legal cost to the Democratic Party would have been high. Kent felt he had already accomplished what he set out to do. The settlement agreed to a permanent injunction and the transfer of $368.50 from the treasury of the "Preservation Committee" to the Democratic state committee—which, with every state constitutional office won and substantial majorities in both houses of the legislature, had preserved the Democratic Party quite nicely. The rest of the issues were submitted to Judge Arnold for final judgment, on the depositions and affidavits, without taking formal testimony in court.

Judge Arnold's final judgment, filed October 30, 1964, was devastating. Portions of it follow (it is reprinted in its entirety in the Appendix).

IT IS HEREBY ORDERED, ADJUDGED AND DECREED that:

1. In October, 1961, Richard M. Nixon announced his candidacy for the governorship of California.

2. In October, 1962, a circular to Democrats was drafted which purported to express the concern of genuine Democrats for the welfare of the Democratic Party and their fear that the party would be destroyed if candidates supported by the California Democratic Council (hereinafter called the "CDC") including primarily Governor Brown, were elected in the November 1962 election. It appealed for the support and money of Democrats in fighting the CDC and certain policies attributed to it and cast aspersions on the Democratic candidates endorsed by it. It was drafted in the form of a postcard poll addressed to Democrats. *This postcard poll was reviewed, amended and finally approved by Mr. Nixon personally in the form attached hereto as Exhibit A.* It criticized the policies of the CDC and the Democratic candidates it supported, notably Governor Edmund G. Brown, and asked the addressee

Democrats to express their preference either for Governor Brown and the other statewide Democratic candidates or their Republican opponents, headed by Mr. Nixon. [Emphasis added.]

Nowhere in Exhibit A or letters mailed by defendant Committee was it stated that the defendant Committee and its mailing of Exhibit A were supported and financed by the Nixon for Governor Finance Committee. *Mr. Nixon and Mr. Haldeman approved the plan and project as described above and agreed that the Nixon campaign committee would finance the project.* [Emphasis added.]

Officials of the Nixon for Governor Committee then made an agreement with defendants Robinson and Company, a corporation, and Joseph Robinson, whereby for the sum of $70,000 Robinson and Company agreed to print, address and mail the postcard poll as described above and to receive and compile the results of the poll as indicated on the return postal cards. . . .

4. . . . All statements for the work performed by defendants Joseph Robinson and Robinson and Company for and on behalf of the defendant Committee were sent for payment to H. Robert Haldeman, Campaign Manager of the Nixon for Governor Campaign Committee.

5. *Richard Nixon in his campaign for the governorship of California, felt that the postcard and poll, Exhibit A would be very helpful to him since it reflected his own position concerning the relationship of Democrats to the CDC.* [Emphasis added.]

The list of seven so-called objectives or viewpoints purportedly held by the CDC, beginning with "Admitting Red China into the United Nations" and ending with "Refusal to Bar Communists from the Democratic Party," as recited in the postcard Exhibit A were substantially the same as charges made repeatedly by Mr. Nixon in his campaign speeches. . . .

8. In October 1962 defendant Committee for the Preservation of the Democratic Party in California and its members, agents and/or employees, . . . directly and indirectly solicited funds upon representations, express and implied, that the funds were being solicited for the use of the Democratic Party.

In truth and fact, such funds were solicited for the use, benefit and furtherance of the candidacy of Richard M. Nixon for Governor of California. . . .

9. Defendants . . . made various misleading statements as specified below in connection with said postcard poll, . . . the letters of October 15, 1962, and October 17, 1962, . . . and the press releases attached hereto. . . .

(a) (Statement) That the Democratic Party or a qualified Committee thereof or members of the Democratic Party sincerely interested in preserving the Democratic Party were mailing postcard Exhibit A to Democratic voters in order to secure a poll of members of the Democratic Party answering the questions on Exhibit A relating to said party and its candidates and wished such

Democratic voters to fill out the poll contained therein and return it to the defendant Committee organized, dedicated and operating for the preservation of the Democratic party and/or to the Democratic Party.

(Fact) Neither the Democratic Party nor plaintiff Democratic State Central Committee nor any qualified officer, official or committee thereof or any member of the Democratic Party primarily interested in its welfare or preservation had any connection with or knowledge of or in any way sponsored or approved the acts or conduct of defendants or any of them. . . .

(b) (Statement) That the Democratic Party and its fundamental and historic policies were and are in opposition to the CDC and its policies.

(Fact) The Democratic Party and the CDC are dedicated to the same basic general objectives and principles. . . .

(c) (Statement and Implication) That the Democratic Party wished said voters to send money for the use and benefit of the Democratic Party and its statewide candidates to the Committee for the Preservation of the Democratic Party in California . . . and the defendant Committee was a bona fide committee of Democrats organized for the sole purpose of preserving the Democratic Party in California. . . .

(Fact) The defendant Committee and its postcard poll and its activities were financed by, for and in aid of the campaign to elect Mr. Nixon Governor of California. . . .

(d) (Statement) That the defendant Committee was a bona fide committee of Democrats organized, dedicated and operating for the sole purpose of preserving the Democratic Party, and desired and was sincerely endeavoring by the postcard Exhibit A to secure a fair and representative poll of all segments of the Democratic Party and to determine by such poll the general sentiment of the rank-and-file members of the Democratic Party toward the CDC, the policies of the CDC and the statewide Democratic candidates. . . .

That the results of the poll would reflect the feelings of rank-and-file Democrats including liberal, progressive and middle of the road Democrats as well as conservative Democrats.

(Fact) The activities of defendant Committee, including its postcard poll, its letters and its publicity releases, were instigated, financed, prepared, implemented, supervised and executed by the Nixon for Governor Campaign Committee and the Nixon for Governor Finance Committee. This is evidenced by these facts:

The invoice dated September 19, 1962, from defendant Robinson & Company, Inc. to Nixon for Governor Campaign Committee, attached as Exhibit G, provided for a "statewide mailing to 900,000 *Conservative* Democrats, also handling and tabulating poll." [Emphasis in original.]

When returns were received from said postcard poll, however, they were publicized by the defendant Committee as representing the "voice of the rank and file Democrat." . . .

Defendant Committee failed to inform the Democrats receiving the postcard poll Exhibit A and the public that said poll actually was mailed to precincts consisting predominantly of conservative Democrats. . . .

(e) (Statement) That "Governor Brown . . . has become their [referring to the CDC] captive." (Exhibit A.)

(Fact) This statement is false. . . .

19. The postcard, Exhibit A, and the letters of October 15, 1962, and October 17, 1962, Exhibits E and E1 respectively, were instigated, written, financed and published by supporters of Richard M. Nixon as a candidate for Governor of California, and their agents. . . .

One more example of Nixon Politics during 1962 needs to be chronicled. Cropped photographs had been used in earlier campaigns by other practitioners, most notably against Senator Millard Tydings of Maryland. A picture of Tydings and of Communist leader Earl Browder had been skillfully blended by aides of his opponent.

In California in 1962 there were two examples of the art. One was distributed by "Democrats for Nixon," as always an in-house group formed, guided, and financed by the Nixon campaign. This manufactured picture showed Governor Brown bowing, smiling, and saying in a caption, "I want this organization, CDC, to flourish and grow." The ethical problem was posed by the fact that Brown never said such words and by the additional fact that the March of Dimes poster girl, at whom Brown was smiling, had been cropped out of the picture. The leaflet went on to attack the CDC in the same language as the postcard poll.

The other cropped photograph showed Brown, hands together in front of him in an Oriental bow. It was an appropriate gesture, for the governor was greeting a Laotian girl who had come to Sacramento on a goodwill mission for her country. The picture was used as part of a leaflet to denounce Brown for Communist sympathies and was made somewhat more effective by cutting the Laotian girl out of the picture and substituting Nikita Khrushchev, with the caption, "Premier Khrushchev, we who admire you, we who respect you, welcome you to California."

Haldeman denied any responsibility for the Khrushchev leaflet, but added in a newspaper interview that both cropped photographs were, after all, "pictures of Governor Brown and were used only as illustrative of actual statements made by him."

Weinberger disowned completely the Khrushchev leaflet as the work of a right-wing extremist (which it was) and didn't bother to defend it at all. (Copies of it, however, had been picked up by some of Kent's people in a Nixon headquarters in Los Angeles.) Weinberger did defend the CDC leaflet as containing "nothing untrue" and said the cropped picture was "irrelevant." It was during this press interview that Weinberger was quoted as denying any knowledge that the Nixon campaign organization was involved in the distribution of the postcard poll.

One last 1962 note: The team was gathering. On a financial statement filed with the California Secretary of State's office after the campaign was over, some familiar names appear. Haldeman and Kalmbach are listed under "campaign managers." John Ehrlichman apparently toiled as Southern California advance chief in an unpaid capacity, or perhaps paid under a general "candidate travel" account, and Finance Chairman Maurice Stans, as in 1972, was officially unpaid. Ron Ziegler was down for $3,218.18 under "Advertising Agencies and Publicity Agents," and Dwight Chapin, who within ten years would be ordering Herbert Kalmbach to pay saboteurs, barely made his letter with $2,059.09, under the general heading of "Stenographers and Clerks."

4. The Exception that Swallowed the Rules

In 1941, as a high school student, I attended a debate in Los Angeles, one of many held across the country that year on the question of whether the United States should get involved in the war in Europe (we didn't call it World War II yet). The contestants were Robert M. Hutchins, president of the University of Chicago, and Norman Thomas, the leader of the Socialist Party.

I have forgotten everything about the debate but Thomas, obviously getting the worst of it from the predominantly liberal and interventionist crowd, rising once to say, in his booming voice, that however noble the cause, America once mobilized and militarized would never be demobilized and demilitarized. "Never" is a long time, but he's been right now for more than thirty years.

The World War II mobilization changed the country. Fifteen million young men of an impressionable age (including Richard Nixon) learned an instinctive respect and fear for high-ranking officers, something many of us unlearned only with difficulty, and others never unlearned at all. Today it is still difficult (but by no means impossible) for me to perceive the foolishness of, let us say, General William Westmoreland or Admiral Thomas Moorer as quickly or as easily as it is to perceive the foolishness of their civilian counterparts.

Men achieved high rank in those years, beyond their abilities and their wildest ambitions, and were understandably loath to return to selling automobiles or settling insurance claims. Fortunes were made selling equipment and weapons to the services by men and companies to whom the swelling figures on the balance sheet compensated for the loss of whatever morals and ethics they may have brought to the enterprise.

Politicians discovered the great truth that if "defense" or

"national security" is involved, or can be made to seem to be involved, rational arguments can be easily overcome. So long as a permanent crisis exists, national priorities can be permanently reversed. Where once a career military man was simply someone who could not get or hold a good job on the outside, the high brass has become exalted, and their words are heeded on all sorts of matters on which they are plainly ignorant, including military concerns.

A hierarchy of issues and budgetary allotments has become firm in Washington. The defense budget is as sacrosanct as pensions or interest on the debt. If cuts are to be made or programs postponed, they come in the "soft" areas of health, social welfare, or education—never from the development of a new weapons system or the expansion of an old one.

The very change of name of the old Departments of War and Navy to a new Department of Defense symbolizes the shift. As Eugene McCarthy has pointed out, once a department of government is called "Defense," it has no effective limit. A war department, after all, is to wage wars, and if there are no wars, it is hard to increase its budget. But defense? There can never, by definition, be enough defense. If one is not for defense, then one must want the country to be defenseless or undefendable. And so, through 25 postwar years, the priorities have grown so distorted that by 1972 two tax dollars out of three were being spent on "defense." And when, with great publicity, a disarmament agreement was negotiated with the other superpower, the Soviet Union, men could rise at the Pentagon, the White House, and the Senate and argue that, as a *result* of the disarmament agreement, the defense budget would have to be *increased* by three or four billion dollars.

All this can be done—and was done—as long as a crisis is either at hand or around the corner. There were real crises—the Soviet threat to Western Europe in the late 1940s; unavoidable crises, such as the Korean Conflict in the early 1950s; and crises both false and avoidable, such as Lebanon in the 1950s, Berlin in the early 1960s, the Dominican Republic in 1965, and finally, the crisis which split the nation as it had not been for a century and changed our image internationally to that of the bully of the world—Vietnam.

Along with all this glory for defense and the military, this national playing at soldier, came a companion development: an increase in the espionage services' influence and popularity. J. Edgar Hoover put on a good show at congressional committees every year, and the FBI became the bulwark against domestic Communism. Men like Richard Nixon and Joe McCarthy used the investigative process of the House and Senate to make it seem as though America was honeycombed with spy networks. The CIA could—and did—become an operational arm of executive policy and toppled governments, undermined currencies, and supported opposition movements throughout the world. By the end of the 1950s, it was hard to tell, at a U.S. Embassy abroad, who was a foreign service officer and who a "spook," as CIA agents were called.

All this made for a sort of "CIA-ization" of domestic life and politics. Industrial espionage occupied the time and money of more spies than the foreign operations of the government. And as the large American trade unions increasingly became conduits for CIA money flowing abroad, they also became propaganda outlets for the Administration in power. In the "civilian" branches of government, the methods of the soldier and the spy became the standard operating procedure. "Secret," "Top Secret," and "Eyes Only" memoranda proliferated in places like the Department of Agriculture. The bureaucrat whose paper could carry no higher a classification than "Confidential" could safely be ignored. Cable traffic to and from posts overseas multiplied and became filled with code, military-sounding abbreviations, and "hard-nosed" technical language. Software, infrastructure, interface, signoff, quantify—everyone wanted to sound like a crisp air traffic control operator or a weary but experienced colonel seeking "intelligence" from a series of dangerous patrols.

Thus, it is the tragedy of the nation that Richard Nixon, a man of no fixed principle, surrounded by aides and old companions who took their cues only from their leader, came to the peak of power in an age already debased by a quarter of a century of growing militarism, by abandonment of power to the executive, and worse, by five years of dehumanizing war. The Nixon methods—Nixon Politics, tested on the California proving ground—became operative at a time when language was already distorted and national policy already dominated by the ugly facts of Vietnam.

It was easy to slide into Vietnam. Twenty years of inflamed rhetoric had smothered both sides of the old debate between "isolationism" and "interventionism"—exemplified by the 1941 debate between Hutchins and Thomas. Now we were all interventionists. Powerful men on both sides saw prosperity

100

and power for all in the permanent crisis. The buttons were available for any President to push; they bore the labels "aggression," "small nations," and "free people." No matter that the words, originally used to describe the battle against Hitler, are now used for some of the least free regimes in the world. During his incumbency as secretary of state, Dean Rusk could invoke "Munich" to defend his policy in Vietnam, even when the mounting horror of American activity made "Nuremberg" a more appropriate reference.

As early as June 28, 1961, President Kennedy's special assistant for national security, Walt W. Rostow, told a graduating class of Special Forces that Vietnam represented "as clear a form of aggression as the North Korean invasion of South Korea in June 1950," and this at a time when no soldier from North Vietnam had yet come south. The direction of guerrilla warfare from the outside, Rostow went on, "was aggression which the whole international community must confront and whose consequent responsibilities it must accept." If it had been made clear that by "international community," Rostow meant the United States and that by "consequent responsibilities" he meant 50,000 dead, 200,000 wounded, and 150 billion dollars spent, it is doubtful that even the graduates would have applauded.

The attempt to avoid the "loss" of Vietnam without a major commitment of American combat troops failed, and President Kennedy died before the failure became apparent. The "loss" of Vietnam was important to avoid—American leaders were regularly accused of "losing" control over countries (and sometimes the countries themselves) the United States had never owned or controlled. John Kennedy was very much aware in 1961 that the opposition party was led by Richard Nixon, a politician whose stock-in-trade for a decade had been to accuse his opponents of having "lost" China and the Iron Curtain countries.

By 1964, Lyndon Johnson, advised that our clients in Saigon could not survive without U.S. military intervention, said, "duty requires, *and the American people demand*, that we give [the free people of Vietnam] the fullest measure of support. The Vietcong guerrillas, under orders from their Communist masters in the North, have intensified terrorist actions against the peaceful people of South Vietnam. This increased terrorism requires increased response."

Defense Secretary Robert McNamara said, "The survival of

an independent government in South Vietnam is so important to the security of all Southeast Asia and to the free world that I can conceive of no alternative than to take all necessary measures within our capability to prevent a Communist victory."

"The fullest measure of support?" "No alternative to all necessary measures?" Did Americans really "demand" all this? Did anyone seriously believe they had? For that matter, did anyone really believe that one corrupt American employee after another—hired to run South Vietnam—was presiding over an "independent government," or that a Vietcong victory could affect "the security of the free world?" Or, for that matter, that the free world was composed of free societies?

To ask these questions is to answer them. These words had been emptied of meaning and had become merely the stimuli for an increased defense effort—that is, more money for more "hardware" to defense contractors looking at shrinking profits, and more flight time, promotions, and ribbons for more generals and admirals who would go to work for the contractors when they "retired." There *was* a military–industrial complex, and its unspoken motto was "Better a bad war than no war at all."

Vietnam was a bad war, one which its captains quickly realized would never have popular support. Korea, after all, was a case of U.S. resistance to real aggression, fought on behalf of a country whose people *wanted* to resist and whose soldiers fought bravely. Even Korea became a most unpopular war and forced from office the President who had chosen to fight it. Vietnam, where there was no aggression and where the successive "governments" we defended mocked our sacrifices as they stole our treasure, could never be sold. This was one war for which Americans, however often the "national security" defense was invoked, would not pay.

So it was arranged they would not have to pay for it—at least not most of them, or at least not the ones who mattered. As the war escalated from 1964 through 1968, as American combat forces grew from an "advisory" force of 17,000 to a swollen combat army of 550,000, as the casualties climbed from zero to 300 dead per week, the cost of the war—financially and emotionally—was limited almost entirely to lower- and working-class Americans.

By the simple device of exempting from military service any young man so long as he was attending a college or university,

102

the government made sure that no influential American had to take on the ultimate risk in order to support the war. Of 535 congressmen and senators, never more than a handful had sons in service, and the same proportion was true of other politicians, bankers, union officials, businessmen, and civic leaders. Hardly anyone in a position of influence or authority needed take into account the possibility that *his* son might be sent to fight.

The result was an emphasis on higher education in the middle and upper classes hitherto unmatched in our history. Young men went to college and university—and stayed. Graduate study thrived and professional schools swelled their enrollment. The Vietnam war was fought by those who could not afford, or whose families, could not afford years in college or university.

(There are interesting results to all this. As the ugliness of Vietnam became more and more apparent, particularly to the young, the attractiveness of representing the United States became more and more remote. Thus, two avenues of postgraduate activity once entered by some of the six best university students—the Foreign Service and the military and naval reserves—were virtually abandoned by those able young men who once would have entered. Divinity school became more attractive. To a young man with a social conscience and to whom Vietnam and much else about America was becoming abhorrent, divinity school seemed a good retreat. One could concentrate on matters less worldly, and in addition, it offered a haven from the draft. The war went on so long that the Vietnam-motivated divinity students, to preserve their deferments, went on to be ordained. Thus the nation may expect, one generation from now, a bad crop of generals, admirals, and ambassadors, but splendid bishops.)

And if the working men and women of America paid for Vietnam with their sons, they paid with their money, too. Since this was a war, as both the Johnson and Nixon administrations understood clearly, that Americans would never pay for, it was decided to let inflation take the tax that otherwise might be exacted. In the peak years of the fighting, the Johnson administration added as much as $3 billion annually to the budget for Vietnam alone, without reducing any other item or calling for any sacrifice, whether in taxes, rationing, or anything else. The result, of course, was inflation but swallowed by so much prosperity at the top that it was felt sharply only toward the bottom of the economic pyramid. Not until the inflation of Vietnam compounded by swollen defense budgets under Nixon, began to touch everybody by 1971 did the administration act, and then it imposed a wage freeze on the very Americans who had already paid the most.

There was protest, to be sure. Many questioned the wisdom of Vietnam—in small groups, in massive marches, in Congress, in churches, in universities, and in the press. The protest reached its height in 1967 and 1968, when it drove Lyndon Johnson first to the fortress of the White House (once he ventured out to speak at a university campus, but one entirely surrounded by an army post) and finally from the presidency itself, thus avoiding defeat in his own party.

To deal with protest, the government used a tool first picked up in the days of the civil rights marches. If thousands of people gather, and particularly if they gather to oppose a government policy, there is always the chance of violence, so the argument runs. Police and military forces must be mobilized, and police and military "intelligence" must seek to infiltrate the protest to identify the "violence-prone." Just as a bombing policy once limited to "surgical strikes" soon became an exercise in random obliteration of what was below, infiltration for a specific purpose led quickly and easily to infiltration for its own sake. If a group is "bad," it can and should be infiltrated, ran the logic which very quickly becomes compelling.

By the time Richard Nixon came to the presidency, the nation had been at war for six years—the longest war period in our history—and what had once been a sound concept of national security had already been cheapened. The techniques for dealing with protest were well established. Local police around the country had refined their methods of what was called "crowd control." Special "political sections" and "intelligence units" had identified, to their satisfaction at least, the ringleaders of the "violence-prone groups." (The measure of the political sophistication and sensitivity of local police "intelligence" operations can be seen in the fact that John Caulfield and Anthony Ulasewicz, hired by John Ehrlichman to do his political second-story work at the White House in 1969, were both high-ranking members of the New York Police Department's security and intelligence unit.)

Young military intelligence agents wearing "hippie" clothing and wigs covered protest meetings, snapping pictures with their tiny cameras. And because many in the generation of young Americans were dropping out of society with drugs and avoiding the draft by the hundreds of thousands, local and national police departments had reason to hire students to identify drug users and draft evaders and to set them up for late night raids.

Thus there began a subtle process in government hitherto known only in the civil law—"the exception that swallows the rule." Lawyers use the phrase to describe some anomaly in the law, an exception to a general rule or norm, that becomes so large or so widely used as virtually to nullify the rule itself. This principle, that there might be an exception which would defeat the command itself, had not previously been thought to apply to the requirements of the Constitution. Slowly but surely, "national security" was becoming such an exception. "Congress shall make no law . . . abridging the freedom of speech or of the press," said the First Amendment, but we were now ready to add, "except in cases of national security." "Persons shall be secure against unreasonable search and seizure," except in cases of national security. "No person shall be deprived of life, liberty or property without due process of law," except in cases of national security. The peacetime draft, an undeclared war, the withholding of government documents, secret testimony before congressional committees, the "classification" of literally millions of documents—all things Americans would once have perceived indignantly as violations of the fundamental charter, and vigorously resisted, now were more or less passively accepted as part of the "national security" exception that had swallowed the rules.

It remained for Richard Nixon, in his pursuit of "victory" in Vietnam—not for the Vietnamese, North or South, but his own *political* victory—to expand the exception of "national security" beyond the Constitution to the Ten Commandments. "Thou shall not bear false witness," went the new Nixon operational code, "except in cases of national security."

There is significance in the fact that Nixon began his term of office by adopting a military course which Johnson had rejected, and that he then deceived Congress and the country about it. The course of action consisted of using Air Force B–52s to bomb the so-called sanctuaries of Cambodia, a step the Air Force had urged on Johnson for years and one he had steadily resisted. Johnson's reasons were many and sound, including a judgment that the action would not stop Vietcong and North Vietnamese infiltration into South Vietnam and that the political price of bringing Cambodia into the war would be too high, both in Cambodia, where Prince Sihanouk had been pursuing a perilous neutrality, and in the United States. Johnson was too good a politician not to realize the storm that the bombing of a neutral, third country would create, and he didn't care to bluff it out.

Whereas Johnson's style with respect to Vietnam was straightforward and at times brutal, Nixon's was devious and ultimately deceitful. If Johnson had decided to bomb Cambodia, he would have announced it and then denounced the "nervous Nellies" who opposed a move which would take the pressure off American troops. Johnson knew it wouldn't go down, and besides, he sensed that, despite the eagerness of his air marshals, it wouldn't work.

Nixon bought the argument of the Joint Chiefs at once, began the bombing of Cambodia, and lied about it. To this very day he refuses to face or tell the truth about the concealment. An elaborate set of double-entry books was set up by the Joint Chiefs and Secretary of Defense Melvin Laird, whereby the Chiefs, Laird, and the White House (Nixon and at least Henry Kissinger) would know which Cambodian targets were being hit, while the rest of the Air Force, the Congress, and the American people were being told of alternate and *false* bombing allegedly going on over Vietnam. The deceit even extended to the next-of-kin of Americans who were killed in this secret war; they were told their sons and husbands died on the "cover" raids which never took place.

The deceit extended until the invasion of Cambodia in 1970, at which time Nixon assured the people we had scrupulously observed the neutrality of Cambodia. When American ground troops left Cambodia in 1970 after an invasion which accomplished no military result except to motivate the North Vietnamese to move into the country in force, Nixon once again assured his countrymen that air support for the Cambodians would be withdrawn as well. It was not true for even one day, and soon the bombing resumed, too.

And as late as the spring of 1973, the Defense Department and the White House were still lying to Congress. Bombing summaries for the war set forth the mock cover missions in order to mask the real missions over Cambodia. As late as August 1973, in a speech to the Veterans of Foreign Wars, Nixon sneered at those who criticized the bombing "of a small neutral country." The criticism had long since passed a concern over the bombing, as he well knew. The criticism was of a president who would conduct a secret war and lie about it to the people and their representatives.

As for Congress, Nixon dismissed the argument quickly in his August address. He said he had told those congressmen "who had a need to know and a right to know" about the Cambodian raids. It summed up the Nixon stance perfectly— it was *his* right to decide which congressmen had a "right to know" about a United States decision to bomb another country. The men who wrote the Constitution thought election to Congress conferred a right to know about decisions of peace and war—indeed, the exclusive right to participate in those decisions. But those men had never heard of the exception of "national security."

The bombing and the invasion of Cambodia was for Richard Nixon only a means to an end, and in his view the 1972 election returns validated it all. And so, after all the deaths and the bloodshed, with most of Cambodia under Communist control and more than one-third of its population homeless as a result of American firepower, with the "sanctuaries" firmly in the hands of the "other side," he could deride the opposition and talk of "peace with honor." The grave questions posed by a secret war, and a futile one at that, came down at the end to a few cheap applause lines to the Veterans of Foreign Wars convention.

Nixon added a new element to the defense of American policy: silence. Like Lyndon Johnson, he assumed that the visible protesters were an insignificant minority, and also like LBJ, he commissioned polls to prove that a majority of Americans supported his policies. During what proved to be the next-to-last gasp of the mass-demonstration part of the peace movement (the Moratorium marches in October and November of 1969), Nixon appealed to the "great silent majority" of Americans and insisted that policy would not be made "in the streets." He boasted that he would ignore the protesters, and his spokesmen let it be known that he watched a football game while half a million of his fellow citizens conducted an orderly protest almost in his backyard.

Predictably, when outrage is ignored by authority, two things happen. Part of the outrage dies away, to be replaced by a kind of passive, sullen resentment. The rest turns to a more dramatic or even violent direction to be heard, and so, as a large part of the peace movement retired from the fray, part of it turned into Weathermen, "Mad Dogs," the "crazies" of the movement.

Like Johnson, Nixon provided a way for his silent majority to tolerate the horrors that the noisy minority were shouting about: a language of military-space-advertising-sports talk that squeezed any humanity out of the words. George Orwell had said in his 1945 essay "Politics and the English Language" that political language had come to consist of "euphemism, question-begging, and sheer cloudy vagueness. . . . Such phraseology [for example, *pacification*] is needed if one wants to name things without calling up mental pictures of them." Not that Richard Nixon and his people invented sterile language—the language had already been corrupted by the war years—but they added markedly to the process.

There is a concept in military thinking called "sanitizing" whereby a document or a briefing may have its "dirty" elements removed for public consumption (laundering money and deleting presidential obscenity from tape transcripts are offshoots of the concept). The Johnson years gave us a sanitized language of war. *Pacification, relocation, strategic hamlets,* and *defoliation* are words that do not conjure up the image of peasants forced from their homes at gunpoint and herded into concentration camps in the midst of scorched earth. *Search and destroy, free fire zones, interdiction,* and *attrition* do not immediately convey the mental picture of the assault on My Lai. *Gooks, slopes, dinks,* and more elegantly, *unfriendlies* are not names for human beings. *Wasting* them and then holding a *body count* does not imply that the bodies have hearts and minds. Conversely, the human name "Fat Albert" does not carry the noise and fire of a bomb that devastates an area 2,000 yards square.

After Nixon took hold of the war, bombing became *protective reaction strikes,* and lest anyone think this represented an interminable policy, they were labeled *limited duration protective reaction strikes*. American soldiers in Cambodia, in violation of congressional policy, were called *end-use observers* for *delivery teams*. *Strategic hamlets* had given way to *pacification,* which now disappeared under the aegis of a CIA operation masked as technical assistance, given the acronym of CORDS, for "Civil Operations, Revolutionary Development Services." CORDS included the *"Phoenix"* program, which did not, as the name might suggest, call for the rebuilding of Vietnamese villages from the ashes to which our bombers and artillery had consigned them. On the contrary, it was a program which had as its objective the elimination of "hostile elements"; that is, the assassination with American assistance of Vietnamese identified for death by agents of their own government. In a world where My Lai could be reported as a successful attack on an enemy stronghold, and the elimination of the village of Ben Tre could be defended by an American major on the grounds that "we had to destroy the village in order to save it," the use of "Phoenix" as a code-name for the nationwide use of assassination squads was a stroke of genius.

The weapons themselves took on an air of unreality. A giant bulldozer, used to destroy a village or a forest or an area of farmland, is called a *Rome Plow* and its function—actually, starvation of the nearby people—is described as "denial to the enemy of access to a sanctuary." The sanctuary, in this case, happened to be their homes.

A *Daisy Cutter* is any weapon designed to explode above the ground, including *Fat Albert,* a huge bomb that descends on a parachute and explodes some yards from earth, killing by concussion and clearing an area large enough for a small landing field. *Daisy Cutter* also includes other above-ground weapons, down to the *Bouncing Betsy,* an M-16 "anti-personnel" mine which, when triggered, jumps to a height of 2 to 4 feet before exploding. It has, according to the army, a "casualty radius" of 35 yards.

Puff, the Magic Dragon, a name taken from a popular folk song, was one of the most fearful weapons in Vietnam. *Puff* is a fighter plane, equipped with three Gatling guns, each capable of firing 1,500 rounds per minute.

Use of these terms answered the need to avoid thinking about real things, but they lacked an appeal to manliness, or what passed for it in America by the end of the 1960s. The Nixon contribution to the language of politics and war was the jargon of sports and the new, impersonal, brisk professions of advertising and computers.

Vietnamization was Nixon's *game plan* for getting out of Southeast Asia with at least his own regime intact. His *team players* would do his *downfield blocking,* or he would throw the *long bomb* or *shoot the gap* or, in any event, be *hard-nosed.* When the computer-advertising gibberish of *input, time frame* (and the tiresome *point in time*), *inoperative, zero defect, downside risk,* and *bottom line* is added, along with the burgeoning space and military penchant for initials (EVA, for *extravehicular activity*, or getting out of the space-ship; MIRV, for *multiple independently targeted reentry vehicles*, the dozens of nuclear warheads forming part of a ballistic missile), it is little wonder that language became so sanitized that the Nixon people didn't know a lie when they saw one, or that the line between right and wrong became blurred and eventually erased.

One digression into a little-known example of Nixon administration double-speak is both warranted and highly exemplary. It is a splendid example of the debasement of language to serve a highly sinister end by masking a gross invasion of privacy in technical language—in this case, the language of marketing.

Early in the Nixon tenure, the Office of Civil Defense came up with an idea, one which has occurred with increasing frequency in authoritarian governmental circles throughout the world, of permitting the leader to speak to everyone at once. OCD called it the Decision Information Distribution System (DIDS) and designed it as a transmitting device to be built into every home television receiver. The transmitter would be automatically triggered from Washington—naturally, in case "national security" was threatened—so as to bring every American with a TV set the voice of the President.

The proposal was not rejected out of hand, probably because it was hardly publicized. By 1972, Charles C. Joyce, Jr., the assistant director of the Office of Telecommunications Policy (an agency otherwise involved mainly in intimidating local television stations into eliminating network news unfavorable to Nixon) was busy promoting the scheme. Here is some of the language he used to justify DIDS:

Studies made several years ago indicated that a warning receiver sold separately would not achieve a very significant market penetration. This led to consideration of the possibility of incorporating the warning receiver into an item of home entertainment equipment. . . . Television sets are the obvious choice as a "carrier" for the DIDS receiver because of the very high penetration of television sets into the home market and because the percentage impact of the DIDS receiver on the overall cost of the television set would be small. Legislation requiring the incorporation of a warning receiver in every television set would, within ten years, achieve a very high penetration of warning receivers and would assure that the economies of mass production would be fully exploited in the manufacture and distribution of warning receivers.

Now, Joyce is not illiterate, and the parallel to Orwell's Big Brother occurred to him at once. He drew a nice distinction: "Big Brother appeared in sound and picture, preempted all other programming, and was capable of listening in on individual households. The DIDS system would provide only voice transmission of warning messages, is clearly limited to one-way transmissions to the home, and does not preempt other programming."

That is hardly reassuring. One imagines that anyone who would use the language of "market penetration" to describe such a plan must be working even now on how to lick the bugs in the system which—as Joyce and his friends would probably put it—"denies the capability of bilateral multisense communication in time frames compatible with executive determination."

The corruption of language was not complete until the agreement was finally signed to end the American fighting presence in South Vietnam. Coming as it did after the Christmas terror bombing of Hanoi, Nixon called it "peace with honor." He called it that after it became clear that there was little peace and, after the terror bombing, no honor at all. He has called it that on many occasions since, once coupling it, incredible as it may seem, with a reference to *his* anguish in deciding on the Christmas attack of the B-52s. All that he has accomplished with the phrase is to ensure that for a generation or more those two good words, "peace" and "honor," will be carried in quotation marks.

Whatever history's judgment of Richard Nixon, beyond the obvious fact that "Watergate" will always be associated with his name, it is clear that he is impatient for the verdict, and that impatience affects his words as well as his deeds. It was thirty years after James Monroe asserted the American determination to keep foreign influence out of the Western Hemisphere that his assertion was referred to as the Monroe Doctrine. Richard Nixon spoke in Guam one morning in 1969 about the desire of the United States that Asian nations solve their own problems with their own military forces, and by that afternoon *he* was calling it the Nixon Doctrine.

Nixon cannot refer to his trip to China without calling it "my historic journey for peace," ignoring the argument that that sort of thing is usually left to the historians. Even Billy Graham was once obliged to abandon his stance as a loyal Nixonian and revert to his position of Baptist minister in order

111

to object to Nixon's characterization of the moon landings as "the greatest week since the Creation."

As a natural complement to the rise of the military and the corruption of the language, America by 1969 was becoming a garrison state.

Alexis de Tocqueville had spoken a century before of an absolute system of government where "the people would become the reflection of the army, and the community regimented like a garrison." In the 1940s and 1950s lawyer-philosopher Harold Lasswell defined the concept for the modern world as a state in which the "specialists in violence" become the most powerful group in society.

The military and the police will come to play the dominant roles in society, Lasswell said, when a society lived in "perpetual crisis." The energy of the nation will be directed toward the production of war materiel, rather than toward the production of goods for the use of the populace. Leaders in the garrison state will feel themselves threatened by the perpetual crisis and will be suspicious of all opposition. This will bring the political police to the fore, and in the modern world (projected for 1954 by Lasswell), it will use the new technological devices of surveillance to insure the safety of the leadership. The leaders will seek to reduce "the hazards of persuasion" and the "uncertainties of response" by the use of "cue words" used to indoctrinate rather than to inform or discuss. The populace will respond to these words in "ritualized ways." The secrecy of state business will lead to the withdrawal of responsible people from the political process, leaving the political field to the new elite of violence specialists and the "agitators." Thus, the creativity of the society will decline, for initiative from the bottom will not be tolerated, and the society will transform itself subtly into the image of its enemy.

In 1949 Lasswell foresaw the use of "defense" as a cue word in our emerging garrison state.

Given the near universal expectation of violence, there is no effective opposition to "defense." The internal consequences of militarization are gradual and far-reaching. Beginning as advisers of the civilian arm of government, soldiers and policemen gain stature even in states which possess strong traditions of civilian supremacy. In the name of security the soldier is permitted to impose restrictions upon the free flow of information and command. The policeman is authorized to look into the loyalty of government employees, and of ever enlarging circles of persons who might under any conceivable set of circumstances prove dangerous to the state. Legal sanctions designed to protect the individual against official interference come to be more honored in the breach than in the observance. Public opinion becomes less well informed and less respected. Political parties decline as instruments of public control. Legislatures and courts decline in relation to the executive arm of government, elections degenerate into plebiscites, local initiative subsides, and civilian agencies give way in effective power to the organs of the military and the police.*

The Ervin Committee hearings in the summer of 1973 exposed what "perpetual crisis" had done to the country. The national security argument reached its final frontier: Burglary was necessary for the safety of the nation. National security was perhaps the only excuse that Nixon might offer to the nation for the Ellsberg burglary and Watergate itself, but suddenly the people were not responding to the cue words anymore. It was too fantastic to argue that national security demanded the break-in at Daniel Ellsberg's psychiatrist's office—to obtain some "dirt" on Ellsberg—or at the Watergate complex—in order to be able to smear Larry O'Brien.

Nixon launched his national security defense on May 22. Leaks of government information necessitated wiretaps; bombings (domestic, not in Vietnam) and demonstrations required a kind of "Rolling Thunder" operation against domestic dissent. But the real evil, Nixon argued, that made all this necessary was the country's reaction to the invasion of Cambodia. The Nixon specialists on violence had apparently been caught off balance. They did not know how to deal with a new technique of protest: campus closings. To make matters worse, the soldiers of the garrison state shot a few students at Kent State and Jackson State.

So in 1973, Nixon wanted the people to believe that in 1970 the country has been on the verge of anarchy. There were, of course, some bad times in 1970. As the sophisticated bombs rained down on South and North Vietnam by the ton, killing thousands and leaving millions homeless, a few amateurs in this country planted homemade bombs at the Defense Department and some other public buildings. On 11th Street in Greenwich Village, novices accidentally blew themselves up along with a $235,000 townhouse, and at the University of

* "The Universal Peril: Perpetual Crises and the Garrison State," by Harold Lasswell, 1949.

Wisconsin a mathematics laboratory was blown up, tragically killing one graduate student, the only casualty of what Nixon now wants us to see as a reign of terror.

Memory is curiously editorial: It registers what it wants to and discards the rest. The Nixon defense of the constitutional abuses in 1969–1970 (as it was expressed in May and August 1973) rested on the hope that the American people would remember those years as the Nixon men did. The President referred to a wave of bombings, burnings, and riots. He blamed the "excesses of Watergate" on the "excesses of the 1960s," as if Jeb Magruder, John Mitchell, and John Ehrlichman had somehow taken their cues from Angela Davis, Jerry Rubin, and Bobby Seale. He scoffed at the civil disobedience of the 1960s, with its "higher morality," and suggested the Watergate criminals had mistakenly adopted its ideas. The implication was clear: the higher morality in Watergate ("Both are wrong. Both should be condemned," Nixon said in August) was loyalty to Richard Nixon.

Throughout the emerging revelations of Watergate, Nixon has swerved from one defense to another—from acknowledging responsibility to offering "national security" as a defense. He has been consistent in urging the public to accept the notion that nothing he or his men have done is much different from what other administrations—usually the Kennedy administration, where the two men who could answer are both dead and thus easier to accuse—have done.

The charge is mean-spirited and, in the best sense of the word, subversive of the ideas which have always informed our society, and it is demonstrably false. Nowhere is it more false, and nowhere is Nixon's use of the argument more knowingly deceitful, than in the comparison between the "higher morality" of the civil rights and Vietnam protesters of the 1960s and the motivations of the Watergate men.

When Martin Luther King violated a Birmingham ordinance and led his people en masse in an attempt to register to vote, he was jailed as he knew he would be. He did so to show his belief that the law was wrong. William Sloan Coffin publicly counseled resistance to the draft and never denied his actions. When young men burned their draft cards at public demonstrations, when members of religious orders celebrated a peace Mass at the Pentagon, they did so openly, in the tradition of civil disobedience—an honorable tradition that includes Christ, Thoreau, and Gandhi.

The resisters and protesters were arrested and tried, and at their trials they did not perjure themselves, deny their acts, or try to cover up what they had done. The difference, and Richard Nixon knows it, is considerable. If the Nixon men were proud of their "higher morality," why did they commit their crimes in darkness, destroy the evidence, collect vast sums of money to persuade others to remain silent, and lie about what they had done?

When Henry David Thoreau was in jail for a principled refusal to pay his taxes, his friend Ralph Waldo Emerson came to visit him. "Thoreau," he asked, "why are you in jail?" Thoreau's reply has become the rallying cry of civil disobedience ever since. "My dear Emerson," he said, "why are you not in jail?"

Nixon and his apologists would have us believe that Thoreau led Emerson to a corner of his cell and, in a low voice, asked if Emerson would suggest that the CIA planned the whole thing, sneak some money from the government to pay his lawyers and his family, and get him some assurances of executive clemency.

The Nixon statement of May 22, stressing "national security" as an overriding justification for most of what John Mitchell would later call "the White House horrors," demonstrates clearly the wisdom of Lasswell's insights in 1949. Substitute "defense" for "national security" and you have the Nixon White House in the years of Watergate, complete to the subtle transformation into the image of its enemy. It should come as no surprise that the only capital in the world where official and press support is heard for Nixon's Watergate explanations is Moscow.

Imagine this dialogue between a perplexed but well-meaning outsider and a knowledgeable White House insider in 1971, as the outsider seeks to understand the reasons for the widespread wiretapping which had been directed against past and present White House employees, journalists, and perhaps others: It was done, the outsider is told, to find the source of serious leaks of information. Very well, he asks, but what information has been leaked? Why, he is informed, the plan for the U.S. delegation at the disarmament talks with the Soviet Union. And why, he wonders, is such a leak so dangerous? Because the Russians will learn of our "fall-back" position. And if they do? Then they will be in a stronger position at the talks, and perhaps maneuver us into accepting an agreement which will leave us weaker. And why then, he asks, should we fear a situation in which the Soviet Union has a stronger military position than it now has? Because, the triumphant answer comes, it might then prevail against us in a test of arms. The outsider remains unconvinced. What then? he asks. Then, says the insider sternly, they could impose their will upon us, and we would have a Communist system here in America. That would be bad, agrees the outsider, finally. Of course it would, says his friend. If that were to happen, the government would be free to burglarize your home and to tap your telephone. None of us would be safe.

5. The White House Horrors

"White House horrors" is what John Mitchell called them, but since he participated in some, it's hard to know just what he meant by the words. President Nixon has referred to them, from time to time, as "deplorable incidents" and "indecent, petty, murky things" in which people might wish to "wallow." George McGovern knew about only some of them, enough to call them a "pattern of deceit and corruption" that contributed to "the most corrupt administration in our history." The Congress may one day, in an assertion of its duty, catalogue them as "high crimes and misdemeanors."

By whatever name, what follows is an account of Nixon White House and administration activities that are only peripherally involved in "Watergate" in the sense that the actors were often the same—including Nixon himself, and that much of it would have remained undiscovered had it not been for the investigation of the Watergate break-in by the press, the police, other law enforcement agencies, and of course, the Ervin Committee. It is significant, I think, that although Nixon three times, by his own statements, launched "sweeping" investigations, none ever turned up wrongdoing of any kind. None of the incidents described in this chapter were brought to light by the White House—indeed, most were initially denied, then partially denied, then "explained," and finally defended on the grounds of "national security," and anyway, everybody else did it and no one complained.

I have made no effort to rank these incidents in the order of their importance, or even by the amount of horror they generate. To many Americans, the effort to slander the memory of John F. Kennedy through the use of a forged diplomatic cable that implicated him in an assassination is the worst crime the Nixon people have perpetrated, particularly since Nixon

117

himself participated in the scheme. Others, particularly professional men and women and their patients and clients, whose livelihoods and reputations largely depend upon confidentiality, think the worst offense was the burglary of the office of the office of Daniel Ellsberg's psychiatrist, Lewis Fielding. Still others, among them lawyers and legislators whose concern is the strict construction of the Constitution, think Nixon's deliberate approval of techniques that violate the Bill of Rights—permissiveness at the summit, as it were—was the worst. There are tax experts who put at the highest levels of the Nixon offenses the use of an incomplete deed—a postdated one at that—to obtain a tax deduction of over $500,000 from the President's personal income.

Whatever the ranking, these offenses happened. They happened while Richard Nixon was president of the United States. These deeds were done either by him or in his behalf by his closest friends and appointees. Even in the few cases where it is difficult to prove his knowledge of them, they all bear the stamp of what the police would call his "M.O.," his *modus operandi*—an amalgam of guile, fraud, and deceit, all toward the goal of his electoral or personal prosperity, which has characterized Nixon Politics ever since the representative of the Committee of 100 placed that fateful phone call from Whittier in 1945.

The Forged Cable

On July 6, 1971, E. Howard Hunt went to work at the White House as a "consultant" and was paid at the rate of $100 per day. Hunt had retired a year earlier after 20 years with the CIA. Some CIA officials now say his employment was something of an embarrassment to them for a while before his retirement. There was, if their accounts are to be believed, a good deal of competition between sections and stations of the agency to avoid being required to "take Hunt."

There is some support to be found for this in Hunt's own account of his role at the CIA prior to and during the "Bay of Pigs" assault on Cuba in 1961. In his recently published book, "Give Us This Day," Hunt describes his work as that of political liaison between the CIA officials in Washington who were running the show and the exiled politicians in Miami who were to form the "provisional government" of Cuba once the island was liberated. Hunt, who has presumably not downplayed his role, comes across in the book as a man "on the

118

shelf"—the last to know important decisions and whose requests were generally ignored in Washington. Finally, as the invasion drew near, the whole political committee was taken out of his hands and moved, physically, to New York, while Hunt was left with no specific assignment in Washington.

In any event, he came aboard at the White House as an employee and protégé of special counsel Charles Colson. Colson was a close friend of Hunt's, and their families had visited socially. (When Hunt's wife died in an air crash in Chicago, and $10,000 in $100 bills was found in her handbag, at a time when Hunt's role in the payoff of the other Watergate defendants was becoming much discussed, Colson worried over whether to attend the funeral and finally decided that discretion dictated that he stay away. Those who recalled that Colson had once written in a memo to his staff that he would walk over his grandmother if it would help reelect Richard Nixon, were not surprised.)

Hunt, who took office space and secretarial help from Colson, began at once to work on the "get Kennedy" project which had previously occupied the time of John Ehrlichman's men Caulfield and Ulasewicz. He did extensive research on all the reports about Chappaquiddick and rapidly became the house expert on the matter. Indeed, his Chappaquiddick file was one of the two files so sensitive that when his safe at the White House was cleaned out by John Dean in the days following Watergate, they were given by Dean and Ehrlichman to acting FBI director L. Patrick Gray, with instructions that they were "never to see the light of day."

The other file was more serious and should, indeed, never have seen the light of day. But it did, and at a presidential news conference. Shortly after Hunt began work for Colson, he requested but did not get from the Pentagon (but did get from the State Department) copies of the cable traffic between Washington and Saigon in the months and weeks prior to the overthrow of Ngo Dinh Diem in South Vietnam in October 1963. All histories of the time, including those by authors with access to the cables in question, agree that although President Kennedy approved the military *coup* which overthrew Diem, he was extremely insistent that no physical harm befall Diem or his brother, a close aide who was equally detested in Saigon.

These were hardly contradictory orders for President Kennedy to give, since the key men on both sides—the Diem regime and the military plotters against him—were on our payroll. It had been only the restraining hand of the United States, exercised by Ambassador Henry Cabot Lodge through our military command and the CIA, that had prevented an overthrow of Diem in the early and middle months of 1963. The rebellious generals were waiting for a signal from their bosses in the CIA as to when and how to act, a signal they had to respect or risk the loss of pay, rank, and the perquisites of corruption which are part of the fee we pay Asian leaders for serving the United States.

Hunt looked through all the cables, and the message was clear—overthrow Diem and Nhu (the conspiratorial brother), but be sure they get to a safe asylum. It also appeared from the cables—many if not all of which were reprinted in the Pentagon Papers—that those were the instructions Lodge passed along. To everyone's shock, Diem and Nhu were captured at their first hiding place (no one yet knows by whom), taken elsewhere, and shot. Hunt's job, and he failed at it, was to find a real cable which could be used to show that President Kennedy, himself an assassin's victim less than one month later, had ordered the killing.

Hunt reported his failure to Colson, according to testimony he later gave, and Colson asked if he couldn't "do better." Hunt said Colson told him he couldn't give him any technical assistance; he would just have to use the tools at hand. So, again according to Hunt, armed with nothing more than a typewriter, a Xerox machine, and a single-edged razor blade, he produced a rather credible forgery. This cable had all the right signatures, including those of Secretary of State Dean Rusk, and National Security Advisor McGeorge Bundy.

Just what happened to the forged cable is in some dispute. It is hard to believe that Colson did not either show it to Nixon or tell him he had it in his possession, and that it would stand up. Because within a few days, on September 16, 1971 Nixon held one of his rare press conferences, and in it he dropped a statement which could not have come from him without the special knowledge that the Hunt–Colson forgery existed.

In answer to a question critical of President Thieu, who had been our client for some time (there were those who regarded Nguyen Van Thieu as the highest ranking holdover appointee of the Johnson administration) and who was about to conduct a presidential election in South Vietnam with only one candidate, himself, Nixon responded: "I would remind all concerned that the way we got into Vietnam was through

Diem . . ." (emphasis added).

that date, the Nixon statement was a bombshell. No president,

In terms of the generally accepted history of Vietnam until overthrowing Diem *and the complicity in the murder of* secretary of state, or historian had ever before suggested American "complicity in the murder of Diem." But the press, preoccupied with the answers to other questions at the session, generally ignored it.

Colson, however, stuck to what must have been the game plan. He showed the Nixon excerpt to some reporters, pointing out to them that it represented a departure from previous accounts of the Diem overthrow and assassination, but there were few takers. Then Colson went further. To one of his special favorites in the press, Bill Lambert, a *Life* magazine investigative reporter and a good one, he showed a copy of the cable which Hunt had manufactured.

Lambert took the cable and studied it. Clearly, if the cable was genuine, it was a big story. The more Lambert looked at the cable, the less authentic it seemed, and finally, after many months, he decided—correctly—that it was a forgery and abandoned the story. It was a decision which must have disappointed Colson. There the matter rests, since the cable and the back-up material presumably went up in smoke at Christmastime in 1972, when Patrick Gray burned it along with the Chappaquiddick file and his holiday gift wrappings.

It is difficult to avoid the conclusion that the President of the United States deliberately participated in a dirty little political trick whose result would have been to alter history, to diminish Ted Kennedy's chances for the presidency by making his brother seem a participant in an assassination, and of course, thereby to enhance Nixon's own chances for reelection.

This theory is strongly supported by an obscure portion of Nixon's famous statement of May 22, 1973. This was a 3500-word statement put out in the President's name by some of his counsel, whose attempts to explain some of it ended in a shouting match between them and the White House press. It was a statement to which Nixon returns time and again and in which he first launched the "national security" defense for practically every White House horror which had then come to light.

I say "had then come to light," because Nixon's statements throughout the Watergate period typically are reactive only; that is to say, he says nothing until a particularly damaging fact becomes public, such as the Ellsberg burglary, his attempt to use the CIA to head off an FBI investigation of the "Mexican laundry" link between the Watergate burglary and his campaign committee, and the existence of the now famous White House tapes.

So it was with his explanation of the Hunt cable. By the time of the May 22 statement, reports had circulated in the press about the existence of the cable, about Colson's attempts to exploit it, about Nixon's use of it at a press conference, and about Patrick Gray's destruction of it at the request of Dean and Ehrlichman.

There had to be an explanation, and there was, buried in the May 22 statement. Of all the Nixon explanations, it is perhaps the lamest and most shameful. Lame because he could hardly have expected anyone to believe the story, and shameful because the silliness of the explanation permits no conclusion other than that the story itself is true. After explaining the reasons for the formation of what he called the Special Investigations Unit—the "Plumbers"—Nixon went on to describe their duties. He said the unit should "as a matter of first priority find out all it could about Mr. Ellsberg's associates and his motives." That was a cover, as we shall see, for the political attempt to smear Ellsberg by rifling his psychiatric file.

Then Nixon went on to describe another duty he assigned to the Plumbers, and this is the curious one which is his only attempt to deal with the forged cable. "I assigned the unit a number of other investigatory matters, dealing in part with *compiling an accurate record of events related to the Vietnam war . . .*" (emphasis added).

Now, really! Who are these men to whom the President of the United States wants us to believe he entrusted the job of compiling "an accurate record of events related to the Vietnam war"?

Of the four men who made up the Plumbers, there was first of all the man in charge, Egil Krogh. A young man, 31 years old, Krogh's work experience had consisted, prior to coming to the White House, of a few months as a young associate in John Ehrlichman's law firm in Seattle.

He was joined as cochairman by David Young, a New York lawyer from one of the proper firms, who had done some campaign work for Governor Nelson Rockefeller. Young came to Washington to work as Henry Kissinger's appointments secretary, but he fell afoul of Kissinger's deputy Alexander

Haig. Haig didn't think Young was capable of doing substantive work on Kissinger's staff, so Kissinger put him to filing documents, without an office, while he waited for an appropriate "slot." He found one as a Plumber.

The other two Plumbers were Hunt and Liddy. One a failed spy, the other a one-time prosecutor with a flair for the dramatic, who had been fired at the Treasury Department because his passion for guns had led him to oppose Treasury policy in favor of gun control. Liddy also came to the White House as an Ehrlichman protégé.

Nowhere in this group is there a historian, a military authority, or anyone with the critical intelligence needed to come up with a notion of *how* to compile a history, let alone *compile* one. It would be like asking Henry Kissinger and Alexander Haig to write a musical comedy about baseball or square dancing—and to do it in secret.

This "history of Vietnam" was to be done, according to the May 22 statement, in secret, without the possibility of consulting anyone in departments of government where knowledge might reside. It is absurd and almost pitiful, if it did not conceal so shabby and demeaning an effort, that this was the best story Nixon and his lawyers could come up with to explain away the cables in Hunt's possession, including the forged one. "The wicked flee when no man pursueth," we are told in Proverbs, and the guilty, apparently, make up cock-and-bull stories about hiring men to write a history when they are caught in the use of a forgery.

What did the President know? That there was at least a "new" cable, changing history, which needed an explanation.

When did he know it? When he used it, on September 16, 1971.

Use of the CIA in the Watergate Cover-up

Here is the major example of Nixon's involvement, direct and personal, in the cover-up of the original Watergate break-in, and it is surprising that more attention has not been paid to it. An analysis by any reasonable man of the testimony on this point—unabashedly pro-Nixon by Haldeman and Ehrlichman, neutral to pro-Nixon by CIA Director Richard Helms, his deputy General Vernon Walters, and L. Patrick Gray—demonstrates clearly enough for any jury the President's complicity.

The facts are hardly in dispute. On June 23, the FBI began

to trace the money found on the Watergate burglars and at their hotel rooms to the Nixon campaign. The cash was in consecutively numbered $100 bills—45 of them—and they had been withdrawn from Bernard Barker's normally inactive Miami bank account. It was short work to trace them to the proceeds of five cashier's checks which Barker had negotiated. Through a process described in detail in Chapter 7, most of the money had been contributed in Texas and then "laundered" in Mexico, so the cashier's checks which Barker had cashed in Miami had originated in Mexico. But all of the cash was Nixon campaign money, and the FBI was about to discover that crucial fact.

At that point, tipped off by someone either at the Campaign Committee or the FBI, Nixon went into action. On June 23 he told Haldeman and Ehrlichman to instruct Helms and Walters to call off the FBI investigation and to use Walters to deal with Pat Gray to that end.

There is no other interpretation possible of the testimony of the men involved. Haldeman says the President was concerned about a possible "national security" conflict between CIA activity in Mexico and the FBI investigation, but there was none, and a direct question to Helms—in person or on the phone—would have yielded that information in ten minutes.

Ehrlichman is less evasive on the point. Trying to minimize his role, he testified that he didn't know what the President wanted, and that he was almost a passive spectator while Haldeman told Walters to tell Gray to call off his dogs. Ehrlichman, in one of his truculent moments of what he believed to be triumph over the Ervin Committee questioners, gave some of the game away. When asked if he didn't think it odd to give instructions to Walters, the deputy, when Helms, the chief, was in the room, Ehrlichman shot back, "Not if the President told you to talk to Walters."

There is every reason for Nixon to have concentrated his firepower on General Walters (Haldeman *and* Ehrlichman is a lot of fertilizer to spread on one little plant). Walters was the deputy director of CIA, but only because he had been a protégé of Richard Nixon's since the vice-presidential days. An accomplished linguist, he had accompanied Nixon on the famous trip to Latin America, and had been with him in the vice-presidential car when it was surrounded and stoned by agitators in Caracas. But Walters wasn't much help this time.

He testified that after the meeting, at which Haldeman had said the FBI investigation into Mexico was "embarrassing" a lot of people and from which he (Walters) got the feeling that what was at stake was "political," he went along and told Patrick Gray to hold off for a while but his loyalty to the CIA and to probity in general was stronger than any gratitude he felt to Nixon. As soon as Helms had assured him that the FBI probe into the Mexican laundering of campaign funds would not compromise in any way any CIA activity, Walters took Gray off the hook and the two men agreed that the FBI investigation should proceed.

It was at this point that Gray, armed with Walters' concurrence, made the famous call to Nixon on July 6. He told the President that people on his staff were trying "to mortally wound" him. Poor Gray didn't understand that Haldeman and Ehrlichman were acting under Nixon's instructions, and so he thought it strange that the President didn't ask him which staff men he was referring to.

Helms also seemed to know what was going on. He thought it odd that the two top White House aides would summon him and his deputy and then instruct his *deputy* to call off an FBI investigation into a purely political matter, on the mere chance that some CIA activity might be compromised. This was particularly true since one question from Nixon (or Haldeman or Ehrlichman) to Helms could have settled the fact that there *was* no CIA activity to be compromised. Helms checked, found there was indeed none, and ordered Walters to so advise Gray. His reward—as he must have known it would be—was to be fired from the CIA directorship as soon as it was safe for a reelected Nixon to do so.

The testimony of Haldeman, Ehrlichman, Walters, Helms, and Gray is consistent with the fact that Nixon wanted the CIA to slow down or preferably to stop altogether, an FBI investigation. This investigation was about to, and later did, establish the unbreakable link between the Watergate burglars and Nixon—they were paid with his campaign funds—and inconsistent with any other set of facts.

That set of facts establishes a crime or crimes, with a variety of descriptions, all coming under the rubric of obstruction of justice. It remains only to examine Nixon's testimony on the matter, which can also be found in the May 22 statement.

By May 22, the White House was aware of the Helms—

Walters–Gray testimony, and something had to be concocted to meet it. As with the forged cable, what came out in the statement didn't help much. "Within a few days [of the burglary], I was advised that there was a possibility of CIA involvement in some way." That statement, as yet unprobed (surprisingly, no newsman at Nixon's press conferences has asked about it), is astonishing, and perhaps its demonstrable falseness establishes Nixon's part in the cover-up more than any other. "Advised" by whom? Certainly not by Helms, according to his own testimony and that of others. If by someone else, then would not the only reasonable course have been to ask Helms if it were true? Nixon never asked Helms if there were any CIA involvement in Watergate; if he had, the answer would have been resoundingly negative.

There is more in the May 22 statement. "I wanted justice done with regard to Watergate, but in the scale of national priorities with which I had to deal—and not at that time having any idea of the extent of political abuse which Watergate reflected—I also had to be deeply concerned with ensuring that neither the covert operations of the CIA nor the operations of the Special Investigations Unit should be compromised. Therefore, I instructed Mr. Haldeman and Mr. Ehrlichman to ensure that the investigation of the break-in not expose either an unrelated covert operation of the CIA or the activities of the White House investigations unit—and to see that this was personally coordinated between General Walters, the Deputy Director of the CIA, and Mr. Gray of the FBI. It was certainly not my intent, nor my wish, that the investigation of the Watergate break-in or of related acts be impeded in any way."

Now that paragraph—with the exception of the claim that the Plumbers were assigned to do a Vietnam history—must stand as the weakest plea to damning information in this whole case. If Nixon were concerned about CIA covert operations, why not ask Helms if any existed? Why ask Haldeman and Ehrlichman to get Walters to do the job—unless it was because he was thought to be the tame loyalist? Finally, why did the concern arise at all, since the FBI was only investigating what appeared to be a purely domestic burglary? How did Nixon know Mexico was even involved? The answer, of course, must be that Nixon already knew of the Mexican connection, but to admit that would be to concede his participation at an early date in a conspiracy to obstruct justice.

What did the President know? That his aides were using the CIA to stop an FBI investigation into an important link between the Watergate burglary and the Nixon campaign.

When did he know it? When he instructed them to do so, on June 23, 1972, six days after the burglary.

The 1970 Intelligence Plan

There is no dispute that on July 23, 1970, Nixon approved an intelligence plan proposed by an interagency committee consisting of the CIA, the FBI, the Defense Intelligence Agency, and the National Security Agency. The White House staff man advising the committee and coordinating its activities was a young man named Tom Charles Huston.

There is also no dispute that Huston drafted the final proposal for Nixon to approve, nor is there any dispute as to what it called for. Put simply, it put a presidential seal on criminal activity by an intelligence group and its components. It recognized that information can be more easily obtained by illegal means than by obeying the law and the Constitution, and it specifically authorized burglary, breaking and entering, theft, unauthorized opening of civilian mail, and wiretapping and other electronic surveillance. The Huston memo, which Nixon initialled, listed all these activities, and stated flatly that they are illegal.

There has been testimony by Haldeman and Ehrlichman, and Nixon concurred in his May 22 statement, that the whole operation was cancelled five days after it was approved, chiefly because of the continuing objection of J. Edgar Hoover. Hoover's opposition, to be sure, wasn't based on any commitment to the restraints of the law and the Constitution (his FBI had apparently burglarized foreign embassies on a regular basis for years and concealed the fact from successive administrations). What Hoover objected to was the bureaucratic downgrading to which the FBI would be subjected under the Huston–Nixon plan—being forced to work under the aegis of an interagency committee staffed from the White House. Hoover threatened to make the plan public if the order was not rescinded, and he won.

There is some doubt as to the actual cancellation. Nixon said on May 22 that ". . . the agencies were notified five days later, on July 28, that the approval had been rescinded."

Everyone involved has been somewhat vague as to how the recision was effected, and all agree that it was not done in writing.

What did the President know? That government officials had been authorized to commit a variety of unconstitutional and criminal acts, and that the authorization had been withdrawn —if at all—because of bureaucratic reasons and objections.

When did he know it? When he authorized the activity, on July 23, 1970.

The Ellsberg Burglary

The facts of this burglary are treated extensively in other chapters. What happened is clear enough—Hunt, Liddy, and a slightly different cast of Cuban refugees did the job, and with somewhat more flair than they handled the Democratic National Committee job. According to one of the Cubans, Felipe DeDiego, they found Ellsberg's file in his doctor's office during a late-night entry, photographed it, and made their way out successfully. Hunt tried the next day to show the evidence to Colson, but the special counsel, who liked to know as little as possible about things he might have to testify to, refused to look.

In assessing the Nixon White House, some attention beyond the facts must be paid this burglary. First of all, it occurred at a time when Ellsberg's "guilt" was clearly established; he had not only admitted giving the Pentagon Papers to *The New York Times,* he gloried in it. It also occurred at a time when the FBI, despite Ehrlichman's attempt to downgrade the agency and its dead director, was manning an all-out attempt to find a crime which could be pinned on Ellsberg. (The problem was that taking of classified documents almost always involves giving them to a hostile power with intent to damage the United States; that is the crime of espionage. Ellsberg took the documents in order that his own countrymen might know the facts; he did it, he said, to *strengthen* the United States.)

Ehrlichman sought to justify the burglary of Dr. Fielding's office on the ground that the FBI would not pursue that avenue of investigation and that, in any event, Director Hoover's closeness to Louis Marx, Ellsberg's father-in-law, was making it difficult for the FBI to investigate at all. Both stories—and the one about Marx was attributed to Nixon himself by Nixon loyalist and aide Richard Moore—were palpably false, and

Ehrlichman as chairman of the board of the Plumbers must have known they were false.

The FBI had already interviewed Dr. Fielding, who had quite properly invoked the doctor–patient privilege and refused to talk about his treatment of Ellsberg more than 18 months before. Marx, a toy manufacturer who had long maintained a friendship with high-ranking generals (Marx's military models were always authentic), was well known to despise his son-in-law and to have cut off his defense fund without a penny. And to top it off, Marx said he had met Hoover only once in his life, thirty years earlier.

The reasons Ehrlichman gave for the burglary were clearly not the real ones. The real ones were set forth quite explicitly in a memorandum dated August 26, 1971, from David Young to Ehrlichman. In an earlier memo, Young and Krogh had proposed the burglary of the psychiatrist's office, and Ehrlichman had approved it "if done under your assurance that it is not traceable."

In the August 26 memo, Young described to Ehrlichman in detail how a "negative picture" was to be developed of Ellsberg and any associates he may have had in the original preparation of the Pentagon Papers, at the Defense Department, so as to make the study itself suspect and the work of men seeking even then to undermine the government. The burglary of the psychiatrist's files was to be only one part of this operation, the objective of which was to discover nasty things about Ellsberg and his friends and leak them to the press. The effort was to be coordinated by J. Fred Buzhardt, then general counsel at the Department of Defense and now the latest in a series of "counsels" to Nixon; Robert C. Mardian (since indicted in connection with the "cover-up"), a Mitchell intimate then in charge of the Internal Security Division at the Department of Justice; and William B. Macomber, a career foreign service officer then serving in an administrative capacity at the State Department.

The three "coordinators" had already met, Young reported, with two Nixon loyalists in the House of Representatives, Representative Leslie Arends (Rep.–Ill.) and F. Edward Hebert (Dem.–La.), for the purpose of starting a congressional investigation to embarrass Ellsberg. The whole operation aimed at Ellsberg, including photographing his file at Dr. Fielding's office, was political, and everyone connected with it knew its political purpose from the beginning.

129

There remains only the question of when Nixon knew a burglary had been committed by White House staff employees. He first said it was on April 25, 1973, when he was informed of it by Attorney General Richard Kleindienst. That was one day before a report of the burglary was given to the presiding judge in the Ellsberg case, who then promptly dismissed the charges because the government's action, he said, had "shocked the conscience" of the court.

Later, after testimony before the Senate Judiciary Committee by new Attorney General Elliot Richardson made it clear that Nixon had known earlier, the story changed—and a later Nixon statement said he had learned of the burglary on March 22. Still later, Assistant Attorney General Henry Petersen told the Ervin Committee that he had told Nixon of the burglary on March 17, at which time Nixon had said to him, "that's national security; you stick to Watergate." Nixon then changed his story again to conform to Petersen's; he now says he knew about the burglary on March 17, forty days before he allowed it to be told to the court where Ellsberg was being tried. Petersen made it clear in his testimony that the information would *never* have reached the Ellsberg judge if he and Kleindienst had not gone to Nixon and said they would resign if the President did not tell the judge.

There is also the curious coincidence of two pieces of hearsay testimony before the Ervin Committee. John Dean said that Egil Krogh had told him the orders for the burglary had come "from the Oval Office." (When Krogh was indicted for the burglary in Los Angeles, he told reporters there that the burglary was "clearly authorized"—by whom?)

Robert Mardian testified that in a conversation with Gordon Liddy, he interpreted something Liddy had said as stating that Nixon had ordered the burglary. Liddy has made it clear that he will never testify, and Krogh declined, on Fifth Amendment grounds, to testify about the crime to a Los Angeles grand jury (the crime was committed in Los Angeles County). Krogh subsequently copped a plea, and was sentenced to six months in prison for conspiracy to violate Dr. Fielding's civil rights, specifically the right not to be burgled by White House aides.

Testimony at the trial of Ehrlichman, Krogh, Liddy and Charles Colson—all of whom have been indicted for conspiracy to commit the Fielding burglary—might yield more truth. At least the grand jury in Los Angeles was not impressed by the "national security" argument.

130

What did the President know? That a burglary had been committed by White House employees on the office of a psychiatrist who had treated Daniel Ellsberg, and that the burglary had nothing whatever to do with national security. He refused, for forty days after he knew, to tell the judge in the Ellsberg case.

When did he know it? At least by March 17, 1973, and perhaps before it was committed.

The Cambodia Bombing

Shortly after Nixon took office, he authorized the bombing of the so-called Cambodian sanctuaries, an area along the Cambodian border used by both sides in the Vietnamese war as a staging and rest area. The bombing went on for more than one year, until the invasion of Cambodia itself in May 1970.

During that time Nixon assured the American people that Cambodia's neutrality was being respected. He was able to get away with it because of an elaborate double entry system of reporting worked out by the Department of Defense and the White House, designed to report bombing of Vietnam which was actually the bombing of Cambodia. The enemy was hardly fooled; he could see the bombs falling, but it was necessary to deceive the Congress, which might not have approved or furnished the funds, and the people, who might have put heat on the Congress.

What did the President know? That the war had spread to a third, neutral country, and that through lies by the nation's top leaders a massive bombing operation was being concealed, not from the enemy, but from the Congress and the people.

When did he know it? When it began.

Income Tax Deductions for Presidential Papers

By 1969, Richard Nixon had already taken advantage, in a thoroughly legal manner, of a provision in the Internal Revenue Code that permitted a taxpayer, within certain limits, to claim a charitable deduction for the value of his own records and papers if given to a charitable institution, college, or university or to the government. This was a common practice for men in public life, and not only politicians. Artists, writers, and others regularly gave their work papers, sketches, drafts, and letters to a variety of institutions. The saving, of course, was substantial, since if the papers were sold and the proceeds donated, a capital gains tax would first have to be paid. In ad-

131

dition, curators and librarians, anxious to obtain such papers, would often put an arbitrarily high value on what were, in fact, almost always items of an uncertain tangible value.

In the Tax Reform Act of 1969, Congress put a stop to the practice and set July 25, 1969, as the date after which such transfers would not qualify for the deductions. On April 15, 1970, the President filed his 1969 tax return, claiming a $570,000 gift of "pre-Presidential" papers to the National Archives before the cut-off date in 1969. Assuming the President is in a 50-percent tax bracket, which his $250,000 annual salary would indicate, this would amount to a tax saving to Nixon of $285,000 spread over the maximum six-year period.

Now no one wants a taxpayer—even President Nixon—to pay more than the law requires. But it appears from the facts put forward by the Nixon people themselves that the gift of the papers was definitely not accomplished before the date of July 25, 1969, after which it was disqualified. In fact, there seems to be strong evidence that the gift has not yet, as of this writing, been made at all.

In April 1969, according to White House spokesmen, counsel to the President Edward Morgan prepared a deed, dated it one month earlier, and signed it himself, leaving a blank signature space for President Nixon. The deed, which Morgan says he deposited with a partner in Herbert Kalmbach's law firm, purported to make a gift to the United States of certain "pre-Presidential papers of Richard Nixon of the approximate value of $500,000, delivered to the National Archives on March 27, 1969. A detailed schedule to be attached hereto upon final sorting, classification, and appraising." The deed has never been found, and investigators for The Joint Committee on Taxation believe it never existed—a most reasonable belief.

On March 27, approximately 1,217 cubic feet of records was shipped to the Archives, but there was no instruction as to which papers were to be retained or whether some or all were merely deposited for temporary storage. It was not until December 1969, well after the cut-off date, that an assessment of the documents was made by a professional in the field, and he selected 392 cubic feet of the records for the "gift," to which he assigned a value of $570,000.

One year after the date of the earlier "deed," the appraiser informed the Archives of his selection. In April 1970, nearly nine months after it had become legally impermissible to make such a transfer but just days ahead of the deadline for filing Nixon's return for the year, a new deed, prepared in 1970 but backdated so as to make it appear to have been prepared in 1969, was delivered to the Archives. It was the first knowledge the Archives had of the existence of any deed.

The deed was not signed by Nixon, although previous deeds, giving earlier documents, had been signed. The Archives has yet to accept the gift, which had not become complete until the receipt of the schedule in March 1970, far too late to qualify.

Nevertheless, Nixon did in fact take the charitable deduction on the return he filed on April 15, 1970, for the value of $570,000 set by the appraiser.

What did the President know? That he had claimed a deduction from income, for tax purposes, of $570,000, based on an unsigned postdated deed describing a transaction which took place, if at all, eight months after the law ended the legality of the practice.

When did he know it? Probably when the transaction was first set in motion; certainly when he signed his tax return, on or before April 15, 1970.

The White House Tapes

The continuing controversy over whether or not Nixon can be compelled, or should be compelled, to yield all or any of the tapes he made of conversations at the White House, either to the Special Watergate Prosecutor to the Ervin Committee (or to the House Judiciary Committee), has tended to obscure the making of the tapes themselves. Here is another "White House horror" which Nixon was apparently quite willing to keep a secret—but to utilize—until it was revealed by someone else. In this case, former White House aide Alexander Butterfield rather dramatically told of the existence of the tapes in the course of some other, rather routine testimony.

Briefly, it appears that beginning in 1970, Nixon arranged that every phone conversation and every conversation he held in person, in the Oval Office, the Cabinet Room, his "hideaway" office in the Executive Office Building, or his office in Camp David, would be secretly taped. At both his offices in Washington, the taping was automatic; at Camp David and in the Cabinet Room the system was activated manually.

For nearly three years, almost everyone who spoke to the President was being recorded without his knowledge but with the President's full knowledge. As Senator Talmadge pointed out, incredulously, every senator, governor, congressman, and private citizen was being taped without his consent.

The present state of the law apparently provides that no crime was committed. The offense to good taste and dignity, to say nothing of the affront to history, is enormous. It is interesting that the President, who says he asked Gordon Liddy and Howard Hunt to compile a history of the Vietnam war, would install hidden bugs, as the faithful Haldeman said, as an "aid to history."

How is history more distorted than by a recording of a conversation where only one party is aware the conversation is being recorded? One imagines the President, confident, statesmanlike, generous but protective of the national interest, gently tolerant of the coarse, personal, often ungrammatical, and occasionally indiscreet politicians and heads of state with whom he talked.

History, however, was probably not served, since it has also been made clear that the tapes are secret and must remain inviolate lest something called "executive privilege" (or is it "separation of powers"?) be defiled. Historians could not have had access to this "historical record." In fact, the tapes are used—and have been used—to refresh the recollection of Richard Nixon and his loyalists when in a tight spot. Haldeman was given a number of tapes to take home and monitor, to see if the Nixon story on the conversations with John Dean could stand up. And it is clear from the May 22 statement that Nixon had already listened to at least one tape, the conversation of July 6 in which Patrick Gray warned him that his aides were trying "to mortally wound" him.

What did the President know? That, unknown to chiefs of state, senators, aides, and ordinary citizens, their conversations were being recorded, and that only the President knew it.

When did he know it? When he ordered the practice begun in 1970.

The Meetings with John Wilson

John Wilson is a Washington, D.C., lawyer with experience in the criminal field. By April 1973, it had become clear even in the White House that both Haldeman and Ehrlichman were targets of the grand jury investigation into the Watergate burglary and the obstruction of justice which followed. Both men engaged Wilson as counsel. Wilson apparently felt no moral or ethical qualms about taking on this dual representation, although many lawyers doubt the propriety of representing two criminal clients whose stories and interests may diverge. Wilson angrily defended himself against this charge during the Ervin Committee hearings by saying that Haldeman's and Ehrlichman's stories contained no conflict, but he could hardly have known that when he took them on as clients.

Nor could he have known that when he held two extraordinary secret meetings with Nixon, in the White House, *after* he had been engaged as the lawyer to both Haldeman and Ehrlichman. Wilson has never claimed to be Nixon's lawyer as well, so the conversations were surely not privileged, and it might be interesting one day to inquire about the content of those conversations. Nixon has never talked to the lawyers of other figures in Watergate, either defendants or potential defendants and he would probably refuse to do so on the grounds that it would be improper while the matter was *sub judice*. He would be right.

What did the President know? That he met secretly, on two occasions, with a criminal lawyer representing two men he had been told by the Justice Department were the subject of a grand jury investigation into criminal activity.

When did he know it? When he did it.

The San Clemente Purchase

On August 27, 1973, Nixon issued the third "full and formal" account of how he bought his house in California. The explanation leaves a number of unanswered questions, and some of them will presumably be answered the next time a "full and formal" explanation is forthcoming.

In May 1969, at a news briefing, it was announced that the Nixons had acquired the house for a down payment of $100,-000. This understated the amount of the down payment by $300,000 and overstated the amount of the Nixon contribution to that down payment by $100,000. What had happened, if the latest statement is to be believed, is that a down payment of $400,000 was made, all paid by Nixon from the proceeds of a loan of $450,000 from Robert Abplanalp, a wealthy friend. Nixon also assumed a mortgage for the balance of one million dollars.

Nothing more was said about the purchase of the property until May 1973, although John Ehrlichman, during his tenure as "counsel" to the President, would say from time to time

135

that the Nixons were anxious to find a "compatible" buyer for that portion of the property which did not include the house or the beach.

In fact, according to the latest explanation, a "compatible buyer" had already been found—Abplanalp. He had also advanced $175,000, making a total of $625,000, to enable the Nixons to buy an adjoining parcel of nearly 3 acres, making the property nearly 29 acres in all. Then, on December 15, 1970, according to the new statement, all but 5.9 acres was sold to Abplanalp and another rich Nixon friend, Miami banker C. G. "Bebe" Rebozo. For their land, Rebozo and Abplanalp paid $1,249,000. This figure assumed $624,000 of Nixon mortgages on the property and forgave the debt of $625,000.

Thus Nixon, who bought 29 acres for $1.5 million, sold 23 acres for $1,249,000, leaving himself with the choice land and the house, 5.9 acres in all, for a total price of $251,000. And since Abplanalp has bought out Rebozo there remains the question of which acres are owned by whom? That will be an important question when tax time—property tax as well as income tax—comes around and will probably be the subject of the next "full and formal" disclosure.

There was one earlier "full and formal" disclosure, in May 1973, when Abplanalp's name first appeared. It was then said that he had formed an "investment company" to take title to the property, but in a subsequent press interview he said there was no investment company. In any event, it will be some time before any of this can be tested by the public record, since the ownership of the property is shrouded in a trust, which shows the Title Insurance and Trust Company of Los Angeles as the record owner.

One further cloud exists. The statement of August 27, 1973, was issued by the White House in the form of a letter to the Nixons from the accounting firm of Cooper and Lybrand. Two partners and one senior associate of the firm were convicted in 1968 of distributing false financial statements and of mail fraud growing out of a false 1962 corporate financial statement. Nixon issued all three unconditional presidential pardons on December 7, 1972. Surely, one imagines, it would have been possible for the White House to have found an accounting firm in which none of the principals had received executive clemency in the preceding year from the man whose affairs they were entrusted to examine.

What did the President know? That three different and conflicting stories had been officially released, describing how he got the money to buy his home in California, and that the third statement was prepared by an accounting firm three of whose former principals he had pardoned within eight months of the preparation of the report.

When did he know it? From the beginning.

The Vesco Case

Two members of the Nixon cabinet were acquitted by a New York jury for perjury and conspiracy to defraud the United States. The indictment against Maurice Stans and John Mitchell alleged that Mitchell and Stans conspired, in return for a $250,000 campaign contribution by Robert L. Vesco ($200,-000 of it in cash), to fix a proceeding by the Securities and Exchange Commission, then under way against Vesco. The SEC had alleged that Vesco "looted" the incredible sum of $224 million from some companies he and his associates controlled. They were acquitted of that charge.

But the Vesco story is sordid all the way. Mitchell, it is alleged, while still attorney general, tried to help Vesco gain control of a defunct bank in Lebanon by using a "legal attaché" (really an FBI man—the CIA objected to FBI agents overseas, so they were attached to U.S. embassies as "legal attachés") to try to influence Lebanese authorities who might have questioned Vesco's character.

John Ehrlichman also lent himself to Vesco's effort to acquire the Lebanese bank. Under the previous ownership, the bank had gambled heavily in American grain futures, with the result that when it crashed, the Commodity Credit Corporation, not ordinarily a large Lebanese bank shareholder, found itself with a large block of shares. Vesco wanted to acquire these shares, and officials of Vesco's organization met with Ehrlichman at the White House to see what could be done. Ehrlichman says he did nothing—the Vesco people say he promised to help—but the meeting in the White House was bad enough in itself. White House Chief Domestic Affairs Advisors simply do not meet—if they have any sense of propriety—with men under investigation by the SEC to discuss their plans to acquire controlling shares of a bankrupt Lebanese bank.

Vesco had heavily involved the Nixon family in his operation as well. He had Donald Nixon, Jr., son of a brother of the

137

President, on his payroll. Vesco wrote to Donald Nixon, Sr., describing the entire transaction one month before the 1972 election, and the President's brother turned the letter over to Mitchell. Vesco's attorney, Harry Sears (who was also the New Jersey chairman of the Nixon campaign), and Vesco came up with $250,000 for the Nixon campaign. Since the money came from what the SEC called "looted" funds, it didn't much matter to Vesco whether the money delivered to Stans was in cash or by check, but he got some good advice. Vesco told Sears that Stans wanted $200,000 of the contribution in cash. Edward Nixon, the other brother of the President, came to Vesco's New Jersey headquarters by helicopter to tell the Vesco people that the Nixon campaign did indeed want the money in cash if Vesco wanted it to remain hidden.

So the $200,000 was delivered—in cash and in the inevitable black bag—and John Mitchell on the same day arranged a meeting with Vesco's lawyers and SEC chairman William Casey. Casey couldn't, or wouldn't, stop the SEC prosecution, but he did delay some vital subpoenas until after the election. In spite of his role in delaying the Vesco case, and for that matter in spite of his having spirited crucial ITT documents over to the Justice Department just as Congressional committees investigating ITT were subpoenaing them, Casey was nominated by Nixon—after Election Day—as under secretary of state.

The other casualty of the Vesco case was SEC Chairman G. Bradford Cook. Cook was general counsel of SEC at the time the Vesco charges were being drawn up. One of the sixty-four charges against Vesco was the illegal and unreported cash contribution of $200,000, made in the expectation of government favors. Cook went hunting for geese late in 1972 with Stans, and Stans, according to Cook, persuaded him to delete reference to the contribution from the charges against Vesco. At the same goose hunt, according to Cook, Stans talked to him about "his future." And shortly after that, Nixon appointed Cook to be Casey's replacement as SEC chairman— the youngest head of the Commission in history.

What did the President know? Nothing, unless he discussed the largest cash contribution to his campaign with either his brother Donald, his brother Edward, John Mitchell, or Maurice Stans.

When did he know it? Not until it became public, unless one of them told him.

The Haig Appointment

General (then Colonel) Alexander Haig served as Henry Kissinger's deputy during Kissinger's first four years as national security advisor to the President. By all accounts, he performed his duties admirably, and Nixon promoted him steadily, finally making him a four-star general and sending him back to the Pentagon as deputy chief of staff.

There, but for Watergate, he might have remained, perhaps in the last two years of Nixon's term becoming one of the youngest chiefs of staff of the Army in our history. But when Bob Haldeman and John Ehrlichman had to leave the White House staff on April 30, 1973, the President thought of Haig. Within a few days, he had installed him in Haldeman's old job as White House chief of staff.

The only trouble was that Haig wanted to stay in the Army, at his General's rank, and keep the White House job as well, and that is forbidden by law. Section 973(b) of Title 10 of the United States Code is quite clear on the point—the acceptance or exercise of a civilian post "terminates" a military appointment.

Confronted with this prohibition, Nixon let Haig stay awhile on a temporary, acting basis, and White House spokesmen let it be known Haig would return to the Pentagon "after a few weeks." But after a few weeks, Nixon announced that the Haig appointment was permanent, and that Haig would retire from the Army in less than three months, by August 1, 1973.

That was still flatly against the law, and Representative John Moss of California pressed Attorney General Elliot Richardson for an answer and a ruling on the apparent conflict. Richardson stalled and raised nonexistent technical problems until August 1 had come and gone. There is no doubt that Haig served illegally in both posts in the interim, but there is little that can be done about it now that he has formally retired from the Army.

But the question remains: Why did they do it? Why not simply obey the law and have Haig retire the day he assumed his civil office? The answer, according to Representative Moss and Representative Les Aspin of Wisconsin, has to do with one of those minor concerns which so preoccupy much of the civil service but which, in this case, demeaned both Haig and Nixon.

It seems that if Haig waited until August 1 to retire from the Army, he could do so at the higher pension paid to four-star generals, whereas if he retired before that date, he would have had to accept the lower retirement pay of a two-star general. The difference is $3,843.60 per year, or $320.30 per month. In order for Haig to earn an extra $320.30 per month in retirement, Nixon was willing to flout the law.

What did the President know? That he was breaking the law openly by keeping Haig in the Army and at the White House, in order that Haig might get a higher pension.

When did he know it? When he did it, from May until August 1, 1973.

After describing each of these "White House horrors," I have used the double question so often asked in the course of the Ervin Committee hearings by the Committee's vice-chairman, Senator Howard Baker of Tennessee. I have done so, not because I agree that the question is important, but precisely because I believe it is not—at least in the narrow way in which Baker uses it. His locution has led otherwise reasonable men to conclude that there is insufficient evidence to "make a case" against Nixon, presumably for impeachment, since that is the only case which can be made against a president.

However, Watergate is more than a burglary and a cover-up. The case against Nixon, if one is to be made, must have a wider ambit. It must contemplate Nixon Politics, now Nixon government. And in those years in power, years of corruption in which the American experiment was degraded and its ideals defiled, the President knew a great deal, and he knew it from the beginning.

6. *The Miami* Ambiente

A foreign land is somewhat like a ship. Hard that sensation of indefinable disgust. One feels the ground rock and shake under his feet. . . . One walks staggering, one's spirit out of balance.

José Martí
Father of Cuban liberation

For an American with preconceived notions of teeming Latin American cities, southwest Miami—"or Little Havana"—is a shock. This is no *barrio* of "Black Orpheus." There is no dancing in the streets, no street vendors or flower girls in colorful native costumes. Nor are there any of the normal signs of a refugee community. There is no huddling together. There are no temporary, makeshift houses. The Cuban Refugee Program is phasing out; the "freedom flights" from Havana have stopped and everyone else is settled. The Office of Economic Opportunity has no interest in the area, and the federal government has withdrawn special privileges for the Cuban exiles in the Florida welfare program. Southwest Miami made the transition from a refugee community to an immigrant community in less than a decade, and the transition is a remarkable story.

One drives for five or six miles along S.W. Eighth Street, the main commercial artery of Little Havana, and except that the signs are all in Spanish, the street is not much different from any commercial street in a well-kept, prospering American neighborhood. To be sure, there are distinctively Cuban aspects to the street. At the cafés along the way, simple windows open to the street for business, and rich, sweet coffee is served in orange juice glasses or in tiny plastic cups of the size in which one might get salad dressing on a flight to Miami. The shot of coffee used to cost three cents in Havana ("used to" is often heard), but in Little Havana, American

141

inflation has raised its price to ten cents. Cuban restaurants and markets proliferate on the street. ("You may think it's funny, sir, but it's important to me to eat Cuban food," said a graduate student at the University of Miami). Recently the Miami *Herald* carried a guide to eating and browsing in the area.

The residential areas off the main street are made up of immaculate bungalows and small apartment houses bunched closely together, for the population density is high. About 150,000 Cubans live in El Centro. The houses sparkle with attention and are appointed with well-clipped lawns and colorful tropical plants and trees. There is a sense of pride and energy about the area. One hears "Could this ever happen in Detroit or Cleveland?" They ask what other city could absorb 450,000 new, ethnic people in ten years as successfully as Miami has, but they know it is mainly a credit to the industriousness of the Cubans themselves.

The Cuban influx into Miami has been a triumph of adaptation, at least on the surface. The first few thousand discredited *Batistianos* came in 1959. Then came the frightened rich. The mass flight in 1960 consisted of professionals—businessmen from large and small enterprises, teachers, bureaucrats, and skilled and semi-skilled workers. Then the first disenchanted *Fidelistas* arrived, feeling that the revolution had been betrayed by their leader in the Sierra Maestra. By the end of 1961, 100,000 Cubans had arrived in the United States. From 1961 to 1973, another 450,000 came, mainly through the "freedom flights" from Havana—the legal way to emigrate after being labeled *gusanos*, or maggots, by Castro; others came more dramatically in boats of all descriptions.

The southwest Miami area was the oldest part of the city, and by 1959 it was declining fast. People were leaving. The refugees flocked to it because it was the cheapest area of the city. They took low-paying jobs at the start, and their diligence drove other minority groups from this lowest level of the job structure, causing considerable resentment in the Miami black community where, with good cause, the installation of the lighter-skinned Cubans was seen as racism. In the past decade, Cubans have started 7,000 new businesses. Sixty percent of the Cubans either have bought or are buying their own homes. Banks lend freely to the Cuban home buyer, and records show that the rate of foreclosure on the Cuban client has been almost nil. Indeed, crime is very low in El Centro.

The Miami Police Department patrols the area as lightly as anywhere in the city, for the incidence of robbery and strong-arm crime is low. Drugs have not caught on here, the Cuban connection in cocaine trafficking notwithstanding. The neighborhood has made a remarkable recovery. Since 1959, Dade County has become the third largest garment-making center in the United States, and Cuban women make up 90 percent of its labor force. There abound success stories of Latin Horatio Algers who began with a loan of $1,000 and four years later had multimillion dollar businesses. Many of the more successful Cubans used El Centro as a jumping-off place, and have moved to swankier neighborhoods. Of the 150,000 Cubans now in Dade County, most have moved away from southwest Miami. The swankiest neighborhood of them all, Miami Beach, which in 1960 might have had a few hundred Cuban residents, now has about 17,000.

At 13th Avenue and S.W. Eighth Street, the heart of Little Havana, there is a memorial "to the martyrs of Assault Brigade 2506." The number was the designation of the first Cuban to lose his life in the effort that became the Bay of Pigs. The young man died learning to drive a jeep near a Guatemalan training camp. The memorial lists 121 names. Atop the marble obelisk there is an eternal flame, presumably not in imitation of the John F. Kennedy grave, for JFK is no hero in the neighborhood. The memorial is cordoned off by a chain strung between artillery shells of the kind denied the assault brigade by the U.S. Navy when the invasion began to sputter.

The memorial was dedicated on the tenth anniversary of the Bay of Pigs invasion, April 17, 1971. That the assault known as the worst fiasco in our post-World War II history should be celebrated joyously attests to the overwhelming unreality of Little Havana.

On the day before the celebration, a half American, half Cuban real estate broker named Bernard Barker left his office in a small shopping center known as *La Vieja de Havana* and returned home. There he found a note tacked to the door. "If you are the same Barker I once knew, contact me at ———— Hotel in Miami Beach. Howard."

This note was like the first step in Richard Condon's novel, *The Manchurian Candidate.* The book's protagonist, Raymond Shaw, had been brainwashed by the Chinese Communists in Korea and had been conditioned to carry out any assignment

143

when he was triggered by two conditions: First, Raymond's controller would say, "Why don't you pass the time by playing a little solitaire." That would "unlock his basic conditioning." The appearance of the queen of diamonds, which was "in so many ways reminiscent of Raymond's dearly loved and hated mother," cleared his "mechanism" for an assignment.

Hunt's note unlocked Barker's basic CIA conditioning. It triggered a complex series of emotions and thoughts deep in the psychology of the Bay of Pigs generation in Miami. Hunt, known as Eduardo by the Cubans, was back in town! They were back in business! It remained only for Hunt to play the queen of diamonds to "clear Barker's mechanism" for an assignment.

The process was begun that would lead to at least five burglary attempts (undertaken in blind loyalty to "Eduardo"), some rough stuff at the funeral of J. Edgar Hoover, an arrest at the Watergate on June 17, 1972, a conviction in a Washington, D.C. court, and a thirty-year jail sentence. The public aspect climaxed on May 24, 1973, when Bernard Barker testified pathetically before the Ervin Committee. Senator Howard Baker of Tennessee, the minority chairman who concerned himself throughout the hearings with questions of motivation and ethics, asked Barker, "What on earth would motivate you, at your station in life, at your age, and with that background, to do something that surely you knew to be illegal?"

"Senator," Barker replied, "E. Howard Hunt, under the name of Eduardo, represents to the Cuban people their liberation. I cannot deny my services in the way that it was proposed to me on a matter of national security, knowing that with my training I had personnel available for this type of operation. I could not deny this request."

The explanation seemed so pitifully inadequate. How could a burglary at the Watergate, with the clear intent of political espionage, that struck at the very heart of the American political process, be to this man a matter of "national security"? What was this training Barker spoke of? Who were his people? How could they all be so pliant in the hands of a schemer like Howard Hunt? The American public, by and large, did not accept the Barker explanation. Cuban liberation was too remote to connect with Watergate. Surely these men were hired criminals, paid handsomely for dangerous work. And yet the statements and actions of Barker's "personnel" do not suggest that they were simply guns for hire, not for hire by *anyone*, that is. And the American people did not understand the power of the queen of diamonds—in this case the national security argument.

□ Virgilio Gonzalez, the locksmith and owner of the Missing Link Key Shop in S.W. Miami, was for 26 years a member of *Organizacion Auténtica,* the group loyal to the last elected president of Cuba, Carlos Prio Socarras (who now lives in a large apartment in Miami Beach). He came to Miami in the early 1950s, and was active in the anti-Batista underground. His house in Miami became a regular arsenal for dynamite and other war supplies for the Cuban rebels. After he turned against Castro, he continued this role for the anti-Castro forces. The most stoical member of the Watergate team, Gonzalez accepts his fate and simply waits for his sentence to be over. At his trial he asserted that he had never received money for his Watergate services and that he involved himself, because "I keep feeling about my country and the way people suffer over there."

□ Eugenio Martinez was described by Barker as one of Cuba's greatest patriots. A Bay of Pigs veteran, Martinez made as many as 150 gun-running and rescue missions to Cuba for the CIA between 1962–69. All were extremely dangerous. The trips were undertaken in ships as small as a motor boat (upon occasion with only enough gas to reach Cuba, but not return) and as large as the *Pueblo.* For these trips the CIA paid Martinez a paltry monthly retainer, at most $500, but usually less. At the time of his arrest at Watergate, Martinez was still on a $100 CIA retainer. Richard Helms described his CIA role as "interviewing emigrés" from Cuba, but more accurately, Martinez served as a conduit for Cuban intelligence to the CIA. Martinez had a CIA superior in Miami to whom he reported regularly. It was not Barker, and Martinez thought that the Ellsberg break-in and the Watergate operations were a CIA test of him to see if he could keep silence. Barker had introduced Martinez to Hunt at the tenth anniversary celebration and Martinez had attempted to recruit other Cubans for Hunt's surveillance team to "watch" the 1972 Democratic Convention. Martinez also recruited Cubans for the Hoover funeral "operation."

Emotional like Barker, Martinez is offended by the talk of their team as "mercenaries." At his trial, Martinez told Judge

145

Sirica, "Money doesn't mean a thing to us, your honor, I own a hospital in Cuba, one of the best hospitals. I own a factory of furniture in Cuba. I was the owner of a hotel in Cuba. I left everything in the hands of the Communists there. So . . . really I lose everything, and really money is not a great deal [sic] in my decision. I never worry for money."

☐ Felipe DeDiego, a Bay of Pigs veteran, was an officer in U.S. Army Intelligence for four years after his release by Castro, participated in the Ellsberg break-in, and was present at the Hoover funeral and at the first Watergate entry on the Memorial Day weekend (though he insists that he did not make an entry himself). Why had he become involved with Barker? "I was led to believe it was an anti-Castro, anti-Communist action that we went to Washington for," he told the Miami *Herald*, "and we didn't ask too many questions. . . . We have been waiting for 14 years to do something against Castro and against Communism. We take any chance we get. It's like a fever that takes hold of you." (Barker had referred to it as a "current that sweeps you away.")

☐ Reinaldo Pico, a Bay of Pigs veteran, from 1962 to 1968 was in the employ of a CIA front called The Cuban Revolutionary Democratic Workers Front (FORDC), disrupted allegedly Communist workers' meetings throughout Latin America in this period, and was present at the Hoover funeral and the first Watergate operation. A large, burly man, probably hired for rough stuff, he punched a "hippie" at the Hoover funeral, was arrested, but was released immediately "at the signal of a man in a grey suit." Pico now thinks he was recruited for a "Poseidon Adventure" (his scornful reference), and even though he was not taken to Washington by Barker for the June 17, 1972, trip, he fled to Venezuela immediately upon hearing that the Barker team had been arrested. Pico calls Barker by his nickname, "Macho," which in Spanish can mean either "brave man" or "pig." He remembers Barker's recruitment pitch this way: "The people who we worked for in the Bay of Pigs are back in town. They want people to work for them again. Are you in a position to help?" Pico replied, "Yes, I'll do anything to help." To which Barker said, "OK, then keep quiet. I'll tell you what to do and when."

☐ Pablo Fernandez, long-time anti-Castro activist, was also in the Barker team that disrupted the Hoover rites. Barker paid his plane fare, hotel, and other expenses, as well as providing $100 spending money on the Washington trip. Fernandez figures most prominently in a totally different case: the trial of The Vietnam Veterans Against The War—the Gainesville Eight. Identified as an informer for the Miami Police Department and the FBI, Fernandez is said to have offered VVAW members 15 machine guns. His involvement in the Gainesville case suggests that the activity of the Barker team was broader than the incidents already revealed.

☐ Finally, Frank Sturgis (born Frank Anthony Fiorini) breaks the pattern somewhat. Of Italian rather than Cuban descent and born in Norfolk, Virginia, Sturgis is a notorious adventurer. A marine in World War II, wounded on Okinawa, he drifted from one escapade to another in the early 1950s: police work in Norfolk, flying planes for the Jewish underground, owning a tavern in Norfolk, rejoining the Army Air Force. In the late 1950s, he was drawn to the Castro revolution, evidently for the fun of it. Friendly with Castro in the Sierra Maestra, a profile of him in *Argosy* magazine in 1961 called him "the greatest soldier in the revolution against Batista" and quoted a rebel leader as saying Sturgis alone was worth 50 men in battle. He still carries scars on his back from whippings in a Batista prison.

Sturgis turned against Castro early, and in October 1959, only ten months after Castro assumed power, Sturgis copiloted a B-25 that dropped 200,000 anti-Castro leaflets over Havana. (Castro subsequently gave a marathon speech about the flight, and Sturgis lost his flying license.) After the Bay of Pigs, he became involved in rescue and gun-running missions into Cuba for the CIA involving both planes and boats. In 1967–1968 he organized a band of highly paid mercenaries, financed purportedly by right-wing Texans and Californians, whose goal was "to fight Communism anywhere in the hemisphere." In the early 1970s Sturgis became active again in Jewish affairs, this time in protest over the treatment of Russian Jews. But then he hooked up with Howard Hunt in 1972 and undertook several jobs relating to narcotics trafficking from Latin America. Sturgis was led to believe that the jobs were the beginning of a supranational police force that was forming and that would expand after the reelection of Richard Nixon. But the narcotics-related missions for Hunt were probably just a test for greater things to come. Bernard Barker described Sturgis to the Senate as "a devoted anti-Communist fighter," and Sturgis himself said at the Watergate trial, "I would do anything to protect this country against a Communist conspiracy."

However, a development after Sturgis's conviction in the Watergate affair seems to make his motives more complicated. In August 1973, Sturgis and five others were indicted by a federal grand jury in Miami investigating a stolen car ring that operated out of Texas in 1968–1970. The cars were stolen in Texas and then taken across the Mexican border for sale. If this alleged crime was committed, it would indicate that Sturgis was not only interested in political adventures.

Toward the end of Barker's testimony before the Ervin Committee, he was asked if he still felt that national security was a proper justification for Watergate. He replied that he did feel the Ellsberg entry and, to a lesser degree, the Watergate break-in were justified by that rationale, but "quite frankly," he continued, "I am just a human being. I get confused about all these things. Sometimes I do not know the answers to these questions. I do not pretend to have all the answers."

At the conclusion of his cross-examination, having appeared up to then a ridiculous and inept figure on national television, Barker's voice cracked with emotion. He and his group would have to live with the label the "world's best known burglars," he said, but "we are not criminal elements. . . . There was no need to buy our silence. We are not for sale. . . . I don't mean that we are not full of all sorts of defects as persons. . . . We are just plain people that very deeply believe that Cuba has a right to be free."

Perhaps it would have been better if they had been truly dispassionate burglars for sale, rather than burdened with a largely counterfeit patriotism. There was a good deal of snide contempt from the intelligence community about these "amateurs," and Richard Helms, ex-director of the CIA, became the spokesman for the cool, superior professional. Before the Senate, Helms called the Watergate break-in "amateurish in the extreme" and suggested that surreptitious entry was something better left to those who did it all the time.

The Miami *ambiente* (the whole physical and emotional environment of the Cuban community) is responsible for the overwhelming naiveté of the Barker team, for their blind loyalty to "la gente" (the people) or "la companía" (the company) as the CIA is referred to among the Cuban exiles, and

148

for their acceptance of such dangers for so little in return. It is in the spirit of the age that flat, technical words are used to desensitize concepts with unpleasant connotations. "Such phraseology is needed," as Orwell wrote in 1945, "if one wants to name things without calling up mental pictures of them." To Barker a burglary is an "operation" for which he was "captured," not arrested; to Melvin Laird, American bombing of Vietnamese villages was "protective reaction"; and to Nixon bombing of Hanoi gave us "peace with honor." If we are to avoid this debasement of language, Barker and his team must be called fanatics. There is a generation of fanatics in Miami, a generation that can be triggered into almost any activity. The American government has played an active role in the development of this fanaticism. To these people the American government in the past fourteen years has been Howard Hunt writ large. Many Barkers have come from the Miami *ambiente*, and they were all *"carne de canon."*

The Barker generation of Cuban exiles is cut off. It is the generation that knew the Cuba of Batista and felt the crackdown of Castro. It experienced the trauma of uprooting and the pain of homelessness. It has been called a mess of "worms" by Castro, which is not exactly conducive to a dispassionate view of the Cuban leader. It has been alternately picked up and used by the Eisenhower and Kennedy administrations and, after the Bay of Pigs, stifled and psychologically castrated by the Kennedy, Johnson, and Nixon administrations. Now, twelve years after the Bay of Pigs, it is being deserted by the young generation of Cuban-Americans who are becoming American citizens, who want to eat *frijoles* in Miami, not in Havana, who study Cuban history, not to prepare for the return to the homeland, but to come to grips with their own identity as ethnic Americans.

The Barker generation still clings to the pre-Castro notion of Cuba, but it is a notion romanticized and glorified. Few said they wanted Fulgencio Batista to return; rather, the prevailing emotion is that Castro betrayed the revolution and sold it to the Russians (this emotion prevailed among the Bay of Pigs invaders). And so over Spanish radio in Miami, one hears, "Fab with Borax cleans your clothes the way the Cuban sun used to," and "Cuban coffee like you used to drink in Havana." Private parochial schools, often expensive and staffed with unqualified teachers, advertise that children will be educated the way they were in Cuba. Debutantes are presented to Little Havana society in dresses cut in the nineteenth-century style. And the chaperone system, where a couple is accompanied on a date by an adult or relative, is still in use.

The Barker generation can see the old customs breaking down. Religion has less of a hold on Cuban youngsters. Girls are moving out of the home before they are married; they often appear as leaders of campus organizations, which conflicts with the traditional concept of the Cuban woman. Fascinating compromises with American culture take place, like the advertisement for an acid rock concert over Spanish radio—"$2 a couple, chaperone free"—quite an inducement to a youngster who wants to attend, but can't afford to pay for the chaperone as well.

Some of the more mature young Cuban-Americans are even amused, in an affectionate way, about the Miami Cuban culture. Said one 22-year-old graduate student at the University of Miami, "When I first came to Miami, I didn't like it. Now I love it. There are two worlds here: the real and the surreal. Life is like a surrealist experience. It's like a painting." In 1972, when a Soviet ship docked in Miami harbor, some exiles hired a helicopter and threw red paint on the ship. The graduate student said she was ashamed of the exiles. "I thought they were childish," she said. Andrés Nasario, the 24-year-old son of the leader of "Alpha 66," known for its raids on Cuban shipping, laughs about the jibes he receives on the street about his beard. " 'That's Castro,' they say." Andrés is concentrating on psychology and would do more political work if he "had the time." But "someone in the family has to make money." Still, Andrés Nasario holds the so-called first paper, defined by Immigration as "on parole," whereas his activist father, who claims responsibility for raids and sabotage within Cuba, holds the second paper, defined as "permanent resident."

Some members of the Barker generation accept this drifting away philosophically. Tomás Cruz, for example, was a commander of a paratroop company in the Bay of Pigs. A picture of him embracing President Kennedy, at the Orange Bowl celebration of the return of the 2506 Brigade from Castro prisons in December 1962, ran in newspapers across the country. He now heads an organization of Bay of Pigs veterans and was the master of ceremonies at the tenth anniversary celebration, with Hunt and Barker in the crowd. Cruz is black and wants to write a book comparing the experiences of the

Cuban and the American black. He is not disappointed that the younger generation of Cuban exiles do not share his passion for a return. He said, "It is the responsibility of our generation." And he referred to José Martí, the "George Washington of Cuba" whose picture is everywhere in southwest Miami. "He [Martí] had to wait thirty years in exile before the liberation of Cuba from Spain." In fact, Martí died in the struggle three years before liberation.

The life of José Martí is one parallel to which the Miami refugeees still cling. Cubans also look longingly at the way in which Jews have maintained their identity and culture in exile, not over fourteen years, but thousands. In the week before Brezhnev's visit to the United States in June 1973, the Miami Cuban community was fascinated by the mass protests of Jews against the Communist leader's visit. The attitude of Carlos Varona is representative, and few have as good credentials in southwest Miami as he. The son of Manuel Antonio de Varona, a member of the Cuban Revolutionary Council which was to be the core of a post-Castro government after the Bay of Pigs, Carlos is himself a Bay of Pigs veteran. (President Kennedy was particularly impressed that three members of the Revolutionary Council had sons in the 2506 Brigade.) When Carlos saw the Jews protesting in Washington, his reaction was, "I said I'm glad. Why can't the Cubans do that?" Then he answered his own question. "The problem is that we are an undisciplined people intellectually. We have the talent and the funds, but not the discipline."

Carlos Varona is a mature and intelligent man. At 32 he is a vice-president of the International Bank (an independent bank) on S.W. 8th Street, fourteen blocks from the Bay of Pigs memorial. He recognizes that both he and Bernard Barker have been trained by the CIA in the techniques of infiltration and espionage and groomed to be fanatics. Of Barker's Watergate break-in, Carlos said, "It's very easy to do a job in your profession," implying that Barker was more professional at burglary than it would appear. Barker was "triggered," says Varona. "Some will say that they will never get involved in such a venture. And then maybe, the CIA guy comes to me tomorrow, and tomorrow night, I go to Washington."

There is a macabre pride in this will to action. Cubans in Miami are intent that Americans understand how Barker's team might have been motivated in the Watergate, and they

151

shrink from labeling the break-in as stupid or naive or fanatical. Even Manuel Artime, the golden boy of the CIA in 1961, the most important figure of the Revolutionary Council, and the conduit for the small amount of hush money sent to the families of the Cuban-Americans by Kalmbach after the Watergate arrest, said, "Look, I want you to understand the Cuban mind. If someone said 'Senator Ervin has in his safe sensitive documents relating to national security, and he's going to turn them over to the Russians, will you do something?' I would blow up Capitol Hill!"

The element of Latin exaggeration is unmistakable in this statement, and yet the history of Cuban exiles in America in the last fourteen years shows, if nothing else, that they are oriented to action rather than rhetoric. Their impulse is to the covert and the conspiratorial. Artime is very close to Howard Hunt and is the godfather of one of Hunt's sons; indeed, Hunt came to Artime's home three days after the tenth anniversary celebration. "We're like brothers," Artime said, "but if anyone's guilty in all this, it's Howard Hunt."

Why should Artime be surprised at Hunt's playing the queen of diamonds? The history of the CIA–Miami symbiosis has been marked by exploitation. Richard M. Nixon was one of the earliest exploiters. In April 1959, Vice-President Nixon received Castro in his office (Ike felt it inappropriate to see Castro and was playing golf in North Carolina). About the meeting, Nixon later wrote, "I was convinced Castro was either incredibly naive about Communism or under Communist discipline and that we would have to treat him and deal with him accordingly." The solution Nixon proposed in a four-page memorandum was to arm and train a group of Cuban exiles to overthrow Castro, even though at that time the only exiles available were discredited *Batistianos*. Historian Theodore Draper wrote of the Nixon stance, "Nixon could think of nothing better than a military operation. . . . His military 'solution' was, in effect, political bankruptcy. It was rejected, and better judgment prevailed at that time. Yet, a residue of Nixon's thinking remained, and it always showed in the wings as an alternative policy if the situation continued to deteriorate."

In the 1960 campaign, after planning for the invasion had begun and Cubans were already recruited and in training in Guatemala, Nixon called the Castro regime an intolerable cancer and suggested that the administration was planning to destroy "economic banditry." "Patience," Nixon said, "is no longer a virtue." Historian Hugh Thomas wrote that U.S. foreign policy was reverting under Nixon's prodding to the spirit of the nineteenth-century Polk and Buchanan administrations, where direct intervention in Latin America was promoted—except that the twentieth century seemed to demand mercenaries as a transparent "cover" for U.S. involvement. The intervention of 1961 had to be "Cubanized."

Although John F. Kennedy had doubts about the Cuban project when he was briefed on it after his election, he authorized the planning to continue, but ordered that the Cuban Revolutionary Council be liberalized to include ex-*Fidelistas*, men who had participated in the 26th of July Movement, but who thought Castro had betrayed the revolution. The liberalization was hard to accomplish in the frenzied, rightist atmosphere of Miami, so Kennedy aides prevailed on the Revolutionary Council to move its headquarters to New York.

As the course of events moved inexorably toward the disaster of April 17, 1961, the disease of exploitation was visited on the exploiters. JFK was wavering on the soundness of the invasion, but CIA Director Allen Dulles said at a meeting on March 11, "Don't forget that we have a *disposal problem*. If we have to take these men out of Guatemala, we will have to transfer them to the United States, and we can't have them wandering around the country telling everyone what they have been doing." The disposal problem persuaded Kennedy, for he repeated it to Arthur Schlesinger, Jr., several days before the landing, "If we have to get rid of these 800 men," the President said, "it is much better to dump them in Cuba than in the United States, especially if that is where they want to go." Kennedy was further pleased in the last days before he gave the go-ahead, when a message came back from Guatemala, "These officers are young, vigorous, intelligent, and motivated by a fanatical urge to begin battle."

Needless to say, the psychological readiness of the invaders was not enough to carry the day against the 200,000 Cuban soldiers and militiamen that began to encircle the 2506 Brigade. The American air power that the invaders had been led to believe would be forthcoming did not arrive. The prevailing sentiment in southwest Miami today is that if only U.S. jets had come from the carrier *Essex*, the miracle of a successful invasion would have happened. Not only did the planes not arrive, but the disaster proceeded too far for an evacua-

153

tion to be attempted by the U.S. Navy. The invaders watched from the beaches as the ships turned and set out to sea.

Three days after the landing, when defeat was clear, President Kennedy asked Richard Nixon to come to the White House. Nixon related the conversation later in a *Readers' Digest* article. Nixon counseled gunboat diplomacy. "Finally he (Kennedy) put the key question to me, bluntly and directly. 'What would you do now in Cuba?'" Nixon wrote "'I would find a proper legal cover and I would go in,' I answered. I suggested three possible legal justifications for taking such action: (1) A new definition of aggression, based on the premise that Soviet bloc equipment was used by the Castro forces and that we had an obligation to see that the Freedom Forces were at least equally supplied. (2) Send American forces in under our treaty right because of the potential threat to Guantanamo. (3) Send American forces in to protect the lives and rights of several thousand American citizens still living in Cuba." Kennedy was not persuaded.

The 1962 Cuban missile crisis brought the world close to nuclear war. Khrushchev has written of those thirteen days that the Soviets had introduced missiles into Cuba because of the Bay of Pigs and the continuing threat of an American invasion. President Kennedy was able to save the Soviet Union from humiliation, and thus prevent a nuclear holocaust, by agreeing not to invade Cuba in exchange for the removal of the missiles. Nixon saw the "no invasion" promise as the result of the "incredibly bad advice" of the liberal Kennedy advisers who had "pulled defeat from the jaws of victory." If the rumored rapprochement with Cuba now follows that with China and the Soviet Union, then one may ask, whose jaws, what victory?

After the missile crisis, the crackdown on the Miami exiles began. The Coast Guard established in Miami an "Operational Intelligence" officer who coordinated the effort among all concerned agencies. Guns were seized, and boats were boarded and searched throughout the Carribbean. In 1963, Miró Cardona resigned in protest as head of the Cuban Revolutionary Council, and the council itself dissolved when the CIA withdrew funds. In 1964 and 1965, CIA-supported Manuel Artime trained more commandos in Costa Rica, but the effort was disbanded when the group attacked a ship that turned out to be Spanish rather than Cuban. Two Spaniards were killed in the attack, and Spain protested to the United States. In addition, a contraband scandal involving Scotch whiskey erupted in the camps and made the papers.

The CIA seems to have ended its active exploitation of S.W. Miami in 1967–68, although "La Companía" maintains a station in the area. According to Tomás Cruz, the agency gave money to some of the exile groups, but not others, in an attempt to divide and thus render impotent the political action role of the exile community. For whatever reason, there is no effective exile group now. Most organizations have become social clubs. Only Alpha 66, called the "last tango" by a Cuban journalist, claims to be active inside Cuba, but the group's claims of sabotage and subversion are inflated and outlandish (five teams of fifty men in the Escambray, according to Andrés Nasarió Segan, leader of Alpha 66). Of that boast Tomás Cruz said, "It's because of big lies like that, the Cubans in Miami have lost confidence in their leaders."

It is upon this history that Richard Nixon gained his standing in the Miami community and John F. Kennedy received bitter scorn. When the presidential campaign of 1972 began, the rhetoric of "last chance" infused the political dialogue of El Centro. When McGovern began his string of primary victories, his association with the bearded young was played up among the Cubans. In his maiden speech in the Senate in 1963, McGovern had argued against "our Castro obsession" and had asserted that it was a mistake to have broken relations with Cuba in the first place. He repeated this in the campaign and promised to end our economic isolation of Cuba. And Edward Kennedy's support made McGovern the candidate who threatened the most basic Cuban illusions. It was easy for the fanatics to jump to the notion that Senator McGovern was a "fellow traveler," and his election a threat to "national security." From there, the road led straight to the District of Columbia jail.

The fantasies of men like Barker began with the uprooting of exile life. They were stimulated by false hopes for liberation of the homeland and bolstered by the "professionalism" that police and CIA training imbues. They were bent by the humiliating relationship with Howard Hunt–type operatives over the years, with their loose tactics and big bankrolls. The fantasies were driven into the subconscious by isolation from active operations and by the growing Americanization of Cubans in Miami, and triggered back into consciousness again

155

by Hunt. In 1972 they were prodded by the desperate realization that Nixon was the last gunboat President the exiles are likely to get.

What went through Barker's mind when he went back into business with Hunt seems clear: Hunt worked at the White House and was at the highest level of government. He said the operation was above the FBI and the CIA and related to national security. Hunt was, by his own statement, handling the "operation," just as the CIA had always operated in Miami. All seemed normal to the other team members. To all Cubans in El Centro, "anything secret is CIA." Finally, and most important, if the operation succeeded, Howard Hunt's star in the White House would rise, and after the President's re-election, Nixon would be obligated to help the cause of Cuban liberation. "I could not deny my services in the way that it was put to me on a matter of national security," Barker had said.

The Barker generation is tailor-made for exploitation, and there is little indication even after Watergate that it will be less susceptible to the fever or the current that "carries one away." Logically, Watergate should discredit once and for all the blind, naive dependence on the Americano. Barker himself said in the Senate hearings, "If I were a wise man, I would not be sitting here today." But in Miami the fantasies continue. Said a Cuban editor, "Here, if a man is in jail, he's a hero one time; if he's in jail and doesn't talk in the interest of Cuban liberation, well then. . . ." And in January 1973, on William Buckley's *Firing Line* program on television Barker's friend Mario Lazo appeared with Howard Hunt and said of the Watergate team, "They're patriots. . . . When we get our country back, get Cuba back, I can assure you that the first government of a free Cuba will decorate this group."

7. The Intelligence Manual as Burglar's Handbook

One of the most curious ironies of the Watergate revelations is the emergence of Nixon's fear of antiwar and student demonstrations. The thousands who marched on the other side of the White House fence, who came loudly and often to petition their government for a redress of grievances, were frustrated in 1969, 1970, and 1971 by the image of a President who watched a football game while half a million people protested his war policies, or who made it a point to be at his Florida or California homes on such occasions. The demise of the peace movement in those years, its abandonment by the bulk of the peace movement "crazies" and even, in Mitchell's term, "violence-prone" groups, was bred of the frustration that "no one would listen, so why protest?"

A very different picture emerged before the Ervin Committee in May and June 1973. Here was a President who could not bear the sight of a protester, who took extraordinary steps to avoid seeing one and extraordinary measures to crush protest generally—a President for whom the extremity of the "threat" required the shredding of constitutional guarantees of free speech and assembly and of the rights of citizens to be secure in their persons and homes. To bend a parallel that Churchill used in relation to Hitler, it was as if "a mouse, a little mouse" of protest had appeared in the chambers of the President, and the potentate had shuddered in terror in a corner.

Nixon's Watergate statement of May 22, 1973, is a document that deserves the full attention I have given it elsewhere in this book. But his view of the nation in 1970, as contained in that document, is clearly the polluted source of what was to become the deluge of Watergate.

157

In March a wave of bombings and explosions struck college campuses and cities. There were 400 bomb threats in one 24-hour period in New York City. Rioting and violence on college campuses reached a new peak after the Cambodian operations and the tragedies of Kent State and Jackson State. The 1969–70 school year brought nearly 1,800 campus demonstrations, and nearly 250 cases of arson on the campus. Many colleges closed. Gun battles between guerrilla-style groups and the police were taking place. Some of the disruptive activities were receiving foreign support.

"Was that really what it was like, grandpa?" one can hear a child asking forty years from now. It might be nice for old peaceniks to muse that war protest was so active, when in fact, it was nearly dead. It had been dead for several years. True enough, the enormity of a new war in Cambodia, the extension of destruction to yet another country in Southeast Asia by a President who had promised to stop it, had revived protest. And true, the closing of college campuses was a new, effective form of protest of which the President had to take note.

At any rate, the protesters that surrounded the White House in response to Cambodia became a hostile army to Nixon; students bearing signs were the enemy. Indeed, goon squads were authorized at some protests to relieve protesters of their signs, on the pretext that a sign could be used as a weapon.

The White House was encircled—in this view—by a hostile army, and the threat meant, in John Dean's phrase, that the occupants needed to "draw the wagons around the White House and defend themselves." Nixon encouraged the development of yet another secret plan. Called "Operational Restraints on Intelligence Collection," the plan, devised by special assistant Tom Charles Huston, proposed burglary, wiretaps, mail openings, and infiltration by civilian and military campus agents to deal with the problem. Protest had become a national security threat, and protesters had become subversives. The full weight of the intelligence establishment was to smother these mice wherever they might lurk.

Given the debased language of bureaucratic communications, the plan sounded very proper. The words were appropriately devoid of Orwell's real mental pictures. Peeping Tomism was called "electronic surveillance" and "mail coverage"; burglary was called "surreptitious entry"; buying students was called "development of campus sources." The plan did not propose that these techniques be used for the first

158

time; it simply proposed that the restraints on them be lifted.

When word of the President's approval of the plan spread through the intelligence community on July 23, 1970, it doubtless was a major happening. The wraps were off. The jubilation must have been similar to that of the commanders of B-52 wings when Nixon removed the frustrating restraints on the targets they could bomb. But, according to the President, J. Edgar Hoover stepped in and launched a protest over the plan. Hoover did not object to the techniques proposed (the FBI had often used them before), but to the power the FBI would lose if the plan were implemented. In effect, a legitimate law enforcement agency squashed Nixon's plan. Nixon then began the process of turning away from legitimate institutions with congressional authority, to private, ad hoc groups under his immediate control.

As early as a few months after Nixon's inauguration in 1969, the White House was developing its private police force. John Caulfield, the man who, according to James McCord, relayed to him an offer of executive clemency in January 1973, was already in place by July 1969 and was targeted against an enemy of high rank, Senator Edward M. Kennedy. Caulfield either carried out or supervised a fairly systematic surveillance of Kennedy, the man Nixon thought would be his opponent in 1972. Caulfield once followed Kennedy to Hawaii and reported reluctantly to Ehrlichman that all Kennedy had done was keep his official engagements.

Chappaquiddick gave Caulfield an opportunity to spread out. Ehrlichman had by this time taken on another ex-New York cop, Anthony Ulasewicz (and hidden him on Herbert Kalmbach's personal payroll). Although Ehrlichman was later to testify piously that he would never "let Herb Kalmbach do anything unethical or improper," he let Kalmbach pay Ulasewicz more than $30,000 a year in salary and expenses to dig for dirt in the drinking, social, and sexual habits of the "enemies" of the President. He knew that Donald Segretti's sabotage operation was being financed by Kalmbach; and he approved Kalmbach's rushing about the country, using public phone booths and automobile drops to raise and dispense hush money to Ehrlichman's former agent Ulasewicz. (What, one wonders, would Ehrlichman have found for Kalmbach to do if he had been willing to let him do something which *was* unethical or improper?)

The Caulfield–Ulasewicz team did a lot for Ehrlichman in

those first two years. They broke into the home of columnist Joseph Kraft to plant a phone tap, and they broke in again to take it out. Kraft himself notes the date (early 1969) and his close professional relationship with Henry Kissinger. He reasons that the tap was not directed so much against him as it was an attempt by Haldeman and Ehrlichman to get some goods on Kissinger. I agree with the reasoning; it was, in any event, an early sign—had it become known—of how Nixon proposed to "bring us together."

It was Chappaquiddick that gave Caulfield and Ulasewicz their busiest time. No sooner did news reach the White House that Senator Kennedy had been involved in an automobile accident which cost the life of Mary Jo Kopechne, a staff aide to the late Senator Robert Kennedy, than the house cops sprang into action. (At whose orders? Colson's? Ehrlichman's? Haldeman's? The Chief's?)

Ulasewicz went to Martha's Vineyard to pose as a newsman and ask "embarrassing questions." Caulfield remained behind to supervise, within the next 24 hours, a phone tap on the apartment Mary Jo Kopechne had shared with three other girls, two of whom had been at the picnic which preceded the accident. There is something not just in bad taste, but nearly obscene, about the haste and the grossness with which the Nixon forces approached Chappaquiddick. The phone tap on the dead girl's apartment was not the limit of bad taste.

Two years after the accident, Ulasewicz (again with the funds furnished by Kalmbach, still protected against unethical and improper conduct by his patron John Ehrlichman) rented an apartment on 46th Street in New York City. Ulasewicz said it was for a detective agency–type office, but the furnishings—velvet walls and fur rugs (courtesy, as always, of Kalmbach)—bespeak another purpose. Federal investigators have been told the apartment was to be used to seduce and then blackmail the "Chappaquiddick girls" into telling, presumably, their dark secrets about "what really happened." One can approach this effort on many levels. The first, of course, is the outrageous sexism and degraded view of women which it implies. The episode is, from any standpoint, disgraceful. The effort, of course, was a failure.

Caulfield and Ulasewicz, during the time when they were "run" by Ehrlichman, performed a number of other "national security" operations. They looked into the private and financial affairs of Speaker of the House Carl Albert; Rep.

Richard Poff (R.–Va.), who was being considered for a Supreme Court appointment until he rather mysteriously withdrew his name from consideration; the Smothers Brothers, a comedy team; and the producers of a semiunderground anti-Nixon movie entitled "Milhouse." There were other tasks, none more savory, and Ulasewicz summed it up in a dialogue with Senator Lowell Weicker before the Ervin Committee. "Would it be fair to say that you dealt in dirt for the White House?" asked Weicker. Ulasewicz, like his boss Ehrlichman a stickler for legal detail, answered, "Allegations of it, yes sir."

When John Dean arrived at the White House in July 1970, Caulfield was placed on his staff and kept on the Kennedy assignment. Though Caulfield was physically on Dean's staff, he received his orders for political intelligence information directly from Haldeman, Ehrlichman, and Charles Colson.

In April 1971, two significant events took place. First, E. Howard Hunt appeared in Miami, played his queen of diamonds, and engaged a principal agent for what was later to be a team of burglars. The meeting was a little like the coming together of two gamecocks. They both knew what they were there for. Barker testified to the Ervin Committee, "I quite frankly waited until Mr. Hunt would tell me if there was any other reason other than social reasons [for his trip to Miami], and I expected him in his good time to tell me if there was anything else, and, eventually, he did." But the elaborate ritual of the intelligence procedure, something akin to courtship, had to be followed. Hunt met with Barker on a number of occasions, which undoubtedly whetted Barker's appetite, but there was no discussion of a mission. The early date of the Barker recruitment (April 1971) remains a mystery, for Howard Hunt was not officially hired by the White House until two months later.

The second significant event of April 1971 was the one hundredth anniversary of the founding of the National Rifle Association, and it invited member G. Gordon Liddy to make a speech at the celebration. Liddy, a special assistant to the Secretary of the Treasury, had become an expert on the "Saturday night specials." Indeed, he had attended many White House meetings on control of cheap handguns as the Treasury Department representative, meetings which were chaired by Egil Krogh, an assistant to chief domestic adviser John Ehrlichman (as he had been at Ehrlichman's Seattle law firm). There was nothing particularly noteworthy about Liddy's speech to the N.R.A., although he did not support Administration policy on gun control. Liddy had failed even to report the invitation to his superior and had not cleared the content of his talk. It was the last straw for his immediate superior, Assistant Secretary Eugene Rossides. Liddy simply did not understand his responsibilities as a staff subordinate, and Rossides wanted him to go, but he did not get his wish for two months. When Liddy was finally fired by Treasury in July, he was immediately rehired by John Ehrlichman at the White House—to the utter astonishment of Rossides.

On June 13, 1971, *The New York Times* began publication of the Pentagon Papers. To Nixon it was a "security leak of unprecedented proportions" (or so he said on May 22, 1973) and posed "a threat so grave as to require extraordinary actions." The full weight and power of the FBI, the defense establishment, and other duly authorized law enforcement agencies apparently was not enough for Nixon. The FBI was "lethargic" in its investigation, Ehrlichman testified later. In the week following, Nixon approved the creation of the "Plumbers," a name with the appropriate double meaning of plugging leaks and bungling jobs. The unit was headed by Krogh and supervised by Ehrlichman. In July, E. Howard Hunt appeared officially on the White House payroll, was assigned to the Plumbers, and was joined by Treasury castoff G. Gordon Liddy.

Nixon said he told Krogh that the "first priority" of the unit was to "find out all it could about Ellsberg's associates and motives." "I did impress upon Mr. Krogh," Nixon said in his May 22 statement, "the vital importance to national security of his assignment."

To Hunt and Liddy, Krogh's professionals in the field, these instructions were in the nature of a specific intelligence requirement. The word "requirement" is important, for in the paramilitary atmosphere of the White House, it is a stronger word than "request." The information *must* be obtained. All intelligence-gathering operations, either in the CIA or in the military, begin with just such a specific "requirement" for information, and each requirement bears a priority rating. Hunt and Liddy went right to work on their Presidential requirement.

Discussions followed as to how the information on Ellsberg might be obtained. A brush at meeting the requirement by

162

legal means was made in July. The FBI interviewed Lewis Fielding, Ellsberg's psychiatrist, about therapy Ellsberg had received in 1968 and 1969, but the doctor acted according to the ethics of his profession and refused to divulge the content of psychiatric sessions, a legal privilege recognized in every state. The CIA was then ordered to prepare a psychological profile on Ellsberg (reportedly over the objections of a CIA doctor who knew quite well that the order contradicted the 1947 law establishing CIA, which prohibits the agency from engaging in domestic operations). But the profile was prepared and found unsatisfactory by the Plumbers.

The unit could only refer back to the Tom Charles Huston memorandum. Of surreptitious entry, the memorandum stated, "Use of this technique is clearly illegal: it amounts to burglary. It is also highly risky and could result in great embarrassment if exposed. However, *it is also the most fruitful tool and can produce the type of intelligence which can not be obtained in any other fashion.*" The President had approved this technique, and its use had been countermanded only because the FBI would not go along (for bureaucratic reasons, to be sure), but now the Bureau wasn't needed.

In his May 22 statement, Nixon wanted it all ways: (1) He desperately wanted information on Ellsberg. (2) He could not get it though legal channels. (3) Of Krogh's authorization, he said, "I can understand how highly motivated individuals could have felt justified in engaging in specific activities that I would have disapproved of had they been brought to my attention" (but he had approved these methods). (4) The last damning admission: "To the extent that I may in any way have contributed to the climate in which this took place, I did not intend to; to the extent that I failed to prevent them, I should have been more vigilant." With such a chief as this, one can be sympathetic with the impossible situation of a simple loyalist zealot like Krogh.

Insofar as the May 22 statement refers to the Ellsberg burglary (as well as in certain other particulars), it is pure hogwash. It is, like other Nixon statements made during the development of the Watergate scandal, defensive—that is, it is a crafty lawyer's attempt to explain away certain damning facts already in evidence. Nowhere is this better demonstrated than in the case of Nixon's explanation of the Ellsberg burglary. There were no national security elements present: Ellsberg had "confessed" to the crime; he had left a wide public trail as he talked to senators, reporters, and friends about making the Pentagon Papers public; he had been arrested, indicted, and had a date set for his trial. Pretrial procedures had begun, and the FBI had begun a massive investigation. The Defense Department was building a witness list to "prove" that the release of the documents could have damaged the United States.

Furthermore, by July 1971, when the Plumbers swung into action, and certainly by August, when the burglary was proposed by Krogh and David Young and approved by Ehrlichman, it was clear that the Pentagon Papers were fascinating history but in no way compromised any American military activity. Indeed, a careful reading—which one assumes *somebody* at the White House must have undertaken—would have demonstrated that had the Pentagon Papers been made public when they were written, the only danger would have been to the *political* security of Kennedy and Johnson Administration officials, including both Presidents.

There is more damning and conclusive evidence. In this period, prior to the burglary at Fielding's office, memoranda were sent to Ehrlichman from his plumber colleagues Krogh and Young. The memos not only described and sought approval for the burglary (approval granted, "only if it is untraceable"), but clearly set forth the reasons for it.

The reason was obvious. It was not national security, not to plug a "national security leak of unprecedented proportions," not because there was information (closely held among those who planned and executed the burglary, it turned out) that the papers had been given to a foreign power. The White House wanted the Ellsberg psychiatric records to smear Ellsberg. Young and Krogh even had a timetable for the release to friendly newsmen of unfavorable information about Ellsberg, so he could be split off from his supporters.

It was, on the whole, one of the most reprehensible of the White House "horrors" because the purpose was so clearly slimy and purely political, the action taken to carry it out so clearly criminal, and the lies told to justify it so lofty and patriotic. God knows what the Plumbers (Ehrlichman included) thought Fielding had written down about his patient of two years before. Psychiatrists rarely treat psychotics in their offices. Some neurosis or other may have sent Ellsberg to Fielding in the first place, but psychiatrists also do not put

164

that kind of information in their files. Clearly, the prurient interest of the Nixon men had been aroused, and they thought they could titillate the rest of the country—especially the peace movement—into changing its view of Ellsberg, perhaps with a few juicy details of whatever may have been bothering Ellsberg.

Thus, covert entry was decided upon; the professionals began to draw up their operation plan, and with the power of the White House behind them, they drew the CIA into complicity. On July 7, 1971, John Ehrlichman called General Robert Cushman, deputy director of the CIA and now Commandant of the Marine Corps. Cushman was the White House's man in the agency, having been Nixon's military attaché in 1959–60, when the Bay of Pigs was underway. He had also shared an office with Howard Hunt at the CIA in the fifties. The Ehrlichman call cleared the way for Hunt, and on July 22, 1971 he met with Cushman at the CIA. Hunt stated that he had been authorized to conduct a very sensitive "one-time interview" operation for the White House and that he needed flash alias documentation and disguises. The following day Hunt met with CIA technicians, and the request was fulfilled. Later the CIA provided disguises and documentation for Liddy, as well as a concealed camera, business cards, and a recorder. In the intelligence business, this is blandly called "furnishing technical assistance"; in law it is called being an accessory to a crime.

In mid-August 1971, Howard Hunt arrived in Miami and again met with his old friend "Bernie" Barker. The expected request for help, pitched to a national security rationale, was made and accepted. Barker sounded out Eugenio Martinez and Felipe DeDiego, both of whom worked in Barker's real estate agency and both ex-CIA men qualified for the mission. Martinez had made scores of clandestine infiltrations into Castro's Cuba on gun-running missions, and DeDiego had been on expeditions to capture Castro documents. DeDiego had also been an intelligence officer in the U.S. Army. They accepted, and "Bernie" called "Eduardo" (Hunt). (Barker had introduced Martinez to Hunt at the Bay of Pigs celebration of April 1971.) Some time later, Barker testified, Hunt called back to say that "the two men had been cleared." How had they been cleared? Who cleared them? There was only one way: checking the CIA dossiers of both men. Krogh was subsequently informed that "certain Cubans" were ready to undertake the mission (according to his affidavit to the Ellsberg trial).

On August 25, 1971, Hunt and Liddy went to Los Angeles to case the joint, or as it is known in intelligence parlance, "survey the denied area." A smiling Liddy was photographed in his CIA disguise outside Fielding's office. On August 26, Hunt passed a roll of film to a CIA accomplice at Dulles Airport, and later in the day he received the developed product.

Hunt's requests to the CIA were getting out of hand. He asked the agency for an office and a secretary. He also wanted an address and a "backstopped" telephone in New York City. ("Backstopped" means that the phone number would be listed in a cover name with all the attendant phony documentation.) This was too much. On August 27, Cushman called Ehrlichman and refused any further assistance to Hunt. Ehrlichman reportedly said that he would attempt "to restrain" Hunt.

Nonetheless, the professionals had what they needed, and on September 3, 1971, the denied area was successfully penetrated. The operation followed certain textbook procedures. Hunt, for example, told his team members no more than they "needed to know" at any particular step in the operation. Hunt told Barker by phone to proceed with his men to Los Angeles and register in the Beverly-Wilshire Hotel. (However much the "Plumbers" may have bungled, they went first-class.) Once there, Eduardo called with the exact address of the target. DeDiego must have been pleased when he heard who the enemy was. Later, when he saw Ellsberg at the funeral of J. Edgar Hoover, he said to a Miami *Herald* reporter, "We saw Ellsberg, that traitor, having a victory demonstration during the Hoover funeral, and it incensed me. Hoover was a hero, and there was this traitor gloating over his death." He should have talked to Ehrlichman about Hoover; if anyone should have been "having a victory celebration," it was Ehrlichman.

The flight back from Los Angeles must have been full of frivolity for Hunt and Liddy, alias "Hamilton" and "Larimer." Hunt chatted with a stewardess and later sent her one of his books, with a note on White House stationery, signed "Hamilton." At the White House, he submitted pay vouchers to Charles Colson for work on September 2, 3, and 4 and was paid routinely at his scale of $100 per day. Later Hunt pre-

166

pared a 28-page report on Ellsberg, which contained phone numbers and addresses.

There was good reason for frivolity on the plane; the Ellsberg break-in was successful in every way. The intelligence cycle had been applied to the task of burglary and had worked superbly. The team had found the Ellsberg file and photographed it, according to DeDiego (though Hunt and Barker deny this). The contention of the Huston memorandum that break-ins are a "most fruitful tool" was justified. "We spend millions of dollars, attempting to break (foreign cryptographic) codes by machine," the memo read. "One successfull surreptitious entry can do the job successfully at no dollar cost." The cost of the Ellsberg operation had been not much more than a few cross-country plane tickets. "Surreptitious entry of facilities occupied by subversive elements can turn up information about identities, methods of operation, and other invaluable investigative information which is not otherwise available," the memo continued. And Ellsberg was a "subversive" of the highest rank. Alas, the "entry" yielded no dirt which could be leaked to the hated press.

Furthermore, the Cubans had been drawn into the Hunt web. Motivated by the national security gimmick, they now had a burglary on their record, and if they got balky, Hunt could threaten to turn them in. DeDiego was not paid for the Ellsberg operation, but was left with the impression that he would get plenty of money from future assignments. In short, Hunt had a firm and secure "handle" on the Cuban team.

In the fall of 1971, a number of unexplained burglaries of leftist groups took place. In the week after the Ellsberg break-in, the New York office of the NAACP's Legal Defense Fund was broken into. The organization at the time was involved in the defense of Bobby Seale in the Chicago Seven conspiracy trial, and of Earl Caldwell, the *New York Times* reporter who refused to turn over notes on the Black Panthers. Meanwhile, the Vietnam Veterans Against the War (VVAW) were becoming troublesome. One VVAW leader, for example, defiled the White House lawn by throwing medals he had won in Vietnam over the fence. On Thanksgiving Day 1971, his home in Gainesville, Florida, was broken into, and membership lists and war crime testimony from Vietnam veterans were taken. Special Prosecutor Archibald Cox began looking into these mysterious episodes and twenty other break-ins (including one at the Embassy of Chile) to see if the White House "professionals" were involved.

Meanwhile, the focus was shifting to the campaigns of 1972. In the early fall of 1971, John Caulfield, the White House wire man and expert on Senator Kennedy, offered a plan, coded "Sand Wedge," for White House consideration. The plan envisaged a private company that would, according to John Dean, be an "extension of the types of things Caulfield had been performing for Ehrlichman." The company, called Security Consulting Corporation, Inc., would have a "covert" capability of providing bag men and wiretappers.

By November, Sand Wedge had failed to engender enthusiasm, and in early December, G. Gordon Liddy moved to CREP, presumably to fill the intelligence vacuum. Howard Hunt, now directly employed by Liddy, was active in Miami in the same month, recruiting a surveillance team for the 1972 Democratic Convention. Bernard Barker contacted the architect of the Miami Convention Hall, whom he knew, and asked for the blueprints of the hall. Barker told the architect that he wanted the plans because he had a friend in Puerto Rico who was building a similar convention hall. The architect refused, and Barker asked if he could have a plan of just the air conditioning system. The architect refused this request even more vehemently, realizing that something very fishy was up.

On January 27, 1972, the process that led to the Watergate debacle began in earnest. On that date, the famous million-dollar meeting took place in the office of Attorney General John Mitchell. In attendance were campaign director Jeb Magruder, presidential counsel John Dean, and campaign chief John Mitchell. G. Gordon Liddy proposed an "intelligence" assault on the Democratic Party. Liddy came armed with six color charts indicating different projects, all with code names. One of the six had the code name "Gemstone," and was a proposal for wide-ranging electronic surveillance, wiretapping, and photography of documents. Other projects included plans for kidnapping radical leaders during the San Diego convention and detaining them in Mexico until the convention was over, and for renting a yacht, hiring prostitutes, and attempting to lure Democratic leaders into compromising situations, to be photographed and later blackmailed. The latter ploy has been used so often in intelligence work that it is something of a cliché, though homosexuals are usually the targets of such blackmail. Liddy put the budget for all plans at one million dollars.

Dean, Magruder, and Mitchell were shocked and embarrassed by the Liddy plan. Mitchell told the Ervin Committee that in retrospect—always in restrospect—"I not only should have thrown him out of the office; I should have thrown him out of the window." But Mitchell did neither, and Liddy was encouraged to return to the drawing board and come up with a more modest proposal. A week later a second meeting took place in Mitchell's office. This time Liddy passed out his charts on 5 x 8 index cards (as an economy measure, no doubt) and the price went down to half a million dollars. The discussion became more specific. The Democratic National headquarters in Washington, the Democratic National Committee headquarters at the Fontainebleau Hotel in Miami Beach, and the headquarters of the Democratic nominee were targeted for wiretapping.

James McCord was told that at this meeting Mitchell apparently raised the possibility of breaking and entering the office of Hank Greenspun, a Las Vegas publisher who, Mitchell claimed, had damaging information in his safe on Edmund Muskie, the Democratic front-runner at the time. According to Liddy, Mitchell asked him to "case" the situation in Las Vegas to see if there was "potential" for burglary. The Las Vegas task may have been a job to keep Liddy happy, for the second meeting ended without approval of the overall plan.

In January and February of 1972, McCord, security director of CREP, was lured into the web. Liddy had come to McCord as early as December 1971 to discuss the state of the art of wiretapping, specifically the types of devices manufactured and their costs. McCord first interpreted these discussions as one professional talking to another about matters of common interest. But in late January, Liddy let McCord know that planning was going on in the attorney general's office concerning political intelligence, and that McCord's expertise would be needed. In early February, Liddy told McCord that he was going to Las Vegas to case the Greenspun office for a possible entry operation and that if there were an alarm system, McCord's services might be needed. A week later Liddy told McCord he had been to Las Vegas, that there was no alarm system, and that McCord's skills would not be needed.

McCord is the source of the fascinating Las Vegas story, and it may well be that it concealed something else. According to his testimony, Liddy told him of Mitchell's suggestion that Greenspun's office might yield damaging information on Edmund Muskie and a questionable campaign contributor. Other details relayed from the meeting with Liddy raise another possibility.

McCord says Liddy told him that the team which did the Greenspun job in Las Vegas would go—with the purloined documents—directly to a small airfield near Las Vegas, where an airplane belonging to Howard Hughes would fly them directly to Central America. That is a strange getaway pattern for successful burglars who want only to turn over their cache to the attorney general of the United States. It suggests another motive and another client.

Greenspun himself, in a newspaper interview the next day, may have provided the clue. He said the Muskie story was nonsense; he had no documents in his safe which faintly involved the senator from Maine. But what he did have, he said, were documents extremely damaging to Howard Hughes, to be used in a forthcoming legal action against Hughes. He also said "he had heard" that Robert Bennett, the son of Utah Senator Wallace Bennett and an associate of Hunt in Washington during those brief days when Hunt wasn't working for the government, had testified somewhere that Hughes had given a blank check contribution to Nixon.

If Greenspun's statement is true—or even partly true—the Las Vegas mission for Liddy and McCord shapes up as a straight favor to Howard Hughes by a grateful Nixon campaign. And in this connection, the "Central America" destination in a Hughes airplane takes on added significance—Hughes himself was at that time in Nicaragua. In any event, the whole Las Vegas mission, Liddy later told McCord, was aborted.

All this was clearly a test of McCord. Liddy was letting McCord know that illegal activities were being discussed, that the White House and the attorney general were involved, and that McCord was included in the plans. If McCord had any moral qualms, he could have announced them at that point, but the President's top legal officer and the attorney general were said to be involved, and McCord evidenced no doubts about involving himself.

In March 1972 the last piece in the puzzle fell into place.

170

Since December the Administration had been squirming under the heat of the ITT affair, in which it was alleged that ITT had agreed to underwrite the Republican National Committee to the amount of $400,000 in exchange for favorable settlements in pending antitrust suits. On February 29, Jack Anderson printed a memorandum from ITT lobbyist Dita Beard which set forth the trade-off. Beard became the center of the storm and mysteriously disappeared. She turned up in a Denver hospital, and the administration sought, unsuccessfully, to discredit her as "irrational" and her memo as a fake. In the course of the Watergate investigation, it turned out that versatile G. Gordon Liddy had been responsible for spiriting Dita Beard out of Washington to Denver, perhaps by kidnap, and that Howard Hunt, in his "ill-fitting" wig, had interviewed the heart patient in her hospital. The important point is that the Nixon men felt particularly stung by the political hay that Democratic chairman Larry O'Brien was making of the case, and they set their sights on him, in retribution.

On March 30, 1972, at Key Biscayne, the Liddy plan was reduced again to a paltry $250,000 and approved by Mitchell, and the elements for a classic intelligence operation against the Watergate headquarters were set.

But how was Liddy to get money to Barker for the operation?

How this happened is extremely important, for the money in Barker's pocket when he was apprehended became the link to the Committee to Re-Elect the President, but more important, the source of funds in the burglars' possession would cause the first confirmed entry of President Nixon into the Watergate cover-up.

Barker's money—$114,000—came to him in two parts: a cashier's check for $25,000 and four for $89,000. The $25,000 had been contributed by Dwayne Andreas, a midwestern soybean tycoon who had largely bankrolled Hubert Humphrey's campaigns in the past and was a heavy Humphrey contributor in 1972. But even before the Wisconsin primary, Andreas either lost confidence in Humphrey's chances or thought it was time to hedge; in any event he got in touch with Kenneth Dahlberg, who was Nixon's Midwest finance chairman and fund raiser. Andreas knew Dahlberg; in fact, the two men were partners in a banking venture for which they had applied for a federal charter. Andreas agreed to give $25,000 to Nixon's campaign, and shortly thereafter the bank charter was granted, and in near-record time, too.

Andreas, for reasons only he knows best, likes to give his campaign contributions in cash, and the contribution to Nixon through Dahlberg was no exception. He delivered it on a Miami golf course on April 9, two days after the deadline set in the Campaign Financing Act of 1972 for unreported contributions. At Andreas' request, Stans did not intend to report the money, and that made it "hot."

Dahlberg converted the cash to a cashier's check in Miami and delivered the check to Stans on April 10. Stans turned it over to Hugh Sloan, his treasurer, and did not report the gift even though it was now three days after the campaign law required its disclosure.

Sloan, who was portrayed in the Ervin hearings as one of the few honest men in the Nixon campaign, did not quite know how to handle cashier's checks. One theory, held by Miami investigators, is that Sloan realized that the Dahlberg check was hot, and therefore he handed it over to the man in the campaign who was engaged in "hot" work. In any event, Sloan gave Liddy the check, and Liddy turned it over to Barker.

Stans had picked up other suspect cashier's checks, four to be exact, totaling $89,000. They represent one of the more celebrated contributions of the campaign—one which enriched the political language, perhaps permanently, with the phrase "Mexican laundry."

The Mexican laundry worked this way. Robert Allen was the president of Gulf Resources and Chemical Corp., a Texas-based conglomerate. He was also Nixon's Texas finance chairman and wished to conceal totally (not just avoid reporting, which he could have done anyway) his—or his corporation's—contribution of $100,000. Allen caused $100,000 to be transferred from Gulf Resources to the account of a defunct Mexican subsidiary of his company. The subsidiary then paid what Allen says was a long-standing legal bill to a lawyer in Mexico City, Manuel Ogarrio. Ogarrio immediately transformed the $100,000 check into four cashier's checks, totalling $89,000, and left $11,000 in cash. Thus, Allen (or Gulf Resources) was presumably obscured as the source of the $100,000. By laundering the money through a foreign country, the Nixon people risked a different violation of the law:

accepting contributions from a foreign national. Obviously, they did not expect to get caught.

Ogarrio, clearly under instructions, never treated the money as his own. He then sent the checks to the office of the Pennzoil Corporation in Houston, whose President, William Liedtke, was serving as a kind of executive funnel for the Nixon campaign. The laundered Mexican checks were put together with other contributions, taken to Washington in a Pennzoil company plane, and delivered to Maurice Stans on the night of April 5. Sloan wound up with the Mexican cashier's checks, too, and again probably because he knew them to be, if not illegal, at least "hot," turned them over to his learned expert, Gordon Liddy. Liddy assured Sloan that he would take care "of the problem." Liddy passed all the cashier's checks on to Barker, whose bank account, normally inactive, now had $114,000 on deposit ($25,000 from Andreas, $89,000 from Mexico). Barker and the others had $1,300 of the Andreas–Allen money on them when arrested, and $3,100 more in their hotel rooms.

The Mexican transaction was clearly illegal. Either the whole thing masked an illegal corporate contribution, or it masked an illegal contribution by a foreign national. A Texas grand jury is investigating the matter, including a fortuitous circumstance for Allen's company. After the contribution, the Environmental Protection Administration dropped a serious air pollution complaint against a Gulf Resources subsidiary in Idaho.

It was the FBI investigation of the trail of those funds through Mexico right after the burglary itself that caused a great White House flurry of activity. Haldeman and Ehrlichman have both testified that Nixon asked them to talk to CIA Director Richard Helms and his deputy General Vernon Walters to try to get them to call off the FBI investigation on the pretext that the investigation might compromise CIA Mexican operations. There were no CIA operations to be compromised; Nixon must have been alerted that the FBI, by following the cash to Mexico, could link the burglary to the Nixon campaign.

Every intelligence operation must have an "operation plan," shortened to "O-Plan" by the professionals. In it the elements of Who? Where? When? Why? How? are answered. The "Why" is the specific intelligence collection requirement referred to earlier. The "How" is the means to be used to fulfill the requirement. At the end, the contingencies or dangers of the operation are addressed. The author of an "O-Plan" must always address himself to the problem of "plausible denial," that concept of intelligence work that had been broadened to general government operations by the Nixon administration: If you are caught and your operation is compromised, how can you make your denial of involvement sound plausible?

If an "O-Plan" were written for the Watergate burglary, it might have looked like this:

- **Who:** Liddy and Hunt, agent handlers; Barker, principal agent; Sturgis, entry and lookout; Martinez, entry and photographer; Gonzalez, locksmith; McCord, wire man; Baldwin, lookout.
- **Where:** Democratic National Headquarters at the Watergate.
- **When:** Memorial Day, May 27, 1972.
- **Why:**

1. Find documents on Democratic contributions, foreign and national; especially proof of contributions from Cuba and Chile. (Barker testimony.)

2. Find documents on relationships between Democrats and violence-prone groups like VVAW, including plans for bombing or demonstration at the Republican National Convention; also any documents relating to the funding of such groups. (McCord testimony.)

3. Find any documents relating to Senator Edward M. Kennedy and Senator George McGovern. (Barker testimony.)

4. Emplace wiretap on telephone of Lawrence O'Brien, to fulfill requirements above, and to discover information to discredit him as an effective spokesman for the Democratic Party. (Magruder testimony.)

- **How:** Infiltration and exfiltration of denied area will be attempted under the cover of a banquet held in the target area; will enter first two individuals as an entry team, then the photographer and the principal agent, and finally, the wire technician. The door will be taped open by the entry team, for easy access of team members following. The principal agent will search for documents and pass selected documents to photographer for reproduction. Wire technician will emplace

174

tap on enemy phone and one other phone chosen at random. The team will exfiltrate by the same route. Contact with agent handlers located in the Watergate Hotel will be maintained on Band 1 of the radio; contact with the lookout in the Howard Johnson Motel across the street from the denied area will be maintained on Band 2.

- **Contingencies:** If the infiltration team is discovered and compromised, operatives will *not* go to Miami for future assignments.
- **Plausible Denial:** In the event of compromise, agent handlers will exfiltrate the denied area as fast as possible. CREP and White House will deny involvement until such denial is no longer plausible.

APPROVED _____

In May, Hunt again went to Miami and informed Barker of an impending "double mission" that would take a week to accomplish. He instructed Barker to get his men in shape for running up and down stairs. The double mission, it turned out, was the burglary of the Watergate headquarters and the McGovern headquarters. But the Watergate proved to be more "denied" than they expected. The team had their Watergate banquet, but a diligent staffer, laboring late at the DNC, forced the team to abort its mission. The team made a successful entry on Memorial Day. Barker was frustrated by not finding documents linking Castro to the Democratic Party, but nonetheless, some documents were photographed, and McCord placed his taps.

A week and a half later Jeb Stuart Magruder received the first "Gemstone" reports. They were in two forms: summary recapitulation of telephone conversations and photographs of documents. Magruder took the packet to his boss, John Mitchell, and to Gordon Strachan, Haldeman's agent. Mitchell found the documents worthless and gruffly called Liddy to his office. He berated Liddy for the results and said the Gemstone documents were not worth the money that had been paid for them. By way of apology, Liddy said that one tap was not working because of the peculiarities of the metal structure of the Watergate building, and another tap was on the wrong phone. Liddy assured Mitchell that these mistakes would be corrected. The tap that was working was on the phone of Spencer Oliver, whose job was to deal with state Democratic party chairmen across the country.

175

On June 15, Joseph Fitzpatrick, the Democratic chairman of Virginia, was a man under the gun. Elected as state chairman only five days before, he had received the list of Virginia delegates to the Miami Beach Convention on the 15th. And yet the 15th was the deadline imposed by the National Committee for a seating chart on the Convention floor. Fitzpatrick knew this was important, both for telephone numbers assignments and for harmony among the Virginia delegates. So he drove to Washington from Richmond with the list, ensconced himself in the DNC headquarters, and began to work on the seating chart.

At closing time, Fitzpatrick was still working, but Spencer Oliver assured him that it would be all right if the chart were ready the following morning. So he stayed on in the DNC headquarters working until 11 P.M., whereupon the foreman of the cleaning detail informed him that either he would have to lock Fitzpatrick in the office overnight or he would have to leave. So the state chairman left and finally finished the chart at 3 A.M. in his hotel room.

The following morning, he returned to the Watergate headquarters, and as he walked by Spencer Oliver's office, Oliver waved him in. Oliver explained that the Committee needed $10,000 quick, as a down payment to the telephone company for the fund-raising telethon scheduled for the night before the convention opened. Richmond was to be a regional center for the telethon, and the telephone company would not start putting in phones until a down payment was forthcoming.

Fitzpatrick agreed to help. Using Oliver's phone, he got the DNC operator, an efficient veteran of 25 years with the committee, identified himself as the state chairman of Virginia, and asked for a long-distance line. The operator said that she was sorry, but all long-distance lines had to be approved by Chairman O'Brien. Fitzpatrick turned the phone over to Oliver. Oliver received the same story, whereupon he said, "Well, get me the chairman." "I'm sorry," came the reply, "but the chairman is in Miami, and that would be a long-distance call." A few heated words were exchanged, and finally Fitzpartick, back on the line, persuaded the operator to connect him with a long-distance operator, and he put the call on his credit card. "Look, lady," Joe remembers saying, "you can listen in, while I give the operator my credit card number, OK?" But someone else was listening as well. This might be the wiretapper's confidential report:

GEMSTONE

source *Ruby 1*

Enemy operative, one Joe Fitzpatrick, identified in rank as State Chairman of Virginia, held telephonic communication to Richmond and spoke to operative designated as "Bonnie." Communication went as follows:

"Bonnie, this is the God-damnedest place you ever saw. I've been haggling with an operator for 15 minutes trying to get a long distance line, and she says I can't make a damn 60-cent call to Richmond without O'Brien's permission and O'Brien's in Miami, so we can't get his permission, cause it would be a long-distance call. Ended up having to use my credit card. I tell ya, Bonnie, if this is the great Democratic Party we're working for, we're in big trouble.

Operative Fitzpatrick went on to request subject Bonnie to call one Jim Cremmins, identified as chairman of "telethon" and ask him to raise $10,000—repeat $10,000—as down payment to the telephone company.

Call indicates disaffection in enemy ranks and possible low morale. Also indicates that enemy is hard pressed for funds.

EXDIS
NO DISEM

WARNING;   THIS INFORMATION IS FOR INTELLIGENCE PURPOSE ONLY. EXPLOITATION MAY COMPROMISE SOURCE AND TERMINATE FLOW OF INFORMATION.

No wonder John Mitchell was dissatisfied. True, the documents were not worth the $199,000 paid for them, but Mitchell thought it was the fault of the improper installation of the "bug."

Today, Joe Fitzpatrick thinks himself lucky that the deadline for the delegates list was June 15, instead of June 16th. He doesn't know what he would do in the same room late at night with four Bay of Pigs veterans and "one of the best wire men in the business." "Good Democrats," Joe says, "don't normally associate with such people."

The source was compromised on June 17, and the flow of

worthless information terminated for other reasons. Bernard Barker had turned down the juice on his walkie-talkie "to save on the batteries," according to Sturgis, and thus never heard the warning from the lookout across the street that the team "had company." McCord had persuaded the team that a mailman must have removed the tapes on the door latches (when it was actually the Watergate security guard). The tape was put there to keep the doors from locking behind them. The mailman, McCord argued, was making deliveries (at 2:30 A.M.!). But worst of all, the "professionals" violated one of the most basic rules of all in intelligence work: Never have anything in your possession, even a laundry tag, that can link you to your real backers. And the Barker team had $4,500 in consecutively numbered $100 bills in their pockets and their hotel rooms—bills that led right to the Committee to Re-Elect the President. The bills may as well have been tagged "Lavanderia Mexicana."

The so-called professionalism, the expenditure of nearly $200,000 of campaign funds given by sincere people who wanted to see Nixon reelected, came down to one polite question by James McCord, "Are you gentlemen from the Metropolitan Police?" and later that night, to the booking of the team as common criminals.

8.   But What if the Truth Won't Sell?

From June 17 to November 7, 1972, the White House was increasingly under siege. The men who had for so long fantasized about their enemies and imagined themselves under attack from the press and its liberal masters found once again that paranoid fantasies can become self-fulfilling. The person who imagines that everyone is against him, whispers about him, and then stops whispering only when he enters a room —and who acts accordingly to defend himself—sooner or later finds that everyone *is* against him, whispers about him, and stops whispering only when he enters a room.

Thus it was in the Nixon White House. Once the Washington *Post* team of Bob Woodward and Carl Bernstein began digging into the burglary at the Watergate on June 17, all the fantasies became reality. The *Post* was accusing the Nixon team of crime, of concealing campaign cash, of sabotage and espionage—and worse, Woodward and Bernstein seemed to have sources inside the government.

On the outside, the McGovern forces (led by the candidate himself) were picking up the charges. McGovern was making "corruption" an issue. All the sly deals, all the chiseling, from extorting campaign contributions in exchange for government favors to the murky details of the San Clemente house purchase, were becoming more believable as they were laid at the door of a man whose campaign now was known to have hired criminals to break and enter.

The options were few. The only question, really, must have been how to cover up, who would cover up, and who would be thrown over the side to save the others. Any other course —as both Jeb Magruder and John Mitchell testified—would have jeopardized Nixon's reelection chances: Perjury, obstruction of justice were clearly preferable and, in any event, necessary.

179

Mitchell's and Magruder's instincts were correct; 1973 polls show that if the facts about Watergate had been fully known, George McGovern would have won the election of 1972. It is not hard to figure out how that could have happened. Suppose, for example, that the burglary at the office of Daniel Ellsberg's psychiatrist had been the one so badly bungled, and not the one at the Watergate? Then the facts would have started coming out in late 1971, instead of mid-1972, and a grand jury, a trial, and perhaps an Ervin Committee might have been news in 1972 instead of 1973.

Truth was never really an option. Not until the spring of 1973, when everything began to come unstuck, did it occur to John Dean, in a memorable phrase, that "only the truth would sell." And those who wondered why Nixon was so secretive, why all the "inoperative" statements had to be put out, why Nixon and Kleindienst were so adamant about not appointing a special prosecutor, now have their questions answered. The truth, whether announced by the White House or discovered by a special prosecutor, would have been devastating. David Frye, the great impressionist whose specialty since 1969 has been "doing" Richard Nixon, said it best in a "Nixon" act at a Washington nightclub in April 1973. "I could have told the truth," said Nixon-Frye, "but there were two objections. In the first place, it would have gravely damaged many people with whom I have worked closely over the years. Second, it would have destroyed me."

The contrary proposition was tried once, hesitantly, by the beleaguered White House. On June 28, 1973, as John Dean's testimony was nearing its conclusion, a long memorandum and a series of proposed questions for Dean were sent to the Ervin Committee by J. Fred Buzhardt, one of the series of lawyers Nixon has employed as his legal counsel. The Buzhardt memo, as read to the witness by Senator Daniel Inouye, turned out to be a disaster, and a disavowel statement was quickly put out in the name of the President. Nobody believed the disavowal because no one seriously believed that any of the President's lawyers would act on his own.

Hidden in the Buzhardt statement was the first White House suggestion that a cover-up wasn't necessary, that Dean was wrong in his assumption that it had, perforce, become "an instant way of life." Buzhardt said, "It would have been embarrassing to the President if the true facts had become known shortly after June 17, but it is the kind of embarrassment that

180

an immensely popular President could easily have weathered."

But could he? What follows is an attempt to *create* a speech Richard Nixon could have delivered to the nation on, let us say, September 15, 1972—after he had had time to discover the facts and if this immensely popular President had decided that at that point in time only the truth would sell.

My Fellow Americans, I have asked for this national network television time tonight to speak to you about an important matter which has arisen in the political campaign. I am sure that my opponents will ask for equal time to answer, and it is their right to do so under our system of government, just as it is *my* right to tell the networks I think they should not grant it. After all, the precious right of free speech is not limited only to those on the liberal side of the issues, or to those who would talk only about what is *wrong* with America. Just this morning, I received a letter from a prisoner of war in Vietnam. "Mr. President," he wrote, "don't *you* have the right of free speech, too?"

Now I want to tell you about what has come to be called the Watergate break-in. In the first place, you should know that it was not the *first* break-in at the headquarters of the Democratic Party. On January 27 of this year, my Attorney General, John Mitchell—a man who in three years has done a great deal to end permissiveness toward crime and to try to balance the struggle between the peace forces and the criminal forces—took over the direction of the Nixon presidential campaign. The first thing he did was to tell our people that we need to gather intelligence about the Democrats. And so the first meeting on this problem was held in his office at the Justice Department because if there is any place in my Administration where the battle against those who would change America is symbolized, it is right there in the Department of Justice in the Nixon Administration.

Now at this first meeting, in addition to Mr. Mitchell, was my legal counsel, John Dean. The legal counsel in the White House is an important man—he is the President's lawyer, and as you know, I am myself a lawyer—and I had chosen Mr. Dean carefully. He had been a lawyer for more than five years, and out of four jobs which he had held, he had been fired from only one for unethical conduct.

Also at that meeting was Mr. G. Gordon Liddy—also

181

a lawyer—who had just been appointed counsel to my campaign committee. The counsel to the campaign committee is an important man in a reelection effort; he must know all there is to know about the election laws and he must be a man of great learning and great loyalty. Mr. Liddy had been selected carefully too. While he knew nothing about election law, he had once been an assistant district attorney in a rural county, he had been defeated in a primary election against a Republican congressman, and out of four jobs *he* had held, he had been fired only once for insubordination.

Finally, Mr. Jeb Stuart Magruder was present at that meeting in the attorney general's office. Mr. Magruder had previously worked at the White House as a special counsel and as an assistant to my chief of staff, H. R. Haldeman. Magruder's qualifications were not quite so outstanding, since he was not a lawyer, but he had never been fired even once for incompetence or insubordination. He had been a businessman and had never really been tested under fire, but when it came time to tell a false story to the FBI and, later, to the grand jury, he came through like a champion, just as if he had been a member of the team all his life. He helped while Mr. Mitchell and Mr. Dean made up the false story for him, and coached him in it, and then he told that false story to the FBI, and he told it to the grand jury, and he told it the same way both times. As a result, he was not indicted, and you can be sure it made us all very happy here at the White House. Mr. Magruder had been made the deputy director of the Nixon campaign—second only to Mr. Mitchell—and he has always justified my faith in him.

At this first meeting, called to discuss ways in which the campaign could obtain more intelligence information about our opponents—or, as we called them, our enemies—Mr. Liddy made a number of suggestions. He proposed that we break into the Democrats' headquarters and plant wiretapping devices, but he also had other ideas. He said we should kidnap the leaders of radical, violence-prone groups and take them to Mexico so they couldn't practice their violent acts during the Republican Convention. And he also proposed that we hire attractive women—I believe the term he used was "call girls"—to be stationed on yachts we would rent at the Democratic Convention. These "call girls" would entertain some of the key delegates and obtain information which they would later tell us.

Now Mr. Liddy's plan certainly proposed a number of worthwhile activities, but it would have cost one million dollars. And I have made it clear—and I shall continue to make it clear—that just because a certain program has a high-sounding title or a worthy humanitarian objective, it will not automatically be approved in this Administration. And so I'm proud to tell you that my attorney general and my counsel and the head of my campaign all turned down that Liddy plan, however fine its objectives, because it simply cost too much money. To have adopted it would have been the easy, popular course, but it would have led to more programs like that, and it was an unwise use of campaign funds.

A week later, on February 4, Mr. Liddy came back with a less costly proposal. This one had eliminated some of the wasteful frills of the earlier plan and would cost only one-half a million dollars. But once again Mr. Mitchell, Mr. Dean, and Mr. Magruder rejected it. They were determined not to spend one penny more than necessary because, strange as it may seem to the big spenders and the budget-busters, they understood that it wasn't *their* money that would be spent. It would be the money of honest, hard-working Republican contributors, some of whom had contributed as little as $50,000—and some of whom had to take that money from corporate treasuries, where it had been slowly accumulating over the years rather than being used to pay lavish dividends to stockholders.

Finally, at a third meeting, held in Key Biscayne, on March 30, Mr. Liddy presented a responsible proposal, one which would meet the needs of the campaign at a price we could afford. For just $250,000, he would arrange for a break-in at the Democratic National Committee, the photographing of certain documents (which I shall not reveal, for national security reasons), and the placing of wiretap devices on telephones.

That plan was approved. My chief of staff, Mr. Haldeman, had been kept steadily informed of these proposals, and he was then informed of the approval. Mr. Charles Colson of my staff—also a distinguished lawyer serving as my special counsel—was particularly pleased because for some time he had been anxiously urging Mr. Magruder and Mr. Dean to approve the Liddy plan—but at a reasonable cost level, you may be sure.

On May 27, Mr. Liddy and his group, which included not only Mr. Liddy but Mr. Howard Hunt, an assistant to Mr. Colson, and four patriotic freedom fighters from Cuba who had been especially assigned to this job by Mr. Hunt, made their first entry into the headquarters of the Democrats at the Watergate. They planted their wiretaps and left quietly. For the next two weeks, reports taken from these phone taps were regularly passed to Mr. Magruder, Mr. Haldeman, and from time to time to Mr. Mitchell.

But Mr. Mitchell, even though he had left the command of the peace forces to take on this important job—at my request—saw almost at once, with his professional skill, that the job was being done poorly. The conversations of Mr. O'Brien, the chairman of the Democrats, were garbled, and we were obtaining nothing of value. Mr. Mitchell called in Mr. Liddy and, I believe the saying is—in fact, I recall it from my days when the bombs were falling in the South Pacific—"chewed him out" for failing to get full value for our money.

So Mr. Liddy arranged to break in again. This time, he took with him not only Mr. Hunt and the freedom fighters, but also Mr. James McCord, who was then the security director of the Republican National Committee and the security director of my campaign committee. Nevertheless, so strengthened had the peace forces become in the past three years—during which time crime in the District of Columbia had actually declined—that all the men were arrested in the Democratic headquarters by the District Metropolitan Police.

That ended the first phase of the Watergate incident and, as you can imagine, it caused quite a bit of consternation at the campaign committee and the White House. At that point in time, the decision was made by my top assistants that, since we had paid to have a crime committed, we must at once proceed to pay to see that no one knew where the funding came from. And it now appears that effort was successful. I have carefully counted it up, and I can tell you tonight that fewer than 100 people knew of the cover-up that has been going on, and I am proud that none of them are in any way connected, at this date, with either the press or the general public. (Of course, two reporters from the Washington

184

Post have learned about it, but the Washington *Post* always attacks the President—that is, of course, their right, and we have learned to live with it—but I have notified the Washington *Post* that further release of this information will be met by me, at a time and by a method of my choosing, in a way which I will consider suitable to protect our interests.)

In order to keep this matter quiet, we realized that large sums of money would be needed. So my personal attorney, Mr. Herbert Kalmbach, was asked to raise as much as he could. He was able to raise almost one quarter of a million dollars, in cash, chiefly by concealing from the donors the purpose of the money. The men in jail, particularly the Cuban-American freedom fighters, are proud men who respect their privacy, and we felt it would be improper and a violation of their cherished individual rights if Mr. Kalmbach were to reveal that the money he was raising was really to be used to pay these men to remain silent and to plead guilty.

In addition to Mr. Kalmbach, Mr. Maurice Stans was most helpful in raising the cash necessary to enable the arrested men to feel secure enough to remain silent. Mr. Stans, who is a respected accountant (and a member of the Accountant's Hall of Fame), unhesitatingly gave to Mr. Kalmbach some cash which was not even his or the committee's. A man from the Philippines, a country with a long history of fighting for freedom against internal subversion, gave Mr. Stans some cash—$30,000 to be exact—to use in my campaign. He was formerly the Philippine ambassador to the United States, so Mr. Stans took his cash with no hesitation. But then Mr. Stans wondered about the law which forbids a contribution from someone from another land, however dedicated it might be to the cause of freedom from foreign aggression. So Mr. Stans put aside the money until he could decide if he held it legally. But when Mr. Kalmbach came to him for cash to pay for the silence of the defendants, Mr. Stans gave him the ambassador's cash with no questions asked. In addition, almost $500,000 which was left over from my 1968 campaign was turned into cash and paid to the defendants. If we had not done this secretly, I am convinced that some of the contributors from 1968 would have heard about it, and a few might have objected.

There was also the question of the documents. After all, there were a number of files which showed all the wiretapping that had been going on. Those transcripts had already been read, and also—you can be sure we paid a lot of attention to this point—we knew that if anyone found those tapes, it could prove quite embarrassing. So the tapes were destroyed, or at least as many of them as could be destroyed. On the very first day, Mr. Liddy, the counsel to the Nixon campaign committee, destroyed a pile of documents almost one foot high by putting them into a shredding machine. Mr. Liddy had been a prosecutor, a member of the peace forces, and he was aware that this material, if not destroyed, could be used as evidence against him—and of course, by the rules of evidence, against all the rest of us, too.

I can't tell you now how much money we raised to pay the Watergate defendants and their lawyers in order for them either to be silent or to commit perjury at their trial, but I can assure you it was a substantial amount. Some people have said—and it is their right to say so under our system of government—that the Nixon Administration has no heart, that we have callously withheld money from those Americans who are poor, and that we oppose prepaid legal services for them. But here is an example of just the opposite. We opened our hearts and our pocketbooks to these unfortunate men. There are only seven of them, and they and their attorneys will receive over $1 million. Now I don't expect the Washington *Post* and other newspapers who can never find anything good to say about America to change suddenly and say "Richard Nixon *does* care about the poor—he *does* care about their legal services"—but I do want the American people to know the facts.

Now of course, it wasn't enough for just the men arrested at the Wategate to remain silent. Separate stories had to be made up for all the people who had participated because the FBI and the grand jury were starting to ask a lot of questions. After all, Mr. Magruder, Mr. Mitchell, and Mr. Stans had approved the payment to Mr. Liddy of $199,000 in cash in order to do the job right, and somehow we had to account for that money. So Mr. Herbert Porter, a young man on my campaign committee who, I'm proud to say, has been working in my campaigns since he was eight years old, came up with a good story. You've heard that story if you listened to the news reports or if you later read about the trial. The

186

story was that Liddy was paid the money so that he, in his capacity as counsel to my campaign committee, could hire some high-spirited young men to infiltrate the peace groups.

So Mr. Magruder and Mr. Mitchell told the story to the FBI, and Mr. Henry Petersen kept in close touch with my counsel John Dean about how the story was going over. And believe me, as a lawyer I know how difficult it is for two men to tell the same story, twice, and to get it right each time. Mr. Petersen, of course, was in charge of the grand jury because he was assistant attorney general in charge of the Criminal Division, so you can be sure he was in a position to know who was going to be indicted and who was not.

Just as an aside, I might tell you an amusing story of how Mr. Petersen came to be assistant attorney general at the Criminal Division, and thus be in a position to advise my counsel John Dean of the skill with which Mr. Magruder gave his perjured testimony to the grand jury. If it weren't for the liberal press, which always talks about what's *wrong* with America, Mr. Petersen couldn't have held that job.

His predecessor, a man I had appointed with great care, was Mr. Will Wilson. But the liberal press decided to discredit Mr. Wilson, and he had to resign. The only thing they raised against him was that he granted immunity from prosecution to a banker who was the central figure in a big banking and loan scandal in Texas. Mr. Wilson *had* taken an unsecured loan of $25,000 from this banker, but I never could see how that was in any way relevant. After all, that's what a banker's job *is*, under our American system of free enterprise, and Mr. Wilson used the money to buy real property, just as I did with my unsecured loan to buy property in San Clemente, which Pat and I call Casa Pacifica, or "Peaceful House." But you can be sure we were glad to have Mr. Petersen on the job.

You will remember that on August 28, I made a statement to the nation, saying that no one presently employed at the White House had been involved in the Watergate break-in. I used those words because Mr. Howard Hunt had been a White House employee at that time, but once he was arrested and put in jail, we took immediate steps to get him off the payroll. As a matter of fact, because he was off the White House payroll, he was one of those we had to pay secretly, otherwise he might have told the whole story—and as you will see, Mr. Hunt had a lot to tell.

In that August 28 statement, I said that Mr. Dean had made a full and complete investigation and cleared everybody. The reason I said that—even though Mr. Dean had never even been asked to make an investigation and certainly never made one—was so that people would think he *had* made an investigation, and then later when the press or anyone else would ask, we could refer to the "Dean Report" in answering their questions. And naturally, there was no danger that Mr. Ziegler, my press secretary, would release the report—which is always a danger when there really *is* a report—because we knew the report didn't exist. That way, the executive branch can discuss a report quite freely, without worrying that some crusading reporter will claim that some phrase or sentence means something else or quote it out of context. (In the case of the Dean Report, there *were no* phrases or sentences—so we didn't worry about the Washington *Post* twisting it around, and we certainly didn't worry about Jack Anderson or *The New York Times* printing it in full because it never existed.) And I'm happy to tell you that there *still* isn't any Dean Report, and there won't be one as long as I'm President of the United States.

Now all this time since June 17, the FBI has been investigating the Watergate break-in. There are a lot of fine investigators at the FBI—I even tried once to be one myself—and we knew that something had to be done or else one of these investigators might find out what had really happened. Worse, he might even tell somebody who had no right to know, such as a member of the public. So we turned to the acting director of the FBI, Mr. L. Patrick Gray. Mr. Gray was a good choice for director of the FBI. He had worked in my campaigns, he had served in the Navy, and he was completely loyal to me.

But Mr. Gray thought—and it was an easy mistake to make—that the job of the FBI was to find out who had committed this crime and who had ordered it and paid for it. So my counsel, Mr. Dean, and my former counsel, a brilliant lawyer named John Ehrlichman, who is one of the two finest government servants I have ever known, decided to compromise Mr. Gray. For some time Mr. Dean and Mr. Ehrlichman had been busy destroying the evidence that was in Mr. Howard Hunt's safe at the

188

White House, and when I tell you later what Mr. Hunt had been doing for us, you will see how important it was to destroy that evidence.

But before they had disposed of quite all of the evidence, Mr. Dean and Mr. Ehrlichman called in Mr. Gray. They handed him two files from Mr. Hunt's safe and told him that the files "must never see the light of day," and Mr. Gray went ahead and destroyed them. Mr. Dean, my counsel, and Mr. Ehrlichman, my counsel before him, understood very well that once you get somebody to help you destroy evidence, he is far less likely to investigate you for a crime.

But there were other problems. As you probably know, the men who were arrested inside the Watergate had $1,300 in cash with them, and $3,100 at their hotel, and the cash had come from funds raised for my campaign. The reason for this was that the Nixon campaign had paid them to do the job. But those funds were special. They had been given to the campaign by a man in Texas who didn't want it known that he had done so. In fact, he had sent the money to Mexico, where a lawyer he owed money to had turned them into cashier's checks—Mexican cashier's checks—and then sent the cash back to Texas. From there, it was sent, with other cash we wanted to keep secret, to Mr. Stans, who gave it to his counsel, Mr. Liddy. Mr. Liddy gave it to one of the Cuban freedom-fighters, and he distributed it to the others.

So we really didn't want the story of that cash to become public. Because, you see, if people knew that, they would not only know that my campaign had hired these men to break into the Watergate, they would also know that my finance chairman in Texas was hiding contributions. Now of course these contributions were perfectly legal—some people just like to send their money to Mexico first and have the cash come from someone else—but we knew there'd be a lot of talk about it, and Ron Ziegler would probably get it wrong. So I decided on a good way to keep it from coming out.

I told Mr. Ehrlichman and Mr. Bob Haldeman, the *other* finest government servant I have ever known, to get the CIA to stop the FBI from looking into the whole question of the Texas money that had come from Mexico. Mr. Gray at the FBI, wholly innocently and without any attempt to expose the crimes in which we were involved, had his agents in Texas looking into the transaction. So I told Mr. Haldeman and Mr. Ehrlichman to get the CIA to tell the FBI to stop looking into it, on the grounds that national security was involved. In this case, of course, there wasn't any national security involved, but I thought General Vernon Walters at the CIA would help anyway. General Walters was the deputy director of the CIA—deputy to Mr. Richard Helms—and as Mr. Ehrlichman later told Mr. Dean, General Walters knew he wouldn't have that job at all if he hadn't been an old friend of mine.

So Mr. Haldeman called in General Walters and Mr. Helms and told them to make Mr. Gray stop looking into the Texas money that had gone through Mexico because the national security was involved, and if it wasn't involved, they should tell the FBI that it *was*. It was probably a mistake, for which I take full responsibility, to invite Mr. Helms to that meeting because Mr. Helms knows a few things about national security, but he let General Walters hold up the FBI investigation for a few weeks anyway. Then Mr. Helms told them to go ahead with the investigation, even though I wanted it stopped. I will say this for Mr. Helms, however. Even if he didn't let our plan go through, he never told anyone about it, and that, of course, was very important. If the word ever got around the Georgetown cocktail circuit that we had asked Mr. Helms to call off part of the FBI investigation of the Watergate affair, in no time at all the voters would have known, and that would have been most destructive to my chances for reelection.

That is where the Watergate matter stands now. The defendants—the men arrested plus Mr. Liddy and Mr. Hunt—have been indicted and will stand trial. But I have been assured that Mr. Kalmbach has raised enough secret cash to pay them so that they will plead guilty at their trial, and I have been assured by my counsel, Mr. Dean, and my former attorney general, Mr. Mitchell, that Mr. Magruder and the others who planned and approved this deplorable incident will tell the same false story at the trial that they told to the grand jury and the FBI. We have every reason to believe that it will stop there. And we will, of course, continue to cite the Dean Report as evidence that no one else is involved.

There will be hard days ahead. Some of my opponents will make charges that we have covered up the commission of crimes. But I am convinced that we have done this so well that we can survive at least until November 7, when public interest will die down. The trial, as you know, has been set for January.

Now I would like to tell you of some other things that have been done during my Administration that will probably be described as "crimes" or "corruption" or "improper conduct" in the press and the networks and by my opponents.

For some time we have had employees at the White House who have been working hard to find out things about our enemies. Naturally, we have kept this secret because most of the things they have done have been illegal, and if it had become public knowledge that fulltime employees of the White House were engaged in such things as burglaries and forging official documents, they would probably have had to stop.

This began in a rather small way in 1969, when Mr. Ehrlichman hired two former New York policemen named John Caulfield and Anthony Ulasewicz. To conceal Mr. Ulasewicz's status, we arranged for Mr. Kalmbach to pay him with money left over from 1968. If anyone asked about their duties, we said they were employed in connection with stopping the terrible traffic in dangerous drugs, and since they had both been policemen, this seemed quite plausible. They were actually performing "investigations" for Mr. Ehrlichman, designed to help my political future and to get me reelected. And, I am sure you will agree, the best way to get reelected is to damage those who might run against you.

In 1969, for instance, Mr. Ulasewicz was sent to Martha's Vineyard, where Senator Edward Kennedy had just had an accident involving the death of a young lady in a car he had been driving. Although Mr. Ulasewicz was an employee of the White House, he was instructed to pretend to be a newspaper reporter and to ask Senator Kennedy as many embarrassing questions as he could at press conferences. While he was doing this, Mr. Caulfield arranged to plant a telephone tap in the apartment in Washington which the dead girl had shared with three roommates. The reason for all this, of course, was that I thought there was a real possibility that Senator Edward Kennedy would run against me in the election of 1972, and we wanted to gather as much scandal about him as we could.

Also, at about the same point in time, Mr. Caulfield

arranged for a break-in at the house of a newspaper man named Joseph Kraft. Mr. Kraft had been very critical of some of the policies of my Administration, and we thought that he might be less so if we were fully aware of everything that he and his family said on the telephone. Furthermore, Mr. Kraft at that time quite frequently spoke with Dr. Henry Kissinger, my national security advisor, and Mr. Ehrlichman and Mr. Haldeman were suspicious of *him.* It seemed a good idea at the time to listen to Mr. Kraft's telephone conversations because there was the possibility that we could not only embarrass Mr. Kraft, but, as far as Mr. Haldeman and Mr. Ehrlichman were concerned, they might be able, as the saying goes, to "get something" on Henry Kissinger, and that would have pleased them very much.

Mr. Caulfield and Mr. Ulasewicz are still working for the government and have more than proved their usefulness in a number of ways. After all the trouble at the Watergate, Mr. Caulfield, for example, was used by my counsel, Mr. Dean, to deal with Mr. McCord. Mr. McCord had threatened to tell the truth, and as I have previously explained, that would have been very damaging to my campaign. Through Mr. Dean, Mr. Caulfield told Mr. McCord that things would go better for him if he did not tell the truth, and Mr. McCord finally agreed.

Mr. Ulasewicz was also useful in other ways. You will recall that my personal attorney, Mr. Kalmbach, raised cash funds to pay the Watergate defendants to remain silent and to commit perjury. Now Mr. Kalmbach is a distinguished member of the bar, and so he naturally did not want to be the one who distributed the money for this purpose. He would meet Mr. Ulasewicz from time to time and give him the money, and Mr. Ulasewicz would then distribute the money to the defendants. In this way, Mr. Kalmbach was able to prevent anyone from knowing what he was really doing, which was an important part of the plan.

By 1970, it seemed to me that the old so-called legal methods of gathering information were no longer suitable. No one has more respect than I for the great men who founded this country, but it is also true that the ideas they had about individual liberties which they wrote into that great document, the Bill of Rights, may have been suitable 200 years ago, but they are not suitable now. So I approved a new way of gathering information which included breaking and entering people's homes and offices, stealing and photographing their documents, planting electronic devices which would overhear their conversations and telephone calls, and opening their mail before it was delivered. Let me assure you, you can learn a great deal more about a person by these means than you can if you just obey the law as the liberal judges have interpreted it, so it seemed to me quite a reasonable thing to do.

The following year we expanded the investigating team that had, up to then, just consisted of Mr. Caulfield and Mr. Ulasewicz. We founded a unit which was called, rather humorously I thought, the "plumbers." They were called the "plumbers" because their job was to stop leaks—in this case, leaks of information to newspapers and to the public.

During this time frame I was very concerned that a number of secret plans having to do with the war in Vietnam were being told to the public. That posed a great danger because it had always been true that if the public knew the real facts about Vietnam, it would be very hard for the Administration—and President Johnson's Administration also knew this—to continue the war. Since under our free system of government the conduct of foreign policy is entrusted to the President, I intended to keep as many of the facts about the war as secret as I could, so we assigned the "plumbers" the job of finding out how the public was learning about Vietnam.

The "plumbers" was a four-man unit. It consisted of Mr. Gordon Liddy, whom I have previously described, Mr. Howard Hunt, Mr. Egil Krogh, and Mr. David Young. Mr. Hunt was a good friend of my special counsel, Charles Colson, and he had been a spy for many years. Mr. Krogh had worked for Mr. Ehrlichman in his law firm in Seattle, and Mr. Young had been Dr. Kissinger's appointment secretary. These four men then worked with Mr. Caulfield and Mr. Ulasewicz in the same kind of work that the other two men had been doing for the previous two years, and they were generally supervised by Mr. Ehrlichman and Mr. Colson.

We were very concerned at that point in time about the fact that Daniel Ellsberg had given the Pentagon Papers to *The New York Times,* and we were most anxious to see that he would be convicted of some crime for having done so.

193

Then it was discovered at the White House that Mr. Ellsberg had once seen a psychiatrist, but the psychiatrist had refused to give the FBI any information about his treatment of Mr. Ellsberg. We then decided it was important to obtain that information in any event. (Permissive, soft-headed judges have refused for a long time to order a doctor to tell what he knows about his patient, but we certainly didn't think that a man as guilty as Mr. Ellsberg should be allowed to hide behind this technicality.) So Mr. Krogh and Mr. Ehrlichman arranged to have a burglary at the office of this doctor in Los Angeles. Mr. Hunt and Mr. Liddy obtained the services of two Cuban freedom-fighters and went with them to Los Angeles, where they broke into the doctor's office and photographed his records of treatment of Mr. Ellsberg. Unfortunately, there wasn't very much in the file. Mr. Hunt and Mr. Liddy, by the way, were paid by the White House only for the actual number of hours required to commit the burglary.

At about the same time, Mr. Colson, my special counsel, was anxious to find out if a man named Morton Halperin, who had once worked for Dr. Kissinger, was involved in making any information public. He thought Mr. Halperin might have some documents that would show this in his office and the Brookings Institution here in Washington. So Mr. Colson proposed to Mr. Caulfield that he break into the Brookings Institution and take the documents from the files. Mr. Colson suggested to Mr. Caulfield that he firebomb the office so that it would appear that someone else had done the job, and in the confusion, Mr. Caulfield could escape with the documents. Mr. Caulfield rather cautiously refused to do this. And so we were never able to find out that information, and Mr. Halperin is still working at the Brookings Institution, which is certainly his right under our form of government.

There was one other job done by the "plumbers" which almost worked and which I want to tell you about tonight. As I have said, I thought in 1971 that Senator Edward Kennedy might be my opponent in 1972. Senator Kennedy's brother, John F. Kennedy, had been President from 1961 to 1963, and Mr. Colson suggested that it would help in the campaign against Edward Kennedy if we could discredit John Kennedy. John Kennedy had been assassinated, and it was thought that if people could be

194

made to believe that he had been involved in the assassination of someone else, it would give Senator Edward Kennedy less of a "sympathy vote."

So Mr. Colson got Howard Hunt of the "plumbers" to create such evidence. Mr. Hunt obtained all of the official State Department cables that went back and forth between Washington and Saigon in 1963 when John Kennedy was President, and he showed these cables to Mr. Colson. Unfortunately, none of them showed that John Kennedy was involved in the assassination of President Diem of South Vietnam, who was killed in October 1963. In fact, the cables showed that President Kennedy was very much opposed to this.

So Mr. Colson told Mr. Hunt to manufacture a cable which did involve John Kennedy, and Mr. Hunt, armed only with a typewriter, a Xerox machine, and a single-edge razor blade, was able to forge a cable which implicated President Kennedy in the assassination of President Diem. Mr. Hunt arranged for all the correct signatures to be on the cable, and it was really quite a good job.

On September 16, 1971, I said at a press conference that we were involved in the Vietnam war because of our complicity in the murder of President Diem. It was the first time any American President had ever suggested that possibility, and Mr. Colson quickly told a number of reporters how important my statement had been.

Mr. Colson then took the forged cable and gave it to a reporter from *Life* magazine with the hope that the reporter would write a major article about it because that would have severely damaged Senator Edward Kennedy and, indeed, the reputation of the whole Kennedy family. Unfortunately, the reporter from *Life* discovered that the cable was a forgery and did not use it.

It was that cable, as well as some of Mr. Hunt's other memoranda about Edward Kennedy, that Mr. Dean and Mr. Ehrlichman gave to Mr. Gray, and which Mr. Gray later destroyed.

Now I would like to tell you some things about how we raised the money with which to conduct my campaign and all these extra activities. As you know, it takes a great deal of money to run a campaign—particularly when you are running for President and particularly when your campaign has as many extra expenditures as mine did. Many people do not want to give money to a political campaign, and in fact will not do so unless it can be made clear to them that there is some financial advantage which they could obtain as a result. So in 1971 and 1972, Mr. Stans and Mr. Kalmbach went around the country making it as clear as they could that contributions to the Nixon campaign, particularly from corporations and from the officers of large corporations, were not just contributions to politics, but were some of the wisest investments that those people and corporations could make.

Mr. Kalmbach, for instance, was not only my personal attorney, but he was also the attorney for United Airlines. When he went to American Airlines and asked them for $100,000, he wasn't just asking for help in providing good government. After all, the President makes the final decision on foreign airline routes, and he also has a good deal to say about who will decide on domestic airline matters. American Airlines thought enough of that argument to give Mr. Kalmbach $100,000.

Mr. Stans and Mr. Kalmbach had the added advantage of being able to tell contributors that they could conceal their names and the amounts that they had contributed if they gave the money before April 7, 1972, or soon thereafter. In this way, they were able to raise nearly $25 million in secret contributions from people who wanted to hide the money they had given.

On March 23, 1971, Mr. Murray Chotiner, a lawyer who had been a part of my campaign organization in California and in my campaign for President, asked if I would meet in the Cabinet Room at the White House with him and some representatives of the dairy industry. At that meeting, we talked, as you might imagine, about the price of milk. The so-called support price for milk was set by the executive branch of the government, usually by the secretary of agriculture. The milk producers explained to me that since the secretary of agriculture had refused to raise the price, they wanted me to overrule him. Now most Americans don't understand about the price of milk. All these men wanted was an increase amounting to a few cents a quart. Since most housewives don't buy more than four or five quarts of milk a week (I checked this with Mrs. Nixon), an increase of one cent per quart would mean that the average American housewife would only spend between $3.00 and $5.00 more per year for milk. But to these men who produced the milk, the increase in profit would be substantial and would run into millions of dollars. And they told me, in Mr. Chotiner's presence, that they would contribute at least substantially to my campaign if I would order the secretary of agriculture to increase the price of milk by just one cent a quart. Now money, particularly in the early stages of a campaign, is very important and represents an important contribution. So, of course, I approved the increase in the price of milk, and I am pleased to say that those dairymen contributed $422,500 to my campaign by the end of 1971.

A few years earlier, Congress had passed a law requiring a higher safety standard for the manufacture of carpets, particularly carpets used in large institutions such as hospitals and nursing homes. The reason for this was that there had been a number of fires caused by burning carpets, and the purpose of the law was to raise the flammability standard. The secretary of commerce was supposed to set this standard, and since Mr. Stans had been the secretary of commerce and was now my finance chairman, it was natural that a group of carpet manufacturers would come to see him. They offered to contribute nearly $100,000 to my campaign if only my Administration would postpone the new flammability standards. The reason they wanted a postponement was that it would cost the manufacturers more money to make their carpets less flammable. And since they believed in the American system of free enterprise, they much preferred not to spend the money until some later time, if at all. Mr. Stans saw the wisdom of this, and he also saw the advantage of a campaign contribution of nearly $100,000, so he agreed.

There were other ways in which we combined good business with good politics and good government. International Telephone and Telegraph in 1971 was seeking to acquire a large insurance company called the Hartford Insurance Company. The head of the Anti-Trust Division of the Department of Justice thought that this would be in restraint of trade and in violation of the antitrust laws. ITT thought that it would be good business for them to acquire the Hartford Insurance Company, since their profits would substantially increase. They offered to pay $400,000 to defray the costs of the Republican convention if we would overrule the Anti-Trust Division and permit the merger. This really was a good business arrangement on both sides, since the Republican party could use the $400,000 to help pay for the convention, and ITT would make far more than $400,000 in additional profit if they were allowed to acquire the insurance company. So my attorney general, John Mitchell, and my deputy attorney general, Richard Kleindienst, overruled the Anti-Trust Division and the merger was approved. And I am pleased to say that our judgment in that matter has proved to be correct. The Republican convention was one of the most successful ever conducted, and the profits of ITT as a result of their acquisition of the insurance company, have exceeded even their fondest expectations.

Now I want to explain fully just what happened in connection with the 1972 sale to the Soviet Union of one-fourth of the American wheat crop. As you know, some people—the ones who can never find anything *right* about America—are calling this a "scandal." They are pointing to some isolated facts—such as that some wheat farmers lost thirty cents a bushel on their wheat crop, that the price of bread will go up a few pennies a loaf, and that the whole transaction cost the taxpayers a few hundred million dollars. But it's easy to criticize if you don't have all the facts, so I want to tell them to you now.

Early this year, after Mrs. Nixon and I took our historic journey for peace to the People's Republic of China, I turned my attention to the relations between our country and the Union of Soviet Socialist Republics and to the historic summit meeting I was to have with Mr. Brezhnev, the first chairman of the Central Committee of the Communist Party of the U.S.S.R. (You will notice that for almost one year, I have been the first American president to use the full names of these countries, which we used to call "Red China" and "Russia." I have taken that historic step because it makes them feel better and because they would not agree to my historic journeys unless I did so. But you will also notice, and this is very important as a part of our larger strategy, that I still refer to the Democratic Republic of Vietnam as "North Vietnam," and sometimes as "the men in Hanoi." And we always refer to the Provisional Revolutionary Government as the "Viet Cong," or sometimes as just "Charlie".)

The forthcoming discussions with Mr. Brezhnev posed some problems. In April, we were making plans to mine the harbor at Haiphong, so as to deny to the men in

198

Hanoi vital war materiel which was being used against our troops in South Vietnam and also being used to keep our POW's imprisoned. Much of this materiel came from the Union of Soviet Socialist Republics, and some Soviet ships would be in the harbor when we closed it. Now I am a student of history—in addition to my profession as a lawyer—and I have observed that when one country's ships are blockaded by another country, it is often taken as a hostile gesture. If your ships are being blockaded in the port of an ally, you usually don't invite the leader of the country which is doing the blockading to come to your capital and join in creating a generation of peace.

And that is what I wanted. Not for just an hour, not for just a day, not for just a year—but a full generation of peace. So before we blockaded the harbor at Haiphong Doctor Kissinger went to Moscow to talk to Chairman Brezhnev. And they agreed that if the historic summit meeting was to take place, something would have to be done for the leaders of the U.S.S.R., so that they could look better to their people while they *seemed* to be abandoning their ally in Hanoi.

I know about the problem. If it weren't for the good feeling we all had, watching the live satellite television coverage from Peking, and if it weren't for all the film we obtained from the People's Republic of China which we are now showing on our regular campaign television messages—if it weren't for that, it would have been hard to answer those people who said we were abandoning *our* ally, Taiwan, by letting them be expelled from the United Nations. So from my own experience in foreign affairs, I knew what the problems were which were facing the men in the Krem—the leaders of the Soviet Union.

Now we knew that there had been a disastrous grain harvest in the U.S.S.R. Our Agriculture Department knew that, and so we weren't surprised when the Soviet leaders told us they wanted to buy enormous amounts of American wheat.

The problem for me and for Secretary Butz, of course, was an agonizing one—namely, whether or not to tell the American wheat farmers. If the normal agricultural bulletin went out, telling the wheat farmers of the great shortages, then when the news came out about the Soviet grain purchase, they would know enough to hold on to their early wheat for a better price.

But if the wheat farmers *didn't* know about how much

199

the Soviet leaders would have to buy, they would sell their early wheat for a cheaper price. It was just simple old-fashioned American free enterprise economics, the kind that has made our country the strongest nation in the history of the world, no matter how much some professors of economics may say about the new economics—which of course, it is their right to do.

So the dilemma was plain. Should we tell the American wheat farmers about the Russian shortage, or should we not? Because, you see, there was another element in the bargain. The Soviets would buy their wheat from five large American grain companies—the Big Five, as they are called. If we told the farmers, then the profits of the grain dealers would be smaller; if we didn't tell the farmers, or if we deceived them, the profits of the grain dealers would be larger.

Now it would have been the easy, popular course to have told the wheat farmers and let *them* make the profit. After all, there are thousands—perhaps hundreds of thousands—of wheat farmers. And they might have voted for us if their profits had been large enough. But it was also true that there was a possibility of large campaign contributions from the grain company officials if we let *them* make the profit. And I'm proud to say that we took the lonely, courageous course and deceived the wheat farmers.

We didn't tell them about the bad Soviet harvest. And when there was talk about a sale to the Soviet Union, we made it appear that it would take at least three years and that other grains would be more important than wheat. Now, the cooperation of the Department of Agriculture was vitally important in all this. Many people say that government bureaucrats are not efficient, that they spend all day drinking coffee and loafing. But I'm proud of those people at the Department of Agriculture. They left the farmers in the dark about the figures, they talked about a three-year sale, with a stress this year on other grains. And, most important of all, they told the large grain companies in advance so they could get the lowest possible price from the farmers and thus maximize their profits.

One of those so-called bureaucrats at the Department of Agriculture not only did a good job for the grain companies, he also did a good job for himself. In the best old-fashioned American tradition of individual initiative, he secured himself an important job with one of the grain companies. He was the assistant secretary of agriculture in charge of the deal with the Soviet Union, and before he went to Moscow, he arranged to be hired by one of the grain companies, and as soon as the trade was negotiated, he went to work for them at their headquarters in New York. Since he knew all the details, I'm sure he was a good executive. And just to show that there was nothing unbalanced about this arrangement, one of the grain company executives went to work as an assistant secretary of agriculture at the same time, so the government would not be deprived of the kind and quality of service these men can provide.

The results were very successful. In addition to the large profits the grain companies made through knowing what the farmers did *not* know, they were able to make even more through a special decision by Secretary Butz. He had been an executive of a large agricultural business himself, and he knew the importance in that field, not only of *secrecy*, but of *subsidies*. Even though he knew the Soviet buyers would pay a premium, and even though he knew that the profits of the large companies were already substantial through the deception of the farmers, he kept in force a large export subsidy of fifty-seven cents a bushel, which allowed the Soviets to pay a lower price and yet keep the grain companies' profits even higher.

Finally, in order to protect the extra profits we had every reason to expect the grain companies would receive, we realized that it doesn't matter very much if you make a large profit—and my parents ran a small business, in which I helped, so I know something about this—if you have to turn right around and pay most of it back in the form of income taxes. If there is one thing that will effectively throttle the American system of free enterprise—which has created over 75 million jobs for Americans of every color and creed—it is a high income tax.

So the grain companies asked to have one-half their special income on this transaction made free of tax. The Treasury can do this in special export situations under the provisions of a law passed last year by the Democratic Congress. Until the election is over, of course, the Treasury will refuse to waive half the tax on the grain companies' profit, but I can assure you tonight that that matter will be corrected just as soon after Election Day as we can.

Now that is the course we have taken, and I'm sure a lot of people will complain. They will say we should have favored the farmers over the grain companies. Some farmers will criticize Secretary Butz and this administration for what we did. But the political future of one man is not as important as the national welfare, and I can tell you that even if that man is the secretary of agriculture, it makes no difference. I have the highest regard for Secretary Butz, but I would rather see him become a one-year secretary than to lose this election and give up my principles.

I have always believed that an American ought not ask what his country can do for him, but what he can do for himself. But before I describe, in all candor and honesty, what I have done for myself, I want to tell you a few things I have done for my friends and associates. I have always believed that one of the greatest virtues is loyalty. I know it isn't very modern. I know the social scientists don't believe it any more. I know it isn't talked about on the Georgetown cocktail circuit, and you certainly won't see a story about loyalty winning a Pulitzer Prize.

But there are millions of hardworking Americans who *do* believe in loyalty—to their families, to their flag, and to their friends. And as long as I am President, *I* will be loyal to my family, my flag, and my friends. As far as my family and my flag are concerned, I have already taken some steps. At only a minimal expense to the taxpayers— less than $3,000 for construction and painting—I have had a flagpole erected at the Western White House, where Old Glory is properly displayed every day. And I am presently in conversation with my old friend Charles Rebozo, who plans, as soon as the election is over, to buy a house in Washington for my daughter Julie and her husband, the grandson of General Eisenhower. The house for my daughter and son-in-law, which Mr. Rebozo will buy, will cost him no more than $150,000 and will enable Julie and David to take an active role in public affairs, as young people should, without the worries so many young people have today about paying the rent. In addition, I will arrange for White House employees—at no expense at all either to myself or to any member of my family—to clean

202

up the house and the grounds, paint it, and otherwise make it ready for their occupancy.

Now let me tell you about loyalty to my friends. I will speak this evening about two dear friends, men who have helped me many times in the past. They have contributed generously to my campaigns, and they were responsible for my becoming the senior partner, in 1962, in one of the most prestigious law firms on Wall Street. Their names are Elmer Bobst and Donald Kendall.

Mr. Bobst has been for many years the head of a forward-looking drug company, Warner-Lambert. In 1970 he wanted to merge his company with another drug company, Parke-Davis. Now in the Justice Department are some men who work in what is called the Anti-Trust Division. Their job is to find out what is *wrong* with American business, just as most Americans, including myself, try to think about what is *right* with American business.

Those men in the Anti-Trust Division decided that Mr. Bobst's company should not merge with Parke-Davis. They think that any business that's big is automatically *too* big. But my attorney general, John Mitchell, happened to be one of those Americans who isn't afraid of someone just because he's a businessman. Unfortunately, he couldn't decide Mr. Bobst's case because when he was my law partner he had also been Warner-Lambert's lawyer, and Mr. Mitchell would not want to be involved in anything which seemed unethical.

So Mr. Mitchell turned the whole matter over to his deputy attorney general, Richard Kleindienst. Mr. Kleindienst decided that the merger should go through, and so it did. And I'm proud to say that everybody involved in that situation has been bettered by it. Mr. Bobst's stock is worth 15 million dollars more than it was worth when it was the stock in only *one* drug company, the head of the Anti-Trust Division is now a federal judge, and Mr. Kleindienst is attorney general.

The other friend I want to talk about is Donald Kendall. Mr. Kendall is the chief executive of Pepsi-Cola, and as you know, when I was a lawyer in New York, I represented Pepsi-Cola in a great many matters. When Mr. Brezhnev raised trade matter with me at the historic summit meeting for peace this summer in Moscow, I was able to discuss Pepsi-Cola with some authority. For a long time, Mr. Kendall had tried to sell Pepsi-Cola within the borders of the Union of Soviet Socialist Republics because he had long observed the poor quality of Communist soft drinks. He was anxious to expand his company's markets, so its profits could increase and thus raise the value of his own stock. I'm pleased to be able to announce tonight that the Soviet leaders agreed that Pepsi-Cola, starting next year, will be the only foreign soft drink which can be sold in that country.

Now I would like to return to what has been called the Nixon doctrine for America: "Ask not what your country can do for you, but what you can do for yourself." I want to tell you some of the things I have been able to do for myself. Most of these things have not yet been made public, but I have been told that reporters are starting to look into the stories, and I am sure they will be reporting all the bad things they find, so I would like to tell you first. As you know, I own what is called the Western White House at San Clemente. We believe that if all our press assistants call it "the Western White House," it will come to be called that by everyone, and that is better than calling it "the Nixon house" because I can tell you after many election contests, that people don't look favorably on a candidate—particularly one who already *holds* high public office—acquiring an expensive house for his own use. So we call it the Western White House, but I want to assure you that I own it.

Now the way I acquired the Western White House is an interesting story. I can't tell you tonight exactly the way in which it was done because my advisers haven't come up yet with a story that fully satisfies me or one that would fully satisfy you. And until we have a story that is absolutely airtight, I will not, as President of the United States, tell that story. I have seen too many cases in the past where Presidents have told a version of how they acquired property, only to have it come out later that it was acquired in a different way, and I think it tends to destroy confidence in the Presidency—not in the President, but in the Presidency—if the occupant of that great office is found to have been telling something which is not the truth.

Now as I said, I'm not going to tell you the *exact* way in which I acquired the property at San Clemente. I will say that the purchase price was $1.5 million, and I have paid very little of my own money, but I cannot tell you who put up the rest of the money because, as I said earlier, we don't have a version yet that will stand the tightest scrutiny. When I bought it, the original owner of the property received approximately $400,000 and agreed to take a mortgage for the remaining $1 million.

Since we didn't know what story we would finally put out as the truth—the official version—we concealed the whole transaction initially and made it appear that the Title Insurance &Trust Company, a Los Angeles company, was the owner. Of course, they didn't own the property; they were just the trustees for me, for the original owners who still were owed $1 million, and for the people who had enabled me to put up the cash down payment. If we had handled this transaction in the usual way in which property is bought in California, everybody would have known the identity of all the parties, and it would have been almost impossible later for me to make people believe that someone else was the real buyer and lender.

Now as soon as I had bought the property and been given the mortgage, the need, of course, was to find someone to pay it off. All that was needed was some person or group which would pay $1 million so that I would not have to owe the money any more. We found that source, and the money was secretly paid to the original sellers. But unfortunately, we can't say who or what it was that paid off the mortgage because the arrangement we had was that it would remain secret—for his benefit as well as mine.

So, for some time, we have been trying to find someone to *say* he paid the mortgage. My friend Robert Abplanalp has a lot of money, and it is entirely possible that we may say, later on and after the election, that Mr. Abplanalp originally loaned me the money and later paid off the mortgage in return for a lot of the acreage. So far, that seems like the most believable story, and I am almost sure that we shall finally settle on that. Unfortunately, if Mr. Abplanalp had really done that, the records would have shown it on the day he was supposed to have done so. Of course, the records *don't* show that, and in California the risk of discovery in tampering with land records after they have been recorded is so great that I shall never agree to try it. If we do decide to say Mr. Abplanalp loaned me the money and that he later bought most of the property in return for paying off the million-dollar mortgage, we will simply refuse to disclose the name of the company he formed, or when he bought the land, or how much land he owns. Some people may complain, but I will not be deterred in my duty. It is wrong for people to believe the President is concealing his own enrichment, and I shall never be a party to encouraging that belief.

Now, in addition to acquiring the Western White House for very little cash—and if any of you have seen the house and grounds you will realize that is a tremendous buy—there was also the question of improving it, of "fixing it up" as we used to say at my parents' home in Whittier. Little by little, we have done so. In addition to the flagpole from which Old Glory proudly flies, we built a bridge so that we will not have to cross the railroad tracks to get to the beach, we have put in a swimming pool with a heater, we have replaced the old furnace, we have done extensive electrical work both inside and outside, we have landscaped the entire estate—all the way from ornamental shrubs to a wind-screen around the swimming pool—and we have built other buildings, including a most attractive gazebo in the garden and a cabana so that guests will not have to change their clothes in the main house. Mrs. Nixon and I want the house to remain an oasis of calm, Casa Pacifica as we call it, and we could not achieve that if guests were continually tracking water and sand through the house.

And I am proud—as proud as I can be—to be able to say to you tonight that almost none of that money spent to fix up the house at San Clemente has come from my pocket or that of any member of my family. Except for the golf course, which was built at a cost of $250,000 by a group of campaign contributors, nearly all of the money at San Clemente has come from government funds. The total is over $700,000, less than the $1,180,522 in government funds used to improve the *Southern* White House at Key Biscayne. The thought of an American President trying to create a whole generation of peace, and at the same time worrying about whether he can pay the bills to have his house improved, is a repugnant idea to me, as I'm sure it is to most honest Americans who work for a living, go to church, send their children to school, and try to get a short vacation in the summer. As long as I am President, you can be sure it will never happen.

And now, as I near the conclusion of this historic recital of truth, I want to talk about something I'm sure all of you share with me, and that is a strong feeling that taxes are simply too high. No matter what good things we think government should do with tax money, it comes from you and me, and if government takes too much in taxes, it will destroy that precious individual initiative that has kept us strong.

I want to tell you tonight how I have managed, over great obstacles, to reduce my taxes in two ways. I have vastly reduced the income tax I would otherwise have to pay, and I have arranged to pay less property taxes, too. Because when we talk about taxes we must remember that it is not only the income tax which takes away money which could otherwise be spent or invested, the property tax is another source of reducing the amount of money Americans can spend on themselves. And the property tax hits only the substantial decent American who owns property, the very person who can help most by investing his capital to make this a stronger and more secure land.

The major property I own is my home at San Clemente—the Western White House. That property is in a county of California with the picturesque name of Orange. And in 1972, the tax assessor of Orange County, a man named Andrew Hinshaw, was anxious to improve himself and run for Congress. Now Mr. Hinshaw had a problem. He was a Republican, and his congressional district was already represented by a Republican, a man named John Schmitz.

Now Congressman Schmitz was not a team player, which, under our American system, he had every right not to be. He insisted, for instance, on continuing to refer to the People's Republic of China as "Red China," and he had begun to blame the Nixon policy of a generation of peace for the fact that Taiwan was no longer a member of the United Nations.

Mr. Schmitz even went so far as to compare the deficit budgets of *my* Administration—which became deficits only because we were spending so much money to defend the free world forces in Southeast Asia—with the deficits of earlier Democratic Administrations, where the deficits had been caused by New Deal boondoggling and wasteful social projects.

So when Mr. Hinshaw, the tax assessor, decided he wanted to run for Congress, we arranged for Nixon supporters in Orange County to support *him* rather than Mr. Schmitz. That way, Republican voters would understand that I wanted Mr. Hinshaw to win, but without the embarrassment of a President's public statement against an incumbent conservative Republican Congressman.

I'm proud to tell you that it worked. Mr. Hinshaw is now the Republican nominee, and he will be the next Congressman from that district. And this year, he assessed the property at San Clemente at a figure far below the level at which he assesses other property. The result is that my property tax will be lower, and I will be able to retain more of my income than if the customary bureaucratic process had been followed, which taxes *all* property, no matter who owns it, at the same rate.

I can also report to you tonight that by taking advantage not only of my position as President of the United States, but also by knowledge of a special feature of the tax laws, I have been able to reduce my federal income tax liability by a substantial amount, probably as much as 250,000 dollars. That means I shall have almost one-quarter of a million dollars more to spend for my own investments than if I had not been able to apply this particular deduction.

For many years, political figures such as myself had been able to give our personal papers to some charitable institution—such as a presidential library or a university or the government—and to treat that gift of personal papers as though it were a charitable gift of the amount of money the papers were worth. The value would be set by someone hired for that purpose. So if I were to give my speeches, or the memoranda I use in my work, or other papers, to a college or to the National Archives, I would get a substantial reduction in my income taxes. Naturally, I did this for many years, as did many other public figures, all of whom are as anxious as any other American to have more money left over after they pay their taxes.

In 1969, the Democrat-controlled Congress decided to put a stop to this practice. They passed a law forbidding public figures to claim a tax deduction for the value of the public papers they gave to charity. The only question in 1969 was the date Congress would select as the cut-off. Naturally, I urged the Congress to set the date as late in the year as possible, so as to give me a maximum amount of time in which to reduce my taxes. And I am proud to say that great American, former President Lyndon Johnson, joined me in that effort.

Congress finally set July 29, 1969, as the date after which the donations would not qualify for a deduction. Later that year, in December 1969, we finally decided which documents I was going to donate, and their value. The deed was delivered later, the next April, in 1970, but it was dated and notarized to make it look as though it had been done in 1969. So for those of you who share my view that income taxes must be reduced because high taxes stifle individual initiative and hold down investment which creates jobs for all Americans, I want you to know that in spite of this Democratic Party law, I was able to reduce my taxes substantially, in this case by $250,000, just by writing the deed *before* the law was made effective, and then by completing it *after* the law took effect, and by *saying* it was done earlier.

Now many people have urged me to ignore the charges of espionage and sabotage which have been raised in this campaign. It would be the easy, popular course simply to deny that it existed. After all, both my press secretary and the director of my campaign have condemned, in unequivocal terms, the irresponsibility of the press in carrying reports that Mr. Haldeman and Mr. Kalmbach have paid campaign money to people whose job it was to sabotage my opponents. So it would be the wisest course, politically, merely to stick to that denial.

But I believe that political wisdom is often not the best guide. I have decided to tell you tonight about that sabotage and espionage because I think it is the courageous thing to do, and because Mr. Kalmbach has told the FBI about it and the Washington *Post* has a report of his confession.

We employed, on a widespread basis during this campaign, people whose sole task was to confuse and divide the opposition. This year several candidates sought the Democratic nomination, and obviously it would be better for me if they were set against each other so it would be more difficult for them to come together after they had selected a nominee.

In addition to ordinary sabotage, such as calling off meetings and sending people to the wrong places, we also used anonymous telephone calls and printed materials to say derogatory things about the Democratic candidates, and made it appear that the candidates themselves were saying those things about each other. Many people have objected to our doing this secretly. Naturally, we could not reveal who was doing this or the whole point of it would have been lost. For instance, we hired people to call voters in New Hampshire, pretending to be members of a "Harlem Committee for Muskie." They called late at night, and they tried to have the voice tone people associate with black people. They suggested that Senator Muskie would help their cause. Now the purpose of this was so the New Hampshire voters would think ill of Senator Muskie, and so Senator Muskie would think ill of his opponent Senator McGovern. I'm pleased to say that is just what happened.

Now in California—and I'm only giving you a very few examples of the kinds of things these men did—we wanted to injure Senator McGovern. We had some pamphlets printed which seemed to come from a "Humphrey Labor Committee" and which attacked Senator McGovern's labor record. Of course, the charges weren't true—if the pamphlet had told the truth there would have been no reason to print it—but it made a lot of labor union members vote against Senator McGovern, and it got Senator McGovern's people mad at Senator Humphrey. We also arranged—I am told—for Mr. Kalmbach's law firm to buy, in secret, naturally, or it would have all been public, the computer firm which was doing the cataloging of voters for Senator McGovern. That way we were able not only to hamper his campaign in the primary—which helped us at least indirectly—but we also were able to obtain, free of charge, a list of all California Democrats and an indication as to which of them favored Senator McGovern and which did not. And believe me, you can't carry that state unless you get some unhappy Democrats to vote with you. It was worth all the trouble to get that list.

Those are just a few examples of the so-called sabotage, but I can assure you there was a great deal more.

Finally, I want to tell you something that has been completely concealed until this time. For nearly two years I have been secretly recording, by means of a voice-activated listening device, every conversation which has taken place in the Oval Office, the Cabinet Room, my office in the Executive Office Building, and my office at Camp David. Of course, I have also recorded on tape every phone conversation during that time.

The interesting thing about this practice, and the most useful, is that the other party to the phone conversation, and everyone in my offices, has been totally unaware that

I have been recording their conversations. This afforded me, as President of the United States, a great advantage over, for example, heads of state, senators, and governors, because they feel quite free to discuss any matter, while I can be quite guarded in my responses. At some future time, I shall, of course, make use of these tapes, or portions of them, but I want to make absolutely clear now that if there is anything on them which could in any way prove incriminating to me, I shall unhesitatingly refuse to make them available. I shall, at such time, invoke whatever Constitutional doctrine seems appropriate or likely to succeed.

So let me sum up what I have told you tonight—as to each of the allegations which has been made against me.

First, there were *two* break-ins at the Watergate, each approved and planned by my counsel, my former attorney general, the head of my campaign committee, and the counsel of that committee.

Second, we did *not* break into the headquarters of my opponent. When the team, including the counsel to the committee, drove by to attempt it, it appeared far too difficult and they would not risk discovery, however worthwhile the purpose might have been.

Third, since June 17, there has been a total effort to cover up the incident which took place on that date. Each of the responsible officials in the White House, including my two top aides, the finest public servants I have ever known, has had a particular task, and each has carried it out perfectly. In addition, important roles have been assigned to men at the campaign committee and to my personal attorney.

Fourth, no one need have any fear that any incriminating evidence will be discovered which might embarrass the Presidency or cause other nations to think us a pitiful, helpless giant. The destruction of the evidence—and there was a lot of it—has been carried out by the acting director of the FBI, my chief of staff, his assistant, and my counsel.

Fifth, there is no possibility that any contradiction will emerge between the facts as they are ultimately determined and the investigation by John Dean on which I relied last month and which I reported in full to the American people. The reason there will be no discrepancies is that there was no such investigation.

Sixth, there have been other wiretappings and burglaries, all with the full approval of high officials in my

Administration. All of it, I assure you, was directed at a man I thought would be a strong candidate against me, and one burglary, of course, was carried out because a doctor refused to talk freely about his treatment of a patient who we thought had committed a crime.

Seventh, I have approved plans to use burglary, opening of mail, and listening in on other people's conversations—all of it to be done only when it has been determined by me or someone I designate that the person or institution involved poses a substantial danger, either to the United States or to my reelection.

Eighth, a cable was prepared which showed that President John Kennedy had approved the assassination of President Diem of South Vietnam, even though he had not done so, because at the time it would have been of great assistance in damaging the Presidential candidacy of his brother Senator Edward Kennedy. Since the senator is no longer a candidate for the Presidency, my statement about President Kennedy at that press conference in September 1971 is hereby declared inoperative. In any event, Mr. Gray has destroyed the cable.

Ninth, the Nixon campaign for 1972 has amassed the largest campaign fund ever raised in the free world. Some of the abundance and job-creating capital of American corporate business has been given to my campaign, much of it in cash, some transferred from foreign subsidiaries.

Tenth, the milk producers have given my campaign nearly half a million dollars, more than one hundred thousand times more than any housewife has had to pay in a *year* because of the increase I ordered in the price of milk.

Eleventh, some technical requirements having to do with the content of cheap commercial carpeting will be postponed for a while, but the carpet manufacturers have contributed more than $100,000 to my campaign as a result.

Twelfth, any contribution ITT may have made to cover Republican Convention costs was more than overcome by the profits they were able to realize once the Justice Department approved its merger with the Hartford Insurance Company. If anything, ITT really snookered us in that deal.

Thirteenth, by choosing to enrich the grain dealers rather than the grain growers, we were able to get some large campaign contributions and please the Soviet leaders who had been prepared to oppose my action in mining the harbor at Haiphong.

Fourteenth, I have been been able to provide a rent-free home for my children, at very little expense to the government, and by the action of the Justice Department and through my expertise in foreign policy, I have been able to enrich two old friends who stood by me when the going was rough.

Fifteenth, as soon as we come up with an airtight story, I will tell you who has been decided upon as the donor of the money to enable me to buy the Western White House for a minimum investment.

Sixteenth, the tax assessor in my home county, who is now my own congressman, was able to reduce the taxes I pay on the Western White House, thus leaving my personal capital free for other and more useful investment.

Seventeenth, by skillfully using the device of a predated deed, I was able to save $250,000 on my income taxes over several years, despite efforts by the Democratic majorities in Congress to deny me that right.

Eighteenth, my campaign workers—supervised closely by high White House officials—have tried wherever possible to slow down and confuse any opponent, whether in the primary elections or in the great contest now before us. They have not done so in any superficial or whimsical way, and they have done so only where there was clear evidence that without such activity on our part, the opposing candidate might threaten my reelection.

Now I know I have spoken for a long time. But I have told you the truth, as I see it. I know that an immensely popular President can easily weather any embarrassment this may cause. I ask you now to forget all of these charges—this smokescreen my opponent has created—and return to a consideration of the real issue in this campaign. And that issue is this: Which of us can best lead this nation to the path of decency and rightness in government? Which of us is best equipped, morally, to stand before you on July 4, 1976, when we celebrate our 200th birthday as a nation, and mutually pledge with you—as our forefathers did on that occasion—"our lives, our fortunes and our sacred honor"?

Thank you, and God bless you, each and every one. Good night."

In 1972, truth was never a real option for Richard Nixon.

9.   *The American* Fuehrerprinzip

When one is considered for a high government job several things must go through his mind. The first is likely to be a judgment of the president. Can I live with this man? Does his view of the country's problems and their solutions coincide with mine? Is he a good man (as opposed merely to a nice guy)? What are his liabilities? His assets? His tenure? From there the questions become more technical: What is the administration's policy toward my particular professional field and my ambitions in that field, and how can I fit into the scheme? The judgment of the boss comes first. What will be the climate of his leadership?

It is generally agreed that John F. Kennedy did better than any president in memory in attracting what seemed at least to be "the best and the brightest" people in the country into his administration. Some might have been elitist or arrogant, and some came to a bad end, but there was no lack of intelligence or imagination, nor was there any reluctance to define and grapple with the real problems of the country.

Kennedy set the tone early. In his first State of the Union Message, on March 30, 1961, he said, "This Administration recognizes the value of dissent and daring . . . we greet healthy controversy as the hallmark of healthy change. Let the public service be a proud and lively career. . . ."

The portion of his message dealing with the public service was printed on posters and placed in every federal agency in Washington, and it lent an air of excitement to those years.

H. R. Haldeman testified to the Ervin Committee that the aim of the Nixon White House was a "zero defect" administration. Apart from the offensiveness of the language itself, the concept is repugnant. Above a certain level of intelligence, it is clear that "zero defect" is nothing more than an ugly phrase

214

used by systems analysts with Masters' degrees in business administration. When one is dealing with the government of human beings by other human beings, there will inevitably be "defects" by the very definition of the task. One of Harry Truman's White House advisers, James Loeb, serving in the Kennedy administration as ambassador to Peru, once summed up the opposite philosophy in a discussion of foreign aid: "If you're not prepared to waste some of it," advised Loeb, "you'll waste it all."

"Dissent and daring"—that was the positive side. Kennedy recognized the negative side to public service as well—the "downside risk" as Haldeman would surely call it. Kennedy knew that with government as big and complex as it is, and with people as close to temptation as they are, standards of ethics in government must be set high. The business of good government depends on it. And so, on April 27, 1961, he sent a special message to Congress on ethics and conflict of interest in government:

No responsibility of government is more fundamental than the responsibility of maintaining the highest standards of ethical behavior by those who conduct the public business. There can be no dissent from the principle that all officials must act with unwavering integrity, absolute impartiality, and complete devotion to the public interest. This principle must be followed not only in reality but in appearance. For the basis of effective government is public confidence, and that confidence is endangered when ethical standards falter or appear to falter.

Richard Nixon entered his first term with a display of confidence in his appointees. He introduced his Cabinet on network television by saying that "this is not a group of yes-men." (He fired Walter Hickel, his secretary of the interior, 15 months later when Hickel said "no" to the Cambodian invasion.)

The President reserved special praise for his new attorney general: "If we are to restore order and respect for law in this country, there's one place where we're going to begin . . . a new attorney general of the United States . . . John Mitchell is more than just one of the nation's great lawyers. I have learned to know him over the past five years as a man of superb judgment, a man who knows how to pick people and to lead them . . . a man who is devoted to waging an effective war against crime in this country. . . . I think he will bring an extra dimension. . . ."

215

Shortly after his installation in office, John Mitchell, bringing that extra dimension to his office, introduced a notion that must be one of the most contemptible in American history: "Don't watch what we say," he told a group of civil rights activists, "watch what we do." In a curious way, this set the tone of the administration's leadership. The public posture was quite different from the private operation, and it put the public on notice—or should have—to disregard anything the President said, for he was probably doing something else in secret.

The President never told the American people, for example, that he was leading a secret crusade against "permissiveness" by any means necessary, including some that were patently illegal. It wouldn't have sounded right. It probably would not "fly in Peoria," to use John Ehrlichman's phrase, especially after Nixon promised Peoria an open administration. "Quiet" was the important word. Nixon wanted to bring quiet to the campuses and quiet to the streets. In his inaugural address, he gave as his understanding of the public mood, "Bring Us Together." A more accurate reading of America, as Nixon would show he knew quite well, would make the national demand "Leave Us Alone." The concept and the contrast were expressed in their most elevated forms by White House aide Tom Charles Huston, the author of the burglary and wiretap plan of 1970. "Repression is the inevitable result of disorder," he said. "Forced to choose between order and freedom, the people will take order."

To end "permissiveness," an ethic of consuming loyalty to the Chief was necessary. To wage a crusade against disobedient, noisy, and occasionally violent youth, obedience and discipline among the crusaders was essential. Nixon hired loyalists, and his White House operation became a perversion of a Ford advertising campaign. Quiet, in this case, became the sound of a well-made administration. But somewhere it went sour; loyalty became synonymous with timidity, compartmentalization, and acquiescence in illegality. Resistance to Watergate at any point required only a little backbone, but there was none.

The problem was that it is not so easy to intimidate Americans exercising their Constitutional rights by legal means, as Lyndon Johnson had found out earlier. He, too, had a visceral distaste for the sight of a demonstrator. In late 1966 he summoned his lawyers and ordered them to find a way to prevent demonstrators from picketing in front of the White House.

The lawyers came back stymied; they did not know how it could be done legally. Johnson kept pressing them, and the debate raged for months. Finally, the inevitable compromise was struck; for "security reasons" demonstrators in front of the White House would be limited to 100 persons.

Nixon could make the leap to illegality more easily. Jeb Stuart Magruder defined the totalitarian impulse to the Ervin Committee: "To all of us in the White House there was that feeling of resentment and of frustration at being unable to deal with issues on a legal basis." When Nixon wanted a demonstrator removed from the White House sidewalk, he ordered Haldeman, and Haldeman ordered Dwight Chapin to have it done, knowing that Chapin had a goon or two on hand. Illegal means, under the guise of providing order to America, became the rule, but it took a collection of weak, unprincipled men to implement those means on so broad a scale.

Through the spring and summer of 1973, a seemingly endless column of satraps and sycophants paraded before the Ervin Committee and the country. Pressed as to why they had acquiesced so easily, often so cavalierly, in illegal activity, they offered one excuse over all others: loyalty to Richard Nixon.

□ Herbert (Bart) Porter, self-described perjurer and head of the CREP surrogate program, said if he were guilty of anything, it was of "excessive loyalty to Richard Nixon." "I did not do it [perjury] for a position. I did not do it to hide anything because I did not think I had done anything. . . . My vanity was appealed to . . . when I was told my name had come up in the highest councils. . . . They said I was an honest man, and that I made a good appearance, that sort of thing. My loyalty to the President was appealed to. Those things, coupled with what I have found to be a weakness in my character, quite frankly, to succumb to that pressure."

□ Charles Colson, chief of the euphemistically called "Department of Dirty Tricks," was described by his father as "viciously loyal" to Richard Nixon. An ex-marine and a successful private lawyer, his brand of humor is exemplified by his "grandma" memo, in which he wrote, "I would walk over my grandmother if necessary" to get Richard Nixon reelected, and by the plaque over his basement bar, "If you've got them by the balls, their hearts and minds will follow." Braggart about being the "White House ass-kicker," he said, "they would lower him away" a Nixon loyalist. His loyalty led him to pro-

217

pose the firebombing of the Brookings Institution, order Howard Hunt to forge a cable linking President Kennedy to the Diem assassination, hire people to pose as homosexuals to tie McGovern to the Gay Lib movement, leak false information about Senator Joseph Tydings to defeat him in a senatorial race, write an advertisement supporting the bombing of Haiphong in 1972 and place it in *The New York Times* over the name of a dummy group, compile and update an "enemies" list, and press the Internal Revenue Service to harass those on it.

☐ John Mitchell, author of so many false doctrines, became the author of the Mitchell principle of perjury and obstruction of justice. With the reelection of Richard Nixon at stake, he testified he would "have to think long and hard" about perjury (but the record makes it clear he did not have to think all *that* long and hard). Obstruction of justice was necessary to save Richard Nixon from making a Presidential decision to "lower the boom"—fire criminals from his campaign committee with the possible negative political consequences—or do nothing and hope the problem would go away. Senator Herman Talmage put the question to the loyalist this way: "Here . . . all around [the President] were people involved in crime, perjury, accessory after the fact, and you deliberately refused to tell [Nixon] that. Would you state that the expediency of the election was more important than that?"

Mitchell replied, "Senator, you have put it exactly correct. In my mind, the reelection of Richard Nixon, compared with what was available on the other side, was so much more important. . . ." In other words, the reelection of the President was more important than the worst and most widespread breakdown of ethical conduct by public officials in the nation's history.

☐ Herbert Kalmbach, paymaster and the President's personal lawyer, could not conceive that the No. 3 and the No. 4 men in the White House would ask him to do anything improper, however illegal his lawyer's instincts must have told him it was. For three months, working with a White House cop, Tony Ulasewicz, using the elaborate devices of code names, secure telephones, and secret drops to deliver hush money to the Watergate defendants, he did not grow suspicious. He thought it all was a moral act, for he had been told, and he did not question it, that the money was for humanitarian purposes, to pay for the lawyers and for the sup-

218

port of the defendants' families. The secrecy was necessary, lest the distribution of the $440,000 be misinterpreted by the press (although there was really only one way to interpret it—hush money). Consistently in his Ervin Committee testimony, Kalmbach repeated, "I was carrying out an assignment." It was reminiscent of so many others who had testified that they were mere "conduits." And then, with childlike disbelief, Kalmbach found out that he had been used—by Haldeman, by Ehrlichman, by Dean, by nearly everyone. What else did he expect?

These and other statements of loyalty indicate that Richard Nixon has introduced a strange new principle into our politics: The American *Fuehrerprinzip*. Although the totalitarian tendencies among a number of Nixon aides is undeniable (how else could such an attack on freedom of speech and the sanctity of the home have been possible?), there is no intent to argue here that there is any precise parallel between Nixon operations and Nazi operations. (Although Haldeman's "good" and "great" in the margin of a memo predicting violence aimed at both Nixon and Billy Graham at a future rally, raises unsettling memories of the Reichstag fire.) Nonetheless, with so shocking a document as the 1970 Huston memo on record, and the Nixon approval of it a fact of history by his own admission, we must be concerned with how democratic institutions are undermined, and we must restudy—in Hannah Arendt's phrase—the origins of totalitarianism.

Albert Speer, Hitler's chief architect and the author of *Inside the Third Reich,* in a letter dated July 3, 1973, though carefully avoiding any judgment on internal American affairs (which, Speer said, would be inappropriate for him to make "with [his] past"), wrote, "The *Fuehrerprinzip* . . . demanded absolute loyalty to the highest leader and those named by him, the uncritical following of orders, even if those orders appeared to be nonsense, the exclusion of all personal considerations toward family and friends."

In the minds of the Nixon men, the good of the whole was the reelection of the president. Of course, all campaign workers feel that; otherwise they would not be in politics. But the Nixon men made another leap to dangerous self-righteousness: "National security" demanded Nixon's reelection. By inference then, McGovern was a security risk and so were his followers.

219

In *The Origins of Totalitarianism*, Hannah Arendt addresses herself to the question of loyalty in totalitarian movements:

. . . their most conspicuous external characteristic is their demand for total, unrestricted, unconditional loyalty of the individual member. This demand is made by the leaders of totalitarian movements even before they seize power. . . . Such loyalty can be expected only from the completely isolated human being who without any other social ties to family, friends, comrades, or even mere acquaintances, derives his sense of having a place in the world only from his belonging to a movement, his membership in the party.

In Nazi Germany the watchword of the SS was "My honor is my loyalty" (*Meine Ehre heisst Treue*). Hermann Goering could say in the early 1930s, "I have no conscience. Adolf Hitler is my conscience."

Hannah Arendt's observation that this kind of loyalty is possible only when "a cause or movement is emptied of all concrete content" is important, but it does not describe all totalitarian movements. Nor would it be appropriate to label the Nixon political group (not really a "party") a totalitarian movement, for the outer and largely open society of the United States often impinges upon the inner, closed Nixon society. It is only when the inner, closed society completely dominates and controls the open, "other" society, as in such states as Nazi Germany or the Soviet Union (or even in such closed and largely self-sufficient societies as the Mafia), that the "totalitarian" label becomes appropriate.

The difference between Nazi and Communist movements is demonstrated by the absence of ideology in one, and its overriding importance in the other. Nazi loyalty was to the *Fuehrer*, and rivalries within the movement were resolved on that question, rather than the "purity" of one's beliefs. In this non-ideological setting (except for shifting theories of "racial purity" there never *was* a Nazi ideology), proximity to the leader largely determined power within the movement, and to be out of the inner circle physically was to be out of the leader's favor and hence out of power.

Struggles in the Communist movement are likely to be over ideology, and a narrow shift in a seemingly obscure doctrinal matter in Moscow can and has led to profound power dislocations throughout the movement. In such a society, purity of ideology rather than physical proximity is the desired status of the rising executive.

When either movement becomes dominant in the "outside world," it produces a society with the major similarities we call totalitarian. The joining characteristic is the politicizing of *all* types of activity and the refusal to permit the existence, let alone the flourishing, of any activity not in conformity with the political goals of the state.

Although the absence of any ideological commitment in the Nixon movement strongly suggests the *"Fuehrerprinzip,"* the preoccupation with policing all kinds of nonpolitical activity is more consonant with other totalitarian societies.

The "enemies" list, for example (whether it was compiled by Dean, Colson, or Nixon himself is unimportant), is wholly compatible with this philosophy. The Nixon movement saw enemies on all fronts—not only in politics. A totalitarian movement considers itself embattled and besieged, and a conspiracy in power assumes the worst—a world teeming with other conspirators.

The presence on the "enemies" list of journalists, actors, athletes, educational leaders, and professors was not a matter of bungling or excessive zeal, but a calculated reflection of an awareness that there is a "Nixon way" of doing everything, from financing schools to making movies (or, for that matter, love). The enemies were not *political* foes who opposed Nixon on issues of government (after all, the Nixon position could, and did, change on the most important of them), but *personal* enemies who opposed Nixon himself or who demonstrated by their life-styles that they would never behave in a Nixon-like or a Nixon-approved manner.

The White House staffers, in short, were compiling lists as though, in harking back to his glory days in the late 1940s, they had become members of an Un-Nixon Activities Committee.

And where they had the power to *act*—as the Committee rarely did—they did so swiftly and often brutally, as in the burglaries, the planting of provocateurs, the physical roughing up of demonstrators, and the white-collar roughing up by the Internal Revenue Service.

The absence of any ideology—Arendt's "emptying of all concrete content"—was well demonstrated during the Nixon term. It had become, to the loyalists, irrelevant to try to balance the leader's activities against the specifics of an ideology or a program. It was not the Nixon men who objected to the rapprochement with what the leader came to call the People's

Republic of China. Haldeman and Nixon, as we have seen, had planned and carried out a major effort against Governor Brown just ten years before, including a fake poll and a phony Democratic Committee, largely on the grounds that Brown favored the recognition of "Red China"; he, apparently, was for "a generation of peace" a generation too early.

On the contrary, the men who felt betrayed were those who had supported Nixon because they believed in what he had said he believed in. William F. Buckley and Representative John Ashbrook led the argument against the Chinese reconciliation, and the White House Nixonites, who had once talked of "Red China" in language otherwise reserved for pornography and the Kennedys, switched over one day and began to care about nothing more ideological than whether their Japanese cameras had enough film to shoot the visit to the Great Wall.

It is now clear that there was almost nothing—certainly no intellectual about-face—that Nixon could do to turn off the loyalists. Price controls, for example, which once were the last refuge of liberals who never met a payroll and who didn't like the capitalist system, are now a "useful tool to stem inflation." Indeed, in at least one case, the Price Commission provided an excellent mechanism with which to reward, with higher prices and profits, a major campaign contributor.

One can imagine Haldeman and Ehrlichman defending a general amnesty or a forthright presidential statement in favor of abortion reform as "contributing to a national reconciliation" or "a lessening of population pressures." One imagines there was little complaint at the Reichskanzlei when the Japanese were proclaimed "honorary Aryans".

Many of the White House loyalists, no doubt, are watching the President bob and weave and fake here and there on the Watergate matter with a kind of awed reverence, as if they were watching the master politician face the biggest crisis of them all (perhaps his last). The loyalists expect a virtuoso performance, and if he makes it through, the shouts of "victory" will be deafening.

It will not matter that the victory will have come at the expense of truth and decency. The Nixonites, including their legion in the press, have stopped caring about exoneration and now cheer only for their leader's survival. Tom Charles Huston sums it up: "The last thing I'd ever do is count Richard

222

Nixon out. He's still the greatest living politician. If anyone can survive, he can."

The Nixon team, at least the team that gave us Watergate, was made up of old cronies whose loyalty had been tested over the years and young, pliant zealots who were ever so grateful to be so close to the seat of power. A team player stepping out of line or, as the Nixon men said, "straying off the reservation," could always be cut from the squad or "go off the screen." Bart Porter was the classic example: "I was not the one to stand up in a meeting and say that this should be stopped. . . . I kind of drifted along." Later he said he was easily shamed into perjury by an appeal to team spirit. Another young team player, Gordon Strachan, Haldeman's 27-year-old assistant, thought it was quite an opportunity to work in the White House and see the President and Henry Kissinger occasionally. He was not one to stand up and object in a meeting when a "sophisticated intelligence-gathering capability costing 300" (read wiretapping, burglary, and sabotage for $300,000) was discussed. Strachan at least was human enough to be embittered by the experience. The age that began with John F. Kennedy saying "Let the public service be a proud and lively career" ended with Gordon Strachan's advice to young people: "Stay away."

Shallow men with an empty political faith, suspicious of the outside world and of each other, tied to an isolated president—this was the closed society of the Nixon court. In his July 3, 1973, letter, Albert Speer directed attention to a passage in his memoirs (*Inside the Third Reich*, page 33): "The ordinary party member was being taught that grand policy was much too complex for him to judge it. Consequently, one felt one was being represented, never called upon to take personal responsibility. The whole structure of the system was aimed at preventing conflicts of conscience from ever arising. *The result was the total sterility of all conversations . . . among those likeminded persons. It was boring for people to confirm one another in their uniform opinions*" (italics added).

The isolation of the President himself greatly contributed to what John Mitchell called the "White House horrors." A leader whose contacts with the public are carefully controlled and whose dealings with his staff are almost never face to face, gathers a certain mystique around him. The power of a staff

223

member in this model of a closed society is measured by the frequency with which he meets with the leader or even catches a glimpse of him. It is that much easier to appeal to the vanity of the staff member, as it was in the case of Porter when he was told that his name had come up "in the highest circles."

Moreover, the top men will be able to speak in the President's name promiscuously when they have no fear that the leader will be called on to interfere, or indeed ever to find out. Under these circumstances, the top men, such as Haldeman, Ehrlichman, and even Dean, totally control what is brought to the leader's attention. Speer wrote in his letter, "It should be taken into account that in Hitler's Germany there was no free press, that therefore in the evaluation of domestic conditions Hitler was forced to rely on reports of his colleagues, which went through Bormann's hands and were filtered by him. With a free press, for instance, scandals instigated by high functionaries would not have remained hidden from the head of state." With a leader totally distrustful of the press, inclined to disbelieve rather than believe anything in the morning paper except the sports pages, who saw the press as constantly out to "get him," who relied on daily news summaries prepared by loyal staff members, does it not amount to the same thing?

With his isolation, it was virtually impossible for Nixon to exercise command responsibility over his staff. This foremost concept of military law, which should certainly apply to the Commander-in-Chief (particularly to a Commander-in-Chief who invokes the title as often as Nixon), means simply that the commander is responsible for the actions of his troops. On the other hand, Nixon relied almost exclusively on Haldeman and Ehrlichman to filter information to him. He emasculated his Cabinet, forcing its members to report through his staff, thereby devastating the sense of worth among the career professionals in the executive departments and agencies. Executive power became exercised by White House janissaries in imperial style—the supercabinets, euphemistically called "ad hoc" committees; the "Plumbers" over the FBI; the Intelligence Evaluation Committee over the CIA and FBI; the DALE program of narcotics law enforcement over the Treasury, Justice, and Bureau of Dangerous Drugs; the National Security Council over State, Defense, and CIA.

The Nixon operation made it possible for scores of White House counselors, assistants, assistants to counselors, special assistants, special counsels, and the like to speak in the name of the President. Whereas Joseph Califano, President Johnson's domestic affairs adviser, had one staff assistant at the beginning of his job and four at the end, Ehrlichman had 82 assistants, and Colson had 20 assistant "ass-kickers." Sycophancy was obviously not enough to control such an uncontrollable situation.

James McCord revealed in his Senate testimony what it was like to be on the receiving end of such a system. "I had been accustomed to working in an atmosphere where such sanction by the White House and the attorney general was more than enough. As with White House staffers, it was not my habit to question when two such high officers sanctioned an activity—it carried the full force and effect of Presidential sanction."

But it was a Nixon system, and it was Nixon's job to control it. As Commander-in-Chief and chief administrator, he bears final responsibility for the actions of his subordinates. Though his words are somewhat suspect now, Nixon seems to accept that notion. "I will not place the blame on subordinates —on people whose zeal exceeded their judgment, and who may have done wrong in a cause they deeply believed to be right," Nixon said on April 30. "The man at the top must bear the responsibility. That responsibility, therefore, belongs here, in this office. I accept it."

But does he really? The concept of command responsibility, of course, was not formed in the My Lai cases, but in the case of a Japanese general in World War II, General Tomoyuki Yamashita. Yamashita had been the commander of Japanese forces in the Philippines when MacArthur landed American forces in 1945. As the Americans pressed forward with the aid of native guerrillas, a group of Japanese forces apparently ran amok and massacred Philippine civilians who would not implicate those who were collaborating with the Americans. Even though Yamashita's communications were cut from the berserk troops, after V-J Day he was tried and convicted for those massacres. The military tribunal asserted that the commander is responsible for the actions of his troops, even if he is not in direct communication with them. It is his duty at all times to see that they are held in check. The decision was later approved by the U.S. Supreme Court. The sentencing in the cases involving the Japanese massacres was stiffer, the higher up the chain of command it went. The lieutenants who had pulled the triggers received the lightest sentences (2 years); Yamashita and his top aides were hanged.

There is no concept of command responsibility in criminal law or public administration that parallels military law. Thus the Nixon climate of leadership which led to such a widespread breakdown in moral conduct and constitutional ethics cannot alone be the basis for impeachment. But the concept keeps priorities straight, as we undergo whatever catharsis and reconstruction may come from the Watergate disaster.

As the Watergate scandal developed, it was hard to find anyone who would take responsibility. Everyone appeared to be only a conduit, from Robert Odle, the office manager of CREP, to Richard Helms, director of the CIA. As a result, the My Lai pattern of criminal prosecution was followed: The lowest men on the scale, the Calleys and the Barkers, men who were the products of the system rather than the authors of it, were the men convicted for wrongdoing. The commanders who designated My Lai or the Watergate complex as "free-fire zones" were left unrepentant, if not unindicted. The men who destroyed evidence to cover up the crime found themselves in position to bargain with the prosecutors. When all the Watergate evidence is in and all the trials have been held, will the lowest agents of the conspiracy again be the ones with the stiffest sentences?

Who can doubt that Watergate was a complex five-stage puppet show, with strings of nearly invisible but strong fiber from top to bottom? The first stage, open to public amusement and scorn, showed the "third-rate burglars" providing us with the "caper." The second stage displayed the agent-handlers, Hunt and Liddy, providing us with the "Affair." Then came the bland, unprincipled, well-tailored young men, Magruder, Dean, Porter, Strachan, et al., giving us a "deplorable incident." The fourth stage revealed the power brokers, the grey eminences, Mitchell, LaRue, Ehrlichman, Stans, Colson, and Haldeman, giving us the worst political scandal in American politics. And finally there is the Grand Puppeteer himself. There is no question that Nixon had the power to stop it altogether, but the question remains: Could the show have gone on without his knowledge?

The point, of course, is precisely that the Watergate disclosures do not reveal the excesses of subordinates acting out of extraordinary and unauthorized zeal. These men were acting squarely within the approved limits of the closed Nixon society, which in turn operated within the larger open society around them. They were not disobeying orders; they were obeying what they correctly saw as the imperatives of the movement. It was not politics, but war; thus those on the "other side" were not opponents, but enemies. The issue was not national priorities but national security, and if John Ehrlichman thought burglary "well within" the legal limits, who was Gordon Liddy or Egil Krogh to say otherwise?

This was not a right-wing movement or a Republican movement—it was a *Nixon* movement, and it had been building and acquiring its moral standards for 25 years.

If any proof is needed, it can be found in the total absence of any criticism, however faint (let alone moral condemnation), of any top Nixon loyalist by any other top Nixon loyalist, whether in the White House or the press. There has been no criticism by Nixon or his defenders of Colson or Hunt for the forged cable, of Haldeman and Ehrlichman for obstructing an FBI investigation, of Ehrlichman or Krogh for the Ellsberg burglary, of Ehrlichman or Ulasewicz for dealing in political slime, of Kalmbach and LaRue for functioning as collection agents to buy silence, nor even of General Haig for illegally serving in two jobs in order to tilt his pension.

The question of Nixon's personal knowledge, either of the Watergate burglary or the cover-up which followed, becomes simply irrelevant. If this were an isolated court case, the question of Nixon's personal knowledge would be crucial, but here we have the fruits of an admitted conspiracy to serve only the interests of the leader, as they had been served through the glorious past.

For the final absurdity of the question of Nixon's precise knowledge and the time of it, imagine the Nuremberg Tribunal, listening to recital after recital of the holocaust as Nazi leader after Nazi leader testified to his role. And then imagine one of the judges, in the accents of Senator Howard Baker, asking of each witness, "But what I want to know is what did the Fuehrer know, and when did he know it?"

10. At the Next Point in Time

Speaking at a college graduation in his home state of Illinois on June 2, 1973, Senator Charles Percy called the unfolding Watergate disclosures "the darkest scandal in American political history," and then touched on the problem that has come to dominate serious discussion of where it all may lead. "If each kernel of truth must be torn away from those who are hiding it, the effort to redeem our national honor could take years," Percy concluded.

The problem is to redeem our national honor. Countries and societies can survive without a sense of national honor, but cannot long remain free and self-respecting. Loss of esteem for the system and the honesty and courage of its leaders quickly leads to loss of self-esteem. In the so-called banana republics it does not matter which constitution is presently in force, or which set of colonels has deposed which other set. There, institutions are degraded—schools, churches, industry, labor—and the people see themselves as weak, powerless, and even crippled. The result is that other societies come to share that view, the currency is regularly devalued, and the outward symbols of authority come to be scorned abroad as well as at home. After twenty-five years of Nixon Politics, four years of a Nixon administration, and one year of Watergate, we are not far from that situation. Even a rich and powerful nation, bristling with weapons with which to bully smaller ones, can become a banana republic.

The President, Vice President, and all civil officers of the United States, shall be removed from Office on Impeachment for, and Conviction of, Treason, Bribery, or other high Crimes and Misdemeanors. (U.S. Constitution, Art. II, Sec. 4)

That is the remedy our charter provides; it is the civil legal remedy, and a stronger case can be made today for its use than at any time in our history. "Impeachment" is the process of indictment, and it is done by the House of Representatives, sitting as a sort of grand jury to hear the evidence. If a "civil officer" (most often, in our history, judges) is impeached by the House, he is then tried by the Senate, sitting as a court. If the president is tried, the chief justice presides.

In our history, many officials have been impeached, and many convicted, but none since the 1930s. The only impeachment of a president resulted in a failure to convict in the Senate, by the margin of one vote. A look at the impeachment and trial of Andrew Johnson shows that the "high Crimes and Misdemeanors" for which he was tried consisted mainly of not supporting the post–Civil War attitudes toward Reconstruction of the Republican majority.

Of the ten charges against Johnson, nine concerned his alleged violation of the Tenure of Office Act, a law passed to prevent Johnson from firing Edwin Stanton, his holdover Secretary of War. The law was of doubtful constitutionality at best and was later declared unconstitutional. The other charge had to do with attacks Johnson had made on Congress during a speaking tour.

The Johnson fiasco has undoubtedly contributed to some of the present legislative and journalistic reluctance to consider impeachment. Impeachment as a political weapon, to be used by the majority at its will, is dangerous. Its use, it is thought, would cheapen the process and lead to government by instant legislative pluralities.

The Nixon administration has not always shared this view. On at least two occasions, Nixon spokesmen have advocated the concept of "impeachment without crime," by majority vote, for whatever reason the majority wishes to assign.

The first advocacy of this theory came from Representative Gerald Ford of Michigan, the Republican leader in the House of Representatives. The issue arose in 1970 over Ford's attempt, with the overt support of Nixon men in the House and the tacit support of the White House (without which Ford would never have moved), to impeach Supreme Court Justice William O. Douglas. Ford had patched together some "evidence" against Douglas, primarily an article he had written on environmental conservation in a magazine said by some to include pornography.

Ford quickly abandoned the notion that any specific "high Crime or Misdemeanor" was provable or even necessary. "What then is an impeachable offense?" he asked. "The only honest answer," Ford continued, in the course of arguing the Douglas case before the Judiciary Committee of the House, "is that an impeachable offense is whatever a majority of the House of Representatives considers it to be at a given moment in history; conviction results from whatever offense or offenses two-thirds of the other body [the Senate] considers to be sufficiently serious to require removal of the accused from office." The committee quickly rejected the Ford view and put forth the rule that there are two bases for impeachment, neither of them the impulse of one day's majority: "criminal conduct" and "serious dereliction from public duty."

These principles were contemptuously brushed aside by Attorney General Richard Kleindienst in March 1973. Kleindienst, even as the Watergate fires grew hotter, went up to Capitol Hill to defend the President's theory of "executive privilege," then about to undergo a test on the question of whether John Dean could be subpoenaed to testify on the question of Patrick Gray's fitness to be director of the FBI.

Kleindienst, in one of the most astonishing performances ever seen before a Senate Committee, told the senators that if a president wished, he could prevent the testimony before a congressional committee of each and all of the more than 2 million employees of the executive branch of the government, from the secretary of state to the newest rookie mailman at the Post Office.

When the senators, particularly Ed Muskie, reacted in anger, Kleindienst said that if the Congress didn't like it, it could always impeach the President. "For what crime?" asked Muskie. "Impeachment doesn't require a crime," Kleindienst replied, "all you need are the votes." And that is the last word we have heard on the subject from the President's chief legal advisor and interpreter of the Constitution.

But when one considers the case for the impeachment, conviction, and removal from office of Richard Nixon, one does not need to depend on the brutal *realpolitik* of Nixon men Ford and Kleindienst. There need only be a consideration of what is already known about the behavior—the actions—of the President and his administration in the years of his incumbency.

☐ We know Nixon ordered his two top aides to try to use the CIA to delay or halt an FBI investigation into the major link between the Watergate burglary and his reelection campaign.

☐ We know that for at least 40 days Nixon withheld knowledge of the burglary of Dr. Fielding's office from the judge who was then conducting the Ellsberg trial. We know that he tried to keep the Justice Department from further consideration of the Fielding burglary on the grounds of "national security" when he knew it was part of a purely political attempt to smear the defendant. We know that he told the judge only when the two top men in the Justice Department threatened to resign if he did not, and two of his appointees have given hearsay testimony that he ordered the burglary in the first place.

□ We know that after Patrick Gray warned him that his top aides were "trying to mortally wound" him, Nixon did not ask who they were (as it turned out, he knew), and by his own account, he waited eight months before beginning an investigation.

□ We know that within months of his inauguration, Nixon began a secret enlargement of the Vietnam war to a neutral country, and participated in a deceitful cover-up of that fact in order to keep the knowledge, not from the enemy, but from the Congress and the people.

□ We know that he has provided three separate and differing accounts of how he bought his private home, and we know that millions of dollars in public funds have been used to furnish it with "security" necessities, ranging from a windscreen around the swimming pool to a leather-topped desk for his den.

□ We know that he knowingly participated in an attempt to make it appear that President Kennedy himself had ordered the assassination of Ngo Dinh Diem, employing for this ugly purpose a cable whose status as a forgery must have been apparent.

□ We know that Nixon approved and set in motion a plan that expressly called for criminal acts by government law enforcement officials, and that if he rescinded the plan at all, it was in response to institutional and administrative pressures rather than to the constitutional mandates it specifically set aside.

□ We know that Nixon claimed a $570,000 deduction from personal income on his tax return through the use of a provision of the Internal Revenue Code which had been repealed months before, and that it was accomplished by a postdated "deed" of gift neither signed by him nor yet acknowledged by the recipient.

□ We know that his special counsel requested the firebomb-

231

ing of private offices in order that another White House employee might steal some papers in the confusion.

□ We know that he approved creation of the "Plumbers" unit, composed of four of his staff aides, whose activities consisted of a number of illegal acts, including the Fielding burglary and the Kennedy cable forgery.

□ We know that for more than two years, his chief domestic adviser ran a two-man political espionage team, one member of which was paid by the President's personal attorney.

□ We know that a systematic plan of espionage and sabotage was carried out against his political opponents, with the approval of his chief of staff, and that the chief saboteur was hired by his appointments secretary and paid by his personal attorney. We know the effort included paying two spies $1,000 a week each to pose as journalists and report to his oldest political associate.

□ We know that his personal attorney secretly raised funds to buy the silence of criminal defendants who had been initially paid for their crime with campaign funds. And we know that the raising of funds for the defendants was approved by his counsel and his chief domestic aide.

□ We know that his appointments secretary, the deputy manager of his campaign committee and at least one other campaign aide committed perjury before the grand jury and at the trial of the Watergate defendants.

□ We know that Nixon ordered his secretary of agriculture to reverse a previous decision and raise the price of milk, after a meeting in the Oval Room between his oldest political associate and representatives of the milk producers, after which the milk groups gave more than $400,000 to his campaign.

□ We know that through the actions of chief officials in the Department of Agriculture, information in the possession of five large grain exporters was withheld from grain farmers, to their detriment, and that subsequently officers of the grain companies made substantial contributions to Nixon's reelection campaign.

□ We know that ITT made an offer of $400,000 to the Republican Party to help defray the costs of its 1972 convention, after which a recommendation of the Anti-Trust Division of the Justice Department was overruled by Nixon's attorney general, and ITT was permitted to acquire a major insurance company. And we know that memoranda in the possession of the Ervin Committee, written by his special counsel, state that the attorney general and the President himself were aware of the offer.

□ We know of another reversal of the Anti-Trust Division, as a result of which Nixon's "honorary father," the chairman of a drug company, was greatly enriched by a merger with another large drug manufacturer.

□ We know that one of Nixon's close friends and benefactors was enriched when the President's foreign policy power was used to permit his soft drink to be sold in the Soviet Union.

□ We know that his chief of staff held office illegally for three months while still an active army officer, apparently so that the aide could earn a higher pension from the army after retirement.

□ We know that Roy Ash, the man he appointed head of the Office of Management and Budget, was the chief executive officer of a company with a major financial dispute with the government, a dispute he said he will not disqualify himself from deciding.

□ We know that Clement Stone, who says he contributed $2 million to the Nixon reelection campaign, received an unlimited price increase on insurance policies his company sells, just seven days after he dined at the White House.

□ We know that Will Wilson, his first assistant attorney general in charge of the Criminal Division, was forced to resign after it was made public that he had received unsecured loans from a man to whom he had granted immunity from prosecution in a bank fraud case.

□ We know that a leading White House aide, Peter Flanigan, pressured the Treasury Department to grant a waiver which benefited a shipping company in which he and his family had a direct interest.

□ We know that Nixon's staff compiled and kept an "enemies" list, and that agencies of the government were used to harass those who were on the list.

□ We know that, in the President's political behalf, his chief of staff proposed to tell the press his Democratic opponent was financing violent revolutionary groups when he knew that the charge had been investigated and found to be false.

□ And worst of all, we know that all this represents merely the exercise, once in power, of what has been for a quarter of a century "politics as usual" for Richard Nixon and, despite his protestations to the contrary, for no one else.

If this recital does not contain anything that could be called "criminal conduct," surely it amounts to the strongest case for "serious dereliction from public duty" ever mounted against a high public official, let alone a President. And yet, there is no public opinion poll—at least as of the writing of this book—and no survey of congressmen which shows more than 50 percent of the respondents willing to seriously consider impeachment.

It is not surprising. Much of this—but without the avalanche of proof and the withering eye television has cast upon the Nixon men as they evade or confess, and sometimes evade *and* confess—was put forth in the 1972 presidential campaign by Senator McGovern. He knew most of it, as is apparent from the speech set forth in the Appendix, and he obtained this information only from the newspapers.

People did not want to act on that information then, as most do not want to act on it now. Even recent polls which show that if the election were held today—that is, if all the facts known today had been known in November 1972—George McGovern would be elected, show no concomitant desire to impeach Richard Nixon. And yet, a change of heart by so many voters can hardly be based on a changed assessment of Senator McGovern. He is the same man now as he was then; those who admired him find him still admirable, and surely those who opposed him because they rejected his ideas have not come to share them.

No, that historically unprecedented shift of public opinion away from a reelected president clearly shows that a substantial number of Americans who voted for Richard Nixon now find him unfit for the office he holds. And yet they reject the course the charter of the nation has laid down for his removal.

That steady refusal to look at the country's "Nixon problem" whole, through 1972 and 1973, is the result of a number of factors, and many are related to the steady debasement of democracy toward empire which I have discussed in an earlier chapter. There is today—and it has been building for two decades—a near reverence for the President, any president.

It is no accident that when Richard Nixon returned from a European tour in his first year in office, he ordered new uniforms for the White House police, which made them seem as though they had stepped directly from the second act of "The Student Prince." When he returns from foreign travel to Andrews Air Force Base, on hand is a group of servicemen known as the "Army Heraldsmen" (typically of the Army, an unnecessary extra syllable has been added to a perfectly good

English word). They wear special uniforms and, lined up along either side of the carpet on which the President leaves the aircraft, blare a fanfare on extra-long posthorns, from which are hanging banners of richly brocaded cloth. One doubts that Henry V received a more royal welcome when he returned from Agincourt.

Harry Truman was probably the last president who fulfilled the notion of the Founders that we would elect someone among us to serve as chief magistrate who would then return to the private life he had left. Truman, when he left the White House for recreation, went to an Air Force Base in Key West, Florida and would never have thought of asking the taxpayers to supply him with millions of dollars of improvements at a "Midwest White House."

After Truman had gone to Eisenhower's inauguration and was no longer president, he took his family to the Union Station in Washington to board a train to Kansas City. Some reporters were there to see him off, and one of them asked him what he would do when he got home. Truman did not have to think long. "Carry the suitcases up to the attic," was his reply. Can anyone imagine any president since saying the same?

It is asking a great deal to expect Americans, now that presidents act like emperors, start wars in secret (but draft young men in public to fight them), summon television networks for their messages to the people, and possess more raw power than any tyrant in history, to think of these men as conspiring to commit shabby crimes. There is no "willing suspension of disbelief"—indeed, there is willing disbelief when it is suggested that this President is no better than the rest of us, and in fact worse than most.

That gradual debasement of our national and personal ideals has produced its share of guilt and cynicism, and it came not only in Vietnam, where the dishonor became so plain that even a historically hawkish Congress finally had to call a halt. A steady deterioration of values, in the marketplace and at work, has made Americans see some of this chiseling, some of this lack of ethics, in themselves. It makes us readier to believe—as Richard Nixon well understands—the argument that "everybody does it."

The cynicism can be found in the way politicians look at impeachment. Too many Democrats are ready to let Nixon keep the job, to finish his term scorned and reviled by the majority of his countrymen who believe him corrupt, so that the next national election will see a turning away from the

Republican party. Many Democrats, who knew as a matter of principle that impeachment was the appropriate remedy, were ready to pass it by merely to avoid the advantage three years of incumbency would give to Spiro Agnew. The example of Calvin Coolidge, who succeeded Warren Harding and was triumphantly relected even as the major Harding scandals were unfolding, was much in their minds.

The "Agnew scare," of course, is over. And even though every poll of public opinion reveals that a President Gerald Ford would be a formidable candidate for re-election, a "Ford scare" does not seem to be developing; no longer do Democrats hint that the party would be better off if President Nixon were left to "twist slowly, slowly, in the wind."

There is an interesting argument in that fact. At this writing, before the House of Representatives has had a chance to vote on the question, it is as clear as anything can be to all political analysts that the short-run cynical advantage to Democrats lies in voting *against* impeachment, just as the short-run cynical advantage to Republicans lies in a vote *for* impeachment. All the special election results since Watergate first came to public consciousness tell us that Nixon is an enormous liability to his party, and that it is no accident that Democratic candidates for Congress are anxious that he come to their districts to campaign, for their opponents, of course.

And yet, it is equally clear that a majority in both parties will vote against the purely political interest of their parties, and will be animated by something else. Perhaps, contrary to those who now denounce politics and politicians, and who assert confidently that "they all do it," and that they are all crooks—perhaps, just perhaps, they will be voting for what they see as the public interest.

But when the Agnew crisis broke, conflicting political motives were apparent. It seemed perplexing, in the fall of 1973, why the Nixon White House was so anxious to make Agnew look bad, and why the President was so anxious that he resign. At first (and so it appeared in an earlier version of this book), it seemed as though the Nixon men only wanted Agnew in trouble, or indicted, since the legal problems he would raise would make the impeachment of Richard Nixon that much more unlikely. After all, it is unthinkable to impeach the President if one does not know whether or not the Vice-President will be in a federal prison when it is time to take the oath.

But as the Agnew crisis developed, it began to appear that both the President and Attorney-General Richardson wanted

Agnew to resign. Richardson, among other reasons, because it would permit the establishment of a clear line of succession —instead of to a putative felon; Nixon, because the impeachment of Agnew would have demonstrated to Congress how the system could work and just how easy the process really was. In any event, once the facts about Agnew had begun to come out, the seven-year history of bribes and extortions set forth in the Justice Department's brief would have demeaned and disgraced not only Agnew, but his sponsor as well.

But whatever the political consequences, a majority of Congressmen—and a bi-partisan majority at that—now seems to understand that impeachment must be considered and undertaken. It is necessary because the alternative of shrugging our shoulders at the appalling acts of this President leads us quickly toward the level of self-esteem of a banana republic, not that of free citizens of a great democracy. If our system cannot call its leaders to account, and punish them for clear misconduct, then it ought not punish anyone. Put another way, "if he can get away with it, why can't I?"

Then corruption will ooze through the rest of the system, private as well as political. There are too many choices and decisions the average man or woman must make in a democracy which require a faith that the law applies reasonably equally to all. Many of those decisions involve a certain self-sacrifice, or at the very least a postponement of gratification in the belief that some common good is thereby served. Why serve in the armed forces, voluntarily disclose income to be taxed, exercise price or wage restraint, avoid easy business frauds, or for that matter, abide by election results, settle differences in court, or even wait in line to be served—if the men at the top neither obey the law nor suffer any penalty for disobedience? Ultimately, the loss of faith in institutions—starting with government—leads to loss of faith in self. In a society where people do not trust their government, where they do not believe it works, they come not to trust each other. And yet, it is that mutual trust which for 200 years has kept the gears of our society from clashing.

There are other, less tangible reasons. Almost every other country in the world is a nation either because of an accident of geography or because its people share a common culture. Usually it is the latter. They are united because their people sing the same songs, teach their children the same stories, eat the same food, and celebrate the same heroes of antiquity. The form of government may be important, but it does not

237

establish nationhood. Greece under a king or a dictator is still Greece. France as a monarchy or a republic, free or under occupation, is still France. But we are unique. Our nation did not come together because our fathers happened to live here —most did not. This country was created and has survived because its people shared a set of ideas, and the diverse background and culture of our citizens—their songs, their food, their heroes—mattered not nearly so much as that they shared those ideas. If we now reject those ideas so that our national emblem is to bear, instead of "E Pluribus Unum," the motto "Sauve Qui Peut," then we have destroyed the basis of the society itself.

We have nearly lost our way. Twenty-five years of empire and ten years of spilling our blood and theirs to force Asians to accept leaders we have hired for them has cost us dearly. And now we learn that our President has betrayed his oath of office, and not only has failed to "take care that the laws be faithfully executed," he has actively connived to break and mock those laws. On July 4, 1976, we will celebrate the 200th anniversary of the Republic. Shall we on that day, remembering George Washington and Benjamin Franklin, Thomas Jefferson and James Monroe, John Adams and James Madison, Alexander Hamilton and George Mason—celebrate Richard Nixon and Spiro Agnew, John Mitchell and Maurice Stans, Howard Hunt and Gordon Liddy, John Ehrlichman and Bob Haldeman, Charles Colson and John Dean, Robert Abplanalp and Bebe Rebozo?

There are those—and they increase in number each day— who say that a Constitution written for a small nation of 4 million people along the Atlantic coast is no longer an appropriate document for a nation of 200 million occupying a whole continent. Perhaps they are right, but it has brought us safe thus far and it is all we have. If we use it, obey its mandate, and move to the impeachment of a President for his "high Crimes and Misdemeanors," that act is sure to divide us, to preoccupy us, and to distract us from the great problems we must solve.

But we are already divided, already preoccupied, and already distracted from those problems. And we will remain divided if we allow our fear of further division to lead us to tell ourselves that the highest among us is above the law. But if we use the law to show that all men are accountable—even the President—we will have started on the road back to self-respect, to the day when it will once again be a source of joy and delight to be an American.

238

Afterword

While this book was being written, the hearings before Senator Ervin's committee were proceeding, and by the time it was published, the focus had shifted to the work of the Special Prosecutor (in which job Leon Jaworski has demonstrated as determined an effort to get at the truth as did Archibald Cox). Since then, impeachment has become a strong possibility—indeed, a probability—and the Judiciary Committee of the House of Representatives has become the White House's perceived danger. Through all of that time, the public has become more and more aware of the nature of Nixon Politics, and Nixon himself—believed by a substantial majority of his countrymen to be morally unfit for the office he holds—has been reduced to finding enclaves of support in Mississippi and Arizona where he may speak. Some events since the earlier publication deserve mention.

⊔ First of all, there now seems to be a reasonable explanation for the Watergate burglary itself, beyond the accumulated political ignorance of John Mitchell and the other Nixon men who ordered it and countenanced it. My earlier speculation that the Nixon administration put the "Plumbers" at the service of Howard Hughes—illegally and with taxpayers' money, of course—has found confirmation in further testimony of Howard Hunt and in a deposition of Hughes' former top administrator, Robert Maheu.

Hunt told the Ervin Committee that the proposed burglary of the office of Las Vegas newspaper publisher Hank Greenspun (see pp. 169–70) was indeed to be as much a favor to Hughes as to find any spurious derogatory information about Senator Muskie. Greenspun had some affidavits in his safe which would be damaging to Hughes in subsequent lawsuits, and it was doubtless these affidavits which the White House men were seeking. The debt to Hughes has also been subsequently established. Maheu has testified that Hughes gave at least $100,000 to Nixon, in 1969 and 1970—in cash, personally delivered to Bebe Rebozo—and Sally Harmony, a secretary who once worked for Gordon Liddy, has told of blank checks from Hughes which were filled in and used at the CREP.

The circumstances of the Hughes gift to Nixon in 1969 and 1970 make it seem most likely that the motive for the Watergate burglary has been found. The gifts were in cash, they were given by a Hughes representative who was a friend of both Nixon and Rebozo, they were handed over to Rebozo at the Nixon home in San Clemente, and there have been confirmed rèports that the gift was preceded by a meeting with both men, and unconfirmed reports that at that meeting Nixon asked for the money.

Furthermore, Herbert Kalmbach—Nixon's personal attorney who has since pleaded guilty to both a felony and a misdemeanor and is cooperating with the authorities while awaiting sentence—has told the Ervin Committee that the Hughes gift of $100,000 was not used—or intended to be used—as a campaign contribution. According to Kalmbach, the money was passed on by Rebozo at least to both Nixon brothers and to the President's secretary, Rose Mary Woods. Rebozo has said he kept all the money—in cash—in a safety deposit box at his Key Biscayne bank for three years, and then returned it unused. The story is highly doubtful. First of all, Robozo is a banker, and bankers do not let large sums of cash lie idle for three years, unless it is "hot." Second, Rebozo's reason for not using the money in the campaigns of either 1970 or 1972 is palpably unbelievable. He says it is because there was turmoil in the Hughes organization. But if the money was a legitimate campaign contribution from Hughes, what difference could it make? However, if it was an *illegitimate* contribution, or if the proceeds were to be used illegally, then there is every reason to worry about various Hughes aides learning of the transaction and using the information either against one another or against the Master himself. Finally, Kalmbach, a much more believable man than Rebozo, flatly contradicts Rebozo's testimony. As Richard Nixon once said of Alger Hiss and Whittaker Chambers, "one of these men is lying." Unfortunately for him, however, this time the perjurer is either his closest friend or his personal attorney.

The Watergate connection for all this lies in Larry O'Brien.

O'Brien, after leaving the Democratic National Committee in 1969, went into the public relations business. In the next two years, before he returned as Democratic chairman in 1971, he had Howard Hughes among his clients. There was nothing hidden about the representation—O'Brien made it public at a press conference when he began the representation, and the identity of his clients was always a matter of public record (it is the nature of the business, and of O'Brien, to operate in the open).

So it is reasonable to believe that to the Nixon men, planning espionage targets in late 1971 and early 1972, it must have seemed likely that Howard Hughes had told Larry O'Brien about his large cash gifts to Richard Nixon in 1969 and 1970, and that O'Brien might have evidence of the gifts in his office at Democratic headquarters in the Watergate building. If Kalmbach is telling the truth, and the money eventually found its way into the pockets of Nixon's two brothers and his secretary, there was every reason for the White House to pay for a burglary to retrieve that information. O'Brien has said he never knew of the Hughes contribution, and there was no such evidence in his files, which may have accounted for the bafflement of the burglars and the fact they came up empty-handed on the initial entry.

□ The results of the curious matter of H. R. Haldeman's change in testimony. When he testified before the Ervin Committee, Haldeman said he had listened to portions of the Nixon tapes, and he said some tapes had been delivered to him in an office at the Executive Office Building, next to the White House. A few weeks after his testimony, he informed the Committee that this was inaccurate, and that in fact a White House aide, Steven Bull, had delivered the tapes to the home of another White House assistant, Lawrence Higby, and that Haldeman had picked up the tapes at Higby's home. Since both Bull and Higby had worked for Haldeman, and since the whole incident had taken place less than one month before Haldeman testified, it is hard to escape the conclusion that the earlier testimony was deliberately false—and corrected only when the truth became known to the Committee through Bull's testimony.

The question is, why would Haldeman deceive the Committee on such a trivial point? The answer seems to lie in the matter of access to the tapes. Nixon is arguing their extreme confidentiality, and Haldeman and Nixon must have thought it damaging to reveal—unless required to do so—that two unimportant White House aides also had access to the tapes.

☐ Hunt is the source of testimony which casts some doubt on the pure patriotism of Bernard Barker's motives. He told the Ervin Committee that he gave Barker the assignment of recruiting "hippies" to pose as McGovern supporters in front of Miami Beach hotels during the Democratic Convention, behave outrageously, and thus bring discredit on McGovern's youthful supporters. It is hard to find in that act anything which might convince Barker he was acting either in the national security interest of the United States or to redeem his homeland.

In any event, the story reinforced a belief held by me and by others in the McGovern campaign at that time that the "hippies" who invaded the lobby of the McGovern headquarters hotel on nomination day were not genuine, but hired for the occasion. If so, it was a dangerous assignment, because only the firm desire of Senator McGovern to avoid a confrontation between the young people and the police—he went down to the lobby and successfully urged the demonstrators to leave peacefully—averted some serious violence. In retrospect, it was probably violent scenes of police battling "hippies" that was the desired result of the whole scheme.

☐ When this book was written, enough was known to determine that President Nixon had grossly underpaid his taxes in 1969, 1970 and 1971, by claiming to have made a gift of pre-Presidential papers to the National Archives three months *before* the date set by Congress after which the deduction would be improper, when in fact the gift was incompletely made nine months *after* the cut-off date, by means of a pre-dated deed.

This information, which was generally known, combined with information leaked by an IRS employee to the Providence (R.I.) *Bulletin* that Nixon had paid only a few *hundred* dollars in federal income taxes for 1969 and 1970, although he had an income of over $250,000 each year, prompted Nixon for the first time in this entire sordid affair to err on the side of disclosure. He made his tax returns public on December 8, 1973, and they demonstrated what can only be described as widespread chiseling. Whether the clear fraud involved in the understatement of Nixon's tax liability by some $450,000 is properly attributed to the President himself or (as he ungenerously stated) to his lawyers and accountants or whether it is properly shared among them all, is a matter the House Judiciary Committee will determine. (The latter hypothesis, a concerted fraud among the taxpayer and his advisors, seems the most likely, particularly since Nixon's tax attorney, Frank DeMarco, has been quoted as saying he "went over each page" of the return with his distinguished client.)

It must be remembered, in assessing the Nixon tax returns, that this was no casual event, such as might be even the filing of a return by any other taxpayer, however complex his affairs. The filing, on April 10, 1970, of the Nixon tax return was the central financial event of his life. It was the keystone in the building of his estate—the precise moment at which he ceased to be merely well-paid, and became rich. One might easily forget—or leave to others to handle—the details of an employment contract paying a substantial annual salary, or the sale of property substantially appreciated in value. But it strains credulity to believe that a poor boy from Whittier, worried all of his life about money, did not know the details by which he succeeded, at one stroke of the pen, in sheltering one million dollars from taxes.

At the time the Internal Revenue Service announced that it generally agreed with the conclusion of the Joint Committee on Taxation that Nixon had underpaid his taxes in three years by more than $450,000 (the Joint Committee put the figure somewhat higher), much was made by the White House that there had been no finding of fraud. To be sure, there was no indication that the matter of fraud (deliberate deception) had even been considered. But the Director of the Internal Revenue Service, in what seemed an extremely arrogant assertion during a television interview, said that while normally the staff of the IRS made such determinations, in this case he himself had decided there was no fraud. Since he was appointed by Nixon, the assertion came as no great surprise, and the Judiciary Committee proceeded at once to its own examination of the evidence. Some of it is most illuminating.

The use of a pre-dated deed, with a false notarial acknowledgment of a signature in an attempt to make it appear that the deed of Nixon's papers had been signed when it was legal, has been discussed elsewhere in detail. But other aspects of the presidential tax returns seem to show fraud even more clearly.

For example, the Nixon apartment in New York was sold after the election of 1968, and at a substantial profit. The tax law is very clear that if something is sold at a profit, there is a tax due on the profit. If the thing sold is not something used in a trade or business, then it is taxed at a lower "capital gain" rate, but still taxed.

The law has a further exception. If the thing sold is a "principal residence," the taxpayer's home, then no tax will be assessed—not even at the capital gain rate—however large the profit, *provided* the proceeds are promptly re-invested in another "principal residence." This provision is clearly designed to encourage taxpayers who can afford to, to upgrade the family housing without penalty. But the law is also clear that the exception is for residences only, and not for property used for business.

The brazenness of the Nixon treatment of this income is hard to equal. For years prior to 1969, he had regularly used his New York apartment for business purposes, or at least so he said, and regularly deducted 25% of the maintenance cost of the apartment as a business deduction. But when he sought to avoid paying the tax on the profit from its sale on the grounds that it had gone into the purchase of a new principal residence in San Clemente, he swore on the return that he had not used the New York apartment for business purposes.

That would have been enough, one would think, since it is truly inconceivable that Nixon in his first months in the White House could not have known, and recalled, that he took substantial business deductions at home when he was Nixon the New York lawyer.

But he did more. He then proceeded to deduct 25% of the cost of running the San Clemente place (down to and including a deduction of 25% of the cost of cleaning the rug in his wife's bathroom—perhaps on the theory that one-fourth of the mud he had tracked onto that rug had been affixed to his shoes during trudges around the property with business associates?), thus destroying totally the residence-for-residence exclusion he had claimed *on the same return*.

Hard as it is to believe, the deception did not end there. Having claimed San Clemente as a non-business "principal residence" to avoid the New York and federal tax on the sale of the apartment, and having then denied that statement by deducting 25% of the cost of running San Clemente on the theory that he spent 25% of his time there as President, he then swore that he was practically *never in San Clemente at all*, in order to avoid paying any California income tax which, as even a part-time resident, he would be required to pay.

It was not only the large-scale chiseling which so annoyed the country (and, presumably, the Congressmen). There was petty stuff, too. Nixon claimed a deduction of $1.80, a "service charge" of interest assessed on his charge account at a Washington department store. He deducted the cost of a "masked ball" thrown for his daughter Tricia. And he demonstrated that, for him at least, charity begins where it is deductible by showing legitimate charitable gifts totalling less than $300, or one-tenth of one percent of his income. That one even drew a complaint, albeit a faint one, from Rev. Billy Graham.

□ The tapes—the famous tapes—have begun to appear more and more the President's undoing. He is widely believed to be concealing incriminating evidence when he refuses to yield them up; he is believed to have countenanced tampering with evidence when they turn up missing or deliberately obliterated, and when they are intact, they convince listeners of his complicity.

Where did it all start? Why would this politically canny man, with such strong instincts for self-preservation and trusting hardly anyone, undertake to put everything on tape, where someday it might be heard? One explanation was given me by John McLaughlin, a Jesuit priest who serves as a Nixon speech-writer at the White House and who appears—at taxpayers' expense—on radio and television "talk shows" to defend the President. It is Fr. McLaughlin's version that the tapes were originally proposed by H. R. Haldeman, a compulsive record-keeper and memo-writer (and the man who thought he was running a "zero-defect" administration). According to McLaughlin, Haldeman thought the Nixon years would be the greatest of any time in history, and he proposed a permanent record be made. The decision to tape all the Nixon conversations, according to McLaughlin, was a compromise agreed to by the President; Haldeman's original proposal was to tape *and film* everything. The theory has the ring of truth; the notion of running the affairs of state as a sort of long-running "Candid Camera" program could only have occurred to a humorless zealot like Haldeman.

In a curious irony, it was Haldeman who was first trapped by the tapes. After listening to them at home, he told the Ervin Committee he had indeed heard John Dean discussing the payment of "hush money" to the original Watergate defendants. He had heard the President then say, said Haldeman, "but it would be wrong." The Grand Jury indicted him for perjury for so testifying, and the Grand Jury heard the same tape.

☐ There have been further developments in the ITT story as well. After then Attorney-General Richard Kleindienst testified under oath that he had had no communication with the President about the case, during the period when ITT had offered $400,000 to the Republican Party and the Justice Department was deciding whether to press anti-trust charges, Nixon remained silent and supported Kleindienst.

But it later developed that the Kleindienst statement was false. The White House admitted that Nixon had indeed called Kleindienst, had called him a "dumb son-of-a-bitch," had wondered whether Kleindienst understood English, and had ordered him to take action favorable to ITT. The occasion for the call was that John Ehrlichman had "ordered" the Justice Department to drop an appeal from a decision in favor of ITT, and Kleindienst had refused. (The "son-of-a-bitch" language is that offered by those who put the best face on it for Nixon; those acquainted with the presidential vocabulary are inclined to think the real language was somewhat more colorful.)

Kleindienst, by spring in 1974, was plea-bargaining in an effort to find some charge less than perjury to which he could plead guilty and avoid disbarment, and that raised interesting questions about Nixon and his lawyers. He has had six from the time he entered the White House until Watergate exploded in his face—John Mitchell and Kleindienst as Attorneys-General; Charles Colson as Special Counsel; John Ehrlichman and John Dean as Counsel to the President; and Herbert Kalmbach as his personal attorney. Of those six, two have pleaded guilty to felonies, three have been indicted for offenses ranging from perjury, through conspiracy to plan the burglary of Dr. Fielding's office, to obstruction of justice in the Watergate cover-up, and one—as this is written—is plea-bargaining. We know what to think of a *lawyer* whose last six clients have gone to jail or are in serious trouble with the law, but what of a *client* whose last six *lawyers* are in similarly bad trouble?

There should be some mention of the developing role played in all this by Alexander Haig, the man who was willing to connive with Nixon (and, for that matter, with then Attorney-General Elliot Richardson) to break the law in order, apparently, to tilt his own pension. As the months passed, Haig became almost the only White House aide with access to Nixon.

It was Haig who planted in the press—in an attempt to salvage something from the "Saturday Night Massacre"—the false story that Elliot Richardson had once agreed to fire Special Prosecutor Archibald Cox and had agreed to the so-called "Stennis compromise." When Richardson challenged Haig on the matter, and when members of the Senate Judiciary Committee called for Haig to tell the story under oath, he declined—and backed down.

Haig's role in the Saturday Night Massacre is told in considerable detail by Aaron Latham in the April 29, 1974, issue of *New York* magazine. As one sees the way in which Haig participated in the successive deceptions of Richardson, Senators Ervin and Baker, and even "Judge" Stennis himself, it is not hard to understand how—with a slender combat record —he was able to rise to the top in the Army.

Haig's view of his Leader is also instructive. When he is not calling him the "Commander-in-Chief" to compel obedience, he uses language which seems to indicate *real* reverence. When a panel of experts—some appointed by the White House —determined in Judge Sirica's court that 18½ minutes of taped conversation about Watergate between Nixon and Haldeman—which took place three days after the burglary—had been deliberately and manually erased, Haig offered the view that it had been done by some "sinister force."

Later, when the Washington *Post* reported that other erasures on other tapes were being investigated by the same experts, Haig at first denounced the story (which later turned out to be true), not as "false" but as "blasphemous." After referring to Nixon's opponents as "sinister" and his detractors as "blasphemous," it came as no surprise to read an interview in the *Christian Science Monitor* in which Haig commented favorably on what he called Nixon's "vicarship." Can Haig believe Richard Nixon rules by Divine right?

In this book, I have not, largely for reasons of space, dealt with a number of matters which some might think should have been included. For example, I have not treated of the relationship between Nixon and James Hoffa, the Teamster leader released from federal prison by a presidential reprieve in time to marshal support for the President's reelection. I have not dealt extensively with the apparently massive program of sabotage and espionage directed at all Democratic candidates

247 ·

largely because many of the incidents have yet to be proved. Nor have I discussed the illegal telephone tap which the President caused to be placed on his brother, Donald, although the reading of the logs might well determine the extent of Nixon's knowledge of the seamier details of the Vesco case, of which Donald Nixon was fully informed. I have tried, if incompletely, to set forth the history of Nixon Politics become Nixon government, in the belief that the unbroken record of fraud, deception, and outright crime might demonstrate at one and the same time both the strength and weakness of our system. The weakness of course is that a man so contemptuous of the limits of decency and morality could reach the presidency (and once there, nearly destroy the system); the strength is that we have demonstrated the capacity to expose that record, and now need only summon the will to act upon what we know.

April 27, 1974

APPENDIX 1.
PRESIDENT NIXON
SPEAKS ON CRIME

On October 15, 1972, President Nixon delivered a campaign address by radio. Following is that portion of the speech devoted to the subject of crime.

Good afternoon.

Four years ago, at the close of a turbulent decade which had seen our Nation engulfed by a rising tide of disorder and permissiveness, I campaigned for President with a pledge to restore respect for law, order, and justice in America. I am pleased to be able to report to you today that we have made significant progress in that effort.

During the 8 years from the end of the Eisenhower Administration until we took office in 1968, serious crime in the United States had skyrocketed by 122 percent, and there were predictions that it would double once again during the following 4 years.

Those predictions have not come true. Instead, we have fought the frightening trend of crime and anarchy to a standstill. The campuses which erupted in riots so often in the late 1960s have become serious centers of learning once again. The cities which we saw in flames summer after summer a few years ago are now pursuing constructive change.

The FBI crime index showed an increase of only 1 percent during the first half of this year. That is the closest we have come to registering an actual decrease since these quarterly statistics began 12 years ago. And in 72 of our largest cities, we have already begun to see a decrease in crime this year as compared to last.

We have moved off the defensive and onto the offensive in our all-out battle against the criminal forces in America. We are going to stay on the offensive until we put every category of crime on a downward trend in every American community.

To reach this goal we must continue to fight the battle on all fronts.

In our courts, we need judges who will help to strengthen the peace forces as against the criminal forces in this country. I have applied this principle in making appointments to the Supreme Court and to other federal courts. As a result, our Constitution today is more secure; our freedoms are better protected.

The two men who have served me as Attorney General, John Mitchell and Richard Kleindienst, have brought real backbone to our national law enforcement effort. Each has demonstrated his determination to see justice done to the overwhelming majority of law-abiding citizens, as well as to those who break the law. Neither has fallen for the naive theory that society is to blame for an individual's wrongdoing.

Tomorrow, Attorney General Kleindienst will make public the first comprehensive report ever compiled on federal law enforcement and criminal justice assistance activities. I commend this report to the attention of every American who is concerned with the rule of the law. It documents the truly massive federal commitment to crime reduction.

The federal role, however, is only a supportive one. As J. Edgar Hoover often used to tell me, it is our local police forces who are the real frontline soldiers in the war against crime. As President over the past four years, I have given all-out backing to our peace officers in their dedicated efforts to make all of us safer on the streets and more secure in our homes, and I shall continue to do so.

In three years we have provided states and localities with law enforcement assistance grants totaling $1.5 billion. That compares with only $22 million in grants during the final 3 years of the previous Administration.

In a single year, 1970, the Congress passed four landmark anticrime bills which this Administration had recommended and fought for—an omnibus crime bill, a bill providing new tools to fight organized crime, a comprehensive reform of the drug abuse statutes, and a new charter for courts and criminal procedures in the Nation's Capital.

The city of Washington had become the crime capital of the United States during the 1960s, but during our term of office we have cut the D.C. crime rate in half.

250

APPENDIX 2.
THE CRIMINAL STATUTES

Criminal statutes which appear to have been violated by members of the Nixon White House staff, or officials of the Nixon campaign:

☐ Improper destruction of classified information and material, Executive Order #11652 and 44 U.S.C. ch. 33.

☐ Accessory after the fact, 18 U.S.C. 3.

☐ Misprision of felony, 18 U.S.C. 4.

☐ Assault by striking and simple assault, 18 U.S.C. 113 (d) (e).

☐ Unlawful conspiracies, 18 U.S.C. 371.

☐ Disclosure of classified information, 18 U.S.C. 798 (3) (4).

☐ Kidnapping, 18 U.S.C. 1201 (c).

☐ Obstruction of justice; influencing witnesses, 18 U.S.C. 1503.

☐ Obstruction of justice; obstruction of proceedings before departments, agencies and committees, 18 U.S.C. 1505.

☐ Obstruction of justice—obstruction of criminal investigations, 18 U.S.C. 1510.

☐ Perjury, generally, 18 U.S.C. 1621.

☐ Subornation of perjury, 18 U.S.C. 1622.

☐ False declarations before grand jury or court, 18 U.S.C. 1623.

☐ Interception and disclosure of wire or oral communications, 18 U.S.C. 2511 (1) (a–d).

☐ Possession of wire and oral communication intercepting devices, 18 U.S.C. 2512 (1) (a).

☐ Powers and duties of the C.I.A., 50 U.S.C. 403 (d) (3).

☐ Attempts to interfere with the administration of the Internal Revenue laws, 26 U.S.C. 7212.

- [ ] Unauthorized disclosure of information from Federal Income Tax Returns, 26 U.S.C. 7213.
- [ ] Bribery of public officials to influence an official act, 18 U.S.C. 201 (b).
- [ ] Bribery to influence the testimony of a witness at a trial or hearing, 18 U.S.C. 201 (d).
- [ ] Acceptance of bribes by defendants, 18 U.S.C. 201 (e).
- [ ] Blackmail, 19 U.S.C. 873.
- [ ] Obstruction of passage of mail, 18 U.S.C. 1701.
- [ ] Opening of mail of others, 18 U.S.C. 1702.
- [ ] Delay of mail by Postal Service employees, 18 U.S.C. 1703.
- [ ] Manipulative and deceptive stock devices, Securities Exchange Act (1934), Rule 10 (b) (5).
- [ ] Promise of employment or other benefit for political activity, 18 U.S.C. 600.
- [ ] Contributions by national banks, corporations, or labor organizations, 18 U.S.C. 610.
- [ ] Contributions by government contractors, 18 U.S.C. 611.
- [ ] Publication and distribution of political statements not containing the names of persons, committees, or corporations responsible for publication or distribution, 18 U.S.C. 612.
- [ ] Accounting of contributions in excess of $10, 2 U.S.C. 432 (b).
- [ ] Segregation of campaign funds from personal funds, 2 U.S.C. 432 (b).
- [ ] Recordkeeping duties of treasurer of political committee, 2 U.S.C. 432 (c).
- [ ] Keeping receipts of every expenditure made by a political committee, 2 U.S.C. 432 (d).
- [ ] Reports by political committees disclosing the amount of cash on hand at the beginning of the reporting period; name and address of each contributor of over $100; and total sum of individual contributions made, 2 U.S.C. 434 (8).
- [ ] Report of any loan to or from any person . . . in the aggregate amount of $100, 2 U.S.C. 434 (5).
- [ ] Report of the total amount of proceeds from the sales of tickets to each dinner, luncheon, rally and other fund-raising event, 2 U.S.C. 434 (6).
- [ ] Report of the total sum of all receipts by or for such committee during the reporting period, 2 U.S.C. 434 (8).
- [ ] Report of name and address of each person to whom expenditures have been made . . . and the purpose of each such expenditure, 2 U.S.C. 434 (9).

☐ Report of the total sum of expenditures made by such committee or candidate during the calendar year, 2 U.S.C. 434 (11).

☐ Reports by persons other than a political committee or candidate of expenditures or contributions in excess of $100, not made to or by the committee, on behalf of the candidate, 2 U.S.C. 435.

☐ Prohibition of contributions made in the name of another, 2 U.S.C. 440.

☐ House-breaking with intent to break and carry away any part thereof, 22 District of Columbia Code 1801.

☐ Attempt at arson, 22 District of Columbia Code 401.

☐ Accessory after the fact, 22 District of Columbia Code 106.

☐ Unlawful possession of intercepting devices, 22 District of Columbia Code 543 (a).

☐ Assault with intent to commit mayhem, 22 District of Columbia Code 502.

☐ Assault with intent to commit any other offense, 22 District of Columbia Code 503.

☐ Unlawful assault or threatening another in a menacing manner, 22 District of Columbia Code 504.

☐ Threats to do bodily harm, 22 District of Columbia Code 507.

☐ Blackmail, 22 District of Columbia Code 2305.

☐ Conspiracy to commit a felony, 44 Florida Code, 833.04.

☐ Conspiracy to wiretap, 44 Florida Code, 822.10.

☐ Conspiracy to commit a misdemeanor, 44 Florida Code, 833.05.

☐ Conspiracy to commit burglary, California Penal Code, Sec. 184.

☐ Burglary, California Penal Code, Sec. 459.

☐ Perjury, California Penal Code, Sec. 118.

☐ Overt acts to effect a conspiracy, California Penal Code, Sec. 184.

☐ Wearing personal disguises to escape recognition in the commission of a public offense, California Penal Code, Sec. 185.

APPENDIX 3.
A LETTER FROM ALBERT SPEER

The following statement by Albert Speer, Hitler's architect and adviser and the author of Inside the Third Reich, *responds to a letter by James Reston, Jr., on the* Fuehrerprinzip. *Reston asked Speer for a definition of the leader principle and also whether Speer saw any parallel between the Nazi underlings and the Nixon loyalists; particularly, whether Haldeman's relationship to Nixon as his chief of staff bore any similarity to Martin Bormann's relationship to Hitler.*

Your letter has unfortunately only just reached me. It is not the first time that the effects of my memoirs have, in a theoretical way, come into connection with explosive political events in the United States. The case of the Berrigan brothers, the Calley trial, and their general effects brought invitations to take a stand publicly on American television. I took the view then, which has remained unchanged, that I feel it would be presumptuous for me, from my particular position, to involve myself in delicate internal affairs of the United States, even if I were only taking a stand in regard to them. That is not fitting for me—with my past.

I hope that you can appreciate this introduction which turned out to be rather long. Now to your questions:

The *Fuehrerprinzip* is certainly explained in some official (Nazi) party program, or other. I myself can only tell you how the *Fuehrerprinzip* was applied. It demanded absolute loyalty to the highest leader, and those named by him, the uncritical following of orders, even if they appeared to be nonsense, the exclusion of all personal considerations toward family and friends, if it was a question of the good of the whole. In my book I did not go into the *Fuehrerprinzip*, but I did go into the other characteristic property of the totali-

254

tarian system: the compartmentalization and the depersonalization of the individual human being. [*Inside the Third Reich*, Macmillan, pp. 32–33]

As I have already explained, far be it from me to involve myself in internal American affairs. I would not be in a position to do so anyhow, since the reporting in the German newspapers (on the Watergate affair) is not thorough enough to give me a picture of the proceedings.

For this reason I will limit myself to the circumstances around Hitler, as they were brought into focus by Bormann. Hitler is known to have lacked the ability to delegate tasks. He believed that he had to carry them out himself if they appeared important to him. Because of this he took a considerable collection of duties on himself, beginning with supreme commander of the *Wehrmacht*, through supreme commander of the army, to chief architect. In such a situation, a secretary to a dictator is always particularly powerful. For he must in the end make decisions on reports or establish communications with the lower echelons.

Probably such powerful secretaries are only found in dictatorships. I would like to remind you that Stalin was Lenin's secretary, and Malenkov was Stalin's secretary, and that Bormann had prospects of becoming Hitler's successor in the same way. In your comparison it should be taken into account that in Hitler's Germany there was no free press. Therefore, in his evaluation of domestic conditions, Hitler was forced to rely on the reports of his colleagues, which went through Bormann's hands and were filtered by him. With a free press, for instance, scandals caused by high functionaries would not have remained hidden from the head of state.

I am not satisfied myself with my answers. . . .

With friendly greetings,
Albert Speer

APPENDIX 4.
SENATOR McGOVERN'S
SPEECH ON CORRUPTION

Following is the text of the television address by Sen. George McGovern on October 25, 1972.

In earlier broadcasts, I have discussed the choices facing the American people on two critical issues: the war in Vietnam and the economy of America.

Tonight, I ask you to consider another issue that troubles the very soul of our country. The issue is integrity. For although we are concerned about our immediate needs, there is a deeper crisis in America—a crisis of the spirit.

As I have listened to the American people and tried to sense what was in their hearts, one message has come through consistently. It is that people are losing confidence in their leaders.

I saw that in the eyes of an elderly woman in Wisconsin, who told me she feels abandoned by her country.

I heard it in the angry voices of men and women on the assembly lines in Detroit, who asked me why so much of their wages go for taxes when some big interests pay no taxes at all.

I heard it from a badly wounded young Marine in Vietnam last year, who told me, "I will never trust the government again." Too many people have told me, "All politicians are crooked."

When I hear that, I fear for the American future. For our free system of government is founded on trust between those who elect and those who are elected. And when that bond weakens, a part of democracy dies.

Restoring that bond of trust may be the greatest challenge facing the next President of the United States.

A few weeks ago, I suggested to the students at Wheaton College in Illinois that the President of the United States has a responsibility greater than running the government. He must also serve as the moral leader of the nation. He can lift the moral vision of America and rekindle our sense of national purpose.

The present administration is failing that responsibility.

Consider, for example, the enforcement of our antitrust laws. They were written to protect consumers against too much economic power in too few hands. And they safeguard our free enterprise system, preserving independent business against excessive concentrations of power.

By swallowing up other companies, ITT has become one of the most powerful conglomerates in the country. When ITT wanted to take over still another corporation—one of the nation's largest insurance companies—the Antitrust Division of the Justice Department said that was too much. So, they prepared to go into court to stop that merger.

But while the case was being prepared, ITT offered several hundred thousand dollars to finance the Republican National Convention. And what happened then? The antitrust case against ITT was dropped, and the company destroyed the evidence of collusion in a shredding machine. Abandonment of that case meant a billion dollar settlement for ITT, higher costs for you, and less freedom in our free enterprise system.

When Mr. Nixon decided to abandon his first economic policy because it was not working, he set up a commission that he promised would control the cost of living.

But the Combined Insurance Company of Chicago is not covered. The chairman of that company gave half a million dollars to Mr. Nixon's 1968 campaign, and he has said he plans to give a million dollars this year. Seven days after he had dinner at the White House, the Price Commission gave his company a special exemption from price controls.

Last year, dairy lobbyists were pressing hard for higher milk prices. The Secretary of Agriculture turned them down. But then, a longtime advisor of Mr. Nixon met in the White House with the dairy lobbyists. They contributed $352,000 to Mr. Nixon's campaign. And within a few days, the Secretary

257

of Agriculture reversed his decision and decreed higher prices for milk.

In 1970, 38 older Americans in Ohio lost their lives in a nursing home fire. After careful investigation, authorities traced the cause of that disaster to a highly flammable carpet. The fire became a raging inferno before the people inside even had a chance to be saved. So, stronger carpet safety regulations were proposed, to see that nothing like that would ever happen again.

But there was another meeting in the White House—between executives of the carpet industry and top officials of the Republican campaign. They gave almost $95,000 for Mr. Nixon's reelection. And the carpet safety regulations were postponed.

These actions do not demonstrate the moral standards that I believe America wants and expects. What they represent is the immoral influence of big money on the public business.

Last year, the Congress decided to do something about that. We adopted a new law that says you have a right to know where the campaign money is coming from, so you can judge whether special favors are involved. We followed the advice of Justice Louis Brandeis: "Sunlight is the best of disinfectants."

Although that disclosure law did not go into effect until April of 1972, my campaign has revealed the name of every contributor since I first became a candidate in January of 1971.

But Mr. Nixon did just the opposite.

Before the disclosure law went into effect, he launched a massive drive to beat the system and to defeat your right to know. By the time of the disclosure deadline, he had collected at least $10 million from powerful supporters.

He has not revealed the name of a single contributor. And that is the secret $10 million fund you have heard about. Mr. Nixon is saying, in effect, that it's none of your business who is bankrolling his campaign.

You have a right to ask candidate Nixon: "Why are you afraid to name your contributors?"

If we knew the names on that secret list, we might have the answers to some other troubling questions about why our government has acted the way it has over the past four years.

Why is it that when there is a tax break, it always goes to those who need it least, and never to you?

Why is it that the inefficient managers of Lockheed got bailed out by a government loan, but nothing is done to save the thousands of small businessmen and family farmers who are going broke every year?

Why did this administration help the big grain exporters take advantage of the family farmers on the Russian wheat deal?

And why is it that this administration puts a lid on wages, but lets prices rise on everything you buy?

These are some of the most important decisions our government has made in the last four years. Each time, the special interests won and you lost.

Is it any wonder that confidence in the moral integrity of government is declining?

Mr. Nixon and I disagree on the proper relationship between money, power, and people.

We disagree, as well, on the conduct of political campaigns.

Four months ago, five men wearing rubber gloves and carrying burglar's tools were arrested by the police inside the Democratic Party Headquarters in Washington. They were there in the middle of the night to remove listening devices they had previously planted on the telephones. And they were there to steal private files on Democratic senators, congressmen, and party officials. One of them had $114,000 in his bank account—money that came from the Nixon campaign fund.

And the Democratic headquarters was not their only target.

We now know that these men were part of a nationwide network of at least fifty agents hired by the Nixon campaign to create confusion and division among the Democratic candidates for President. Part of their job was to distort your impressions of those candidates—what kind of men they were and what they stood for.

You may recall the incident in Manchester, New Hampshire, in this year's first primary, when Senator Muskie showed his outrage at the unfair things that were printed about him in that city's newspaper. Many people believe that event had a decisive impact on Senator Muskie's chance for the nomination.

The whole affair started with a letter, supposedly from a voter in Florida, accusing Senator Muskie of using insulting language. But that Florida voter was never found. And now

259

we know why. The letter was a forgery. And it has been traced to a White House aide.

This same army of Republican sabotage agents released false statements to the press in the name of Democratic candidates. They tried to place listening devices in my campaign office. They attempted to throw campaign schedules into disarray. They forged letters. They followed our families. They even plotted a disruption of their own Republican convention in Miami Beach so they could blame it on the Democrats.

And all of this was paid for out of a secret $700,000 espionage fund kept in the safe of Mr. Nixon's finance chairman and controlled by John Mitchell, even while he was still Attorney General of the United States.

Not one of these facts has been refuted or explained. The only response has been to attack the reporters who searched out the truth.

During 18 years in politics, I have never seen such efforts to poison the political dialogue. These Republican politicians have fouled the political atmosphere for all of us who see public service as a high calling.

They do not seek to defeat the Democratic Party; they seek to destroy it.

And in the process, they would deny one of the most precious freedoms of all—your freedom to judge which candidate will better serve your interests and truly reflect your view of America.

If our free system is to survive, we must recall that just as you set standards of decency and fair dealing in your own lives, there are accepted limits on what is right in a political contest.

But on the few occasions when they even acknowledge these actions, administration officials use terms like "caper" and "prank." They want you to believe that all Presidential candidates accept contributions with strings attached. They want you to believe that all politicians wiretap and sabotage and spy, and they always have. That is simply not true.

Special favors and secret funds cannot be ignored.

The crime of burglary cannot be excused by calling it a "caper."

And $700,000 worth of political espionage is no "prank."

The men who have collected millions in secret money, who have passed out special favors, who have ordered political sabotage, who have invaded our offices in the dead of night—

all of these men work for Mr. Nixon. Most of them he hired himself. And their power comes from him alone. They act on his behalf, and they all accept his orders.

Yet, Mr. Nixon has even promoted some of the officials implicated in the scandals.

And he has blocked any independent investigation. He refused to answer questions from either the press or the people. He stays hidden in the White House, hoping you will mistake silence for innocence.

In 1961, when the Bay of Pigs invasion turned into disaster, President Kennedy did not duck the issue. He accepted full responsibility for everything that went wrong.

When Harry Truman sat in the White House, he had a sign on his desk: "The buck stops here."

That is the kind of men they were. And that is the kind of responsible Presidential leadership we must restore.

Our present leadership has not only failed the test, it has undermined the personal freedoms of Americans and the Constitutional framework of our government.

We have seen a demeaning of our judicial system with Supreme Court nominations that shocked the nation. Two of those appointments were rejected by the Senate. Two others were stopped short by the American Bar Association. But four of Mr. Nixon's appointments now sit on the Supreme Court. And another four years could easily permit him to dominate the entire Court for the rest of this century.

Likewise, the Congress has been undermined by the encroachment of arbitrary Executive power. American forces were committed across the Cambodian frontier without so much as a telephone call to leaders of the Congress. Mr. Nixon said of Senator Mansfield's resolution calling for an end to the war, that the Administration would ignore any such expression by the Congress. Secret arrangements have been negotiated with foreign powers without the consent or even the knowledge of the Senate Foreign Relations Committee. The war-making power which the Founding Fathers lodged in the Congress has been preempted by the Chief Executive. And this abuse of power was made all the more dangerous when a military commander went unpunished even after he conducted bombing raids without the approval of civilian authority.

The executive abuse of power is further compounded by the shift of foreign policy decisions to the basement of the White

House, where the President invokes executive privilege to prevent those aides who make foreign policy behind closed doors from being cross-examined by the people's representatives in the Congress.

And now we are confronted with executive efforts to assume the Constitutional responsibility of the Congress to decide how public funds should be expended. In the tradition of an emperor rather than a public servant, the President has said to the Congress, "Give me $250 billion and I will decide what is best for the American people."

But this is not the whole story of the abuse of power by the Administration. The First Amendment, which protects the people's right to a free press, has been weakened by a savage effort to intimidate the press. For the first time in American history, newspapers have been ordered not to print information embarrassing to the government, and reporters have been told they must produce their private notes before grand juries.

The government has asserted the right to tap telephones without a court order; a strange new doctrine called "qualified martial law" was used at a Washington peace gathering to lock up 13,000 people—the innocent along with the guilty —all of this in plain defiance of the Constitution.

Other dangerous new practices, such as preventive detention, no-knock searches of our homes, and a requirement that telephone companies and landlords must assist in planting eavesdropping devices—all of these are unprecedented threats to our personal freedoms.

We want to think that our Department of Justice applies the law with an even hand. But conspiracy laws were used to prosecute nuns and priests involved in a war protest, whereas no action was taken when students were killed at Kent State or Jackson State.

We are confronted, in short, with both a moral and a Constitutional crisis of unprecedented dimensions. Ambitious men come and go, but a free society might never recover from a sustained assault on its most basic institutions. And one can only ask, if this has happened in four years, to what lengths would the same leadership go in another four years, once freed of the restraints of facing the people for reelection?

The next President will inherit this crisis and this legacy of distrust that has been accumulating over the last four years. It will take time to convince people that they can believe in their government once again. It is not easy to teach respect for law and order when the government itself has scorned the moral and Constitutional foundation of law and order.

But it can be done. I believe that a President who keeps faith with the American people will, in time, revive that confidence.

The next President can summon the American people to a higher standard—but only if he sets a higher standard for himself.

He can persuade Americans to care about their fellow human beings—but only if he cares himself.

And the next President can rekindle our love of freedom—but only if he loves freedom more than power.

The next President must understand that freedom is not indestructible. He must heed the warning of Benjamin Franklin, as he stepped out of Independence Hall on the day that America was born.

"What kind of government is it?" someone asked.

"A republic," he said, "if you can keep it."

Benjamin Franklin and the others present in Philadelphia that day had risked their lives to secure their liberty from an oppressive government. They were not about to hand it over to more oppression.

They understand what we must remember—that freedom lost is seldom restored.

And like those early patriots, we must stand as watchmen, guarding our liberty from the advance of over-reaching political power, just as we would defend it from an advancing foreign army.

I believe we will keep our Republic. We will save the ideals we have cherished for nearly 200 years.

I believe that because I have been out among the people campaigning.

And this is what I have learned.

The people are not left or right or center. Rather, they seek a way out of the wilderness.

They want a President who will restore their trust in government by trusting them—a leader who will neither distort the truth nor loan away the government.

They ask for a President who will tell them, not just what they want to hear, but what they have a right to know.

They want a leadership that will return a basic sense of fairness to government—that will set not one standard for the powerful and one for those without power; but a single standard for us all.

They hunger for that clarifying vision of national purpose that only a President can provide—a President who will lift our eyes above the daily entanglements to a more distant horizon, to the time when, as Thomas Paine said, "No land on earth shall be as happy as America."

That is the kind of President I want to be.

A President who will ask the best of our people, so we can glow with a new love for America—and America can lift a new light before the world.

Then our children and their children after them will love this land, not merely because they were born here, but because of the great and good country that you and I together have made it.

Thank you and good night.

APPENDIX 5.
JUDGMENT OF THE SUPERIOR COURT CASE NO. 526150, OCTOBER 30,1964

GERALD J. O'GARA
O'GARA and O'GARA
1200 Mills Tower
San Francisco 4
Attorneys for Plaintiffs

GERALD D. MARCUS
593 Market Street
San Francisco

WEBSTER V. CLARK
111 Sutter Street
San Francisco 4
Of Counsel for Plaintiffs

IN THE SUPERIOR COURT OF THE STATE OF CALI-
FORNIA, IN AND FOR THE CITY AND COUNTY
OF SAN FRANCISCO

DEMOCRATIC STATE CENTRAL COMMITTEE,
et al.,

Plaintiffs,

vs.

COMMITTEE FOR THE PRESERVATION OF
THE DEMOCRATIC PARTY IN CALIFORNIA,
an unincorporated association,
et al.,

Defendants.

The above entitled matter came on regularly for hearing on

October 22, 1962, at which time the above entitled Court issued a temporary restraining order against the defendant Committee for the Preservation of the Democratic Party in California, hereinafter called the defendant Committee, Joseph Robinson, Robinson & Company Inc., a corporation, William Marlin, Ed Fitzharris, Herry J. Boyle, Austin Healy, Crocker-Citizens National Bank, formerly Crocker-Anglo National Bank, Recorder Printing and Publishing Company, a corporation, and Bernhard A. Hansen, individually and as vice-president of said Recorder Printing and Publishing Company. Thereafter the matter was continued from time to time to November 2, 1962, at which time the Court issued a preliminary injunction against the defendants above named. Pursuant to court order the matter was then continued while plaintiffs herein took depositions of persons not parties to this action. The matter then came up for hearing before this Court, Department 5 thereof, Honorable Byron Arnold presiding without a jury, and upon the complaint (as amended to insert the names of certain appearing defendants sued as fictitious defendants) and the above defendants' demurrer, and Gerald J. O'Gara, Esq., Webster V. Clark, Esq., and Gerald Marcus, Esq., appeared as counsel for plaintiffs and Ralph Golub, Esq., appeared as counsel for the defendants Joseph Robinson, Robinson & Company Inc., William Marlin, Ed Fitzharris, Austin Healy and Harry J. Boyle, and Almon B. McCallum, Esq., appeared for defendant Crocker-Citizens National Bank, formerly Crocker-Anglo National Bank, and Brobeck, Phleger & Harrison by Robert Metz appeared for defendants Recorder Printing and Publishing Company, and Bernhard A. Hansen, individually and as Vice President of Recorder Printing and Publishing Company. The Court having read the depositions of six witnesses taken in San Francisco and Los Angeles and all said depositions having been admitted in evidence and the Court having examined the proofs, both oral and documentary, offered by the respective parties, and further evidence having been presented and admitted from time to time until October 30, 1964; and the cause having on that date been submitted for decision, and the Court having fully considered all the evidence and arguments of counsel;

NOW, THEREFORE, the parties having waived notice of time and place of trial and findings of fact and conclusions of law herein except as specifically set forth herein and the Court being fully advised in the premises hereby finds as facts the matters set forth herein and from the facts so found makes the conclusions of law set forth herein.

IT IS HEREBY ORDERED, ADJUDGED AND DECREED that:

1. In October 1961, Richard M. Nixon announced his candidacy for the governorship of California.

In October 1962, a circular to Democrats was drafted which purported to express the concern of genuine Democrats for the welfare of the Democratic Party and their fear that the party would be destroyed if candidates supported by the California Democratic Council (hereinafter called the "CDC") including primarily Governor Brown, were elected in the November 1962 election. It appealed for the support and money of Democrats in fighting the CDC and certain policies attributed to it and cast aspersions on the Democratic candidates endorsed by it. It was drafted in the form of a postcard poll addressed to Democrats. This postcard poll was reviewed, amended, and finally approved by Mr. Nixon personally in the form attached hereto as Exhibit A. It criticized the policies of the CDC and the Democratic candidates it supported, notably Governor Edmund G. Brown, and asked the addressee Democrats to express their preference either for Governor Brown and the other statewide Democratic candidates or their Republican opponents, headed by Mr. Nixon.

Nowhere in Exhibit A or letters mailed by defendant Committee was it stated that the defendant Committee and its mailing of Exhibit A were supported and financed by the Nixon for Governor Finance Committee. Mr. Nixon and Mr. Haldemann approved the plan and project as described above and agreed that the Nixon campaign committee would finance the project.

Officials of the Nixon for Governor Committee then made an agreement with defendants Robinson and Company, a corporation, and Joseph Robinson, whereby for the sum of $70,000 Robinson and Company agreed to print, address, and mail the postcard poll as described above and to receive and compile the results of the poll as indicated on the return postal cards.

In accordance with that agreement defendants Robinson and Co. and Joseph R. Robinson mailed more than 500,000 postcards to registered Democratic voters in California in the month of October 1962. That mailing continued until this Court enjoined further mailings and enjoined compilation or publication of any poll resulting from the distribution or mailing of the postcards.

As shown by the report of the Nixon for Governor Finance Committee filed with the Secretary of State of California and attached as Exhibit B, and by the testimony of members of the Nixon Finance Committee and Campaign Committee, the Nixon campaign paid $70,000 to defendant Robinson and Company for its work in connection with the distribution of the postcard attached as Exhibit A and with the taking of this poll in the name of the Committee for the Preservation of the Democratic Party in California.

The financial support for the defendant Committee consisted of the above sum contributed by the Nixon for Governor Finance Committee and approximately $368.50 which was contributed by Democratic voters in response to the postcard and appeals circulated and made by the defendants Robinson and Company, Joseph Robinson, the defendant Committee, and other defendants.

The executive secretary of the defendant Committee was defendant William Marlin. He was paid $750 for his services by defendant Committee.

Defendant Ed Fitzharris was one of the publicists employed by the defendant Committee. He was paid $1,000 for his services on behalf of defendant Committee.

2. Plaintiff the Democratic State Central Committee, also known as the California Democratic Party in California. The Democratic State Central Committee exists pursuant to the Elections code of California and conducts the business and campaigns of the Democratic Party in California. It is the only official statewide Democratic organization in the State of California.

3. On December 10, 1962, John Robert White, as treasurer of the Nixon for Governor Finance Committee 1962 General Campaign caused to be filed with the Secretary of State of California a General Campaign Statement. This statement Exhibit B contained under heading "Expenditures for Payment of Personnel, Item (d)" an entry as follows: "Robinson and Co.—$70,000."

This payment was the largest single item of expenditure for payment of personnel in the statement.

Defendant Robinson & Company received the above sum from the Nixon for Governor Finance Committee for the mailing of the double postcard attached hereto as Exhibit A and related services. Payment was received by Robinson & Company in the form of two checks drawn on the Nixon for Governor Finance Committee account, one dated October 5, 1962, check No. 3530 for $35,000, and one on October 22, 1962, check No. 3837 for $35,000.

Said checks are attached hereto as Exhibits C and C1 respectively.

4. All accounts and ledger sheets which defendants Joseph Robinson and Robinson and Company Inc. carried on behalf of the defendant Committee were carried in the name of "Nixon for Governor Campaign (Committee for Preservation of Democratic Party in California)" as reflected by the ledger sheet attached hereto as Exhibit D.

All statements for the work performed by defendants Joseph Robinson and Robinson and Company for and on behalf of the defendant Committee were sent for payment to H. Robert Haldeman, Campaign Manager of the Nixon for Governor Campaign Committee.

5. Richard Nixon in his campaign for the governorship of California, felt that the postcard and poll, Exhibit A would be very helpful to him since it reflected his own position concerning the relationship of Democrats to the CDC.

The list of seven so-called objectives or viewpoints purportedly held by the CDC, beginning with "Admitting Red China into the United Nations" and ending with "Refusal to Bar Communists from the Democratic Party," as recited in the postcard Exhibit A were substantially the same as charges made repeatedly by Mr. Nixon in his campaign speeches.

6. The defendant Committee for the Preservation of the Democratic Party in California consisted at most of 20 or 30 members. Defendants Austin Healy and Harry J. Boyle were and are cochairmen of said Committee.

7. Defendant Joseph Robinson, president of defendant Robinson and Company, Inc. is a professional political pollster and fund raiser for campaigns. Defendant Robinson and his corporation arranged for printing and handled the distribution of the postcard Exhibit A.

8. In October 1962 defendant Committee for the Preservation of the Democratic Party in California and its members, agents and/or employees, . . . defendants Joseph Robinson, Robinson and Company, Inc., a corporation, William Marlin, Harry J. Boyle, Austin Healy and Ed Fitzharris, directly and indirectly solicited funds upon representations, express and

implied, that the funds were being solicited for the use of the Democratic Party.

In truth and fact, such funds were solicited for the use, benefit and furtherance of the candidacy of Richard M. Nixon for Governor of California.

None of the following persons gave their consent to the Committee for the Preservation of the Democratic Party in California to solicit funds for or on behalf of the Committee for the Preservation of the Democratic Party in California or the Democratic Party in California:

Stanley Mosk, Democratic National Committeeman from California

Elizabeth Rudel Gatov, Democratic National Committee Woman from California

Eugene Wyman, Chairman of the California Democratic State Central Committee

Roger Kent, Chairman of the Northern Division of the California Democratic State Central Committee

John Kerrigan, Chairman of the Southern Division of California Democratic State Central Committee

Nor did any executive committee of any Democratic county central committee wherein the solicitation was made give such consent.

9. Defendants . . . made various misleading statements as specified below in connection with said postcard poll, . . . the letters of October 15, 1962, and October 17, 1962, . . . and the press releases attached hereto as Exhibits H and H1.

(a) (Statement) That the Democratic Party or a qualified Committee thereof or members of the Democratic Party sincerely interested in preserving the Democratic Party were mailing postcard Exhibit A to Democratic voters in order to secure a poll of members of the Democratic Party answering the questions on Exhibit A relating to said party and its candidates and wished such Democratic voters to fill out the poll contained therein and return it to the defendant Committee organized, dedicated, and operating for the preservation of the Democratic party and/or to the Democratic Party.

(Fact) Neither the Democratic Party nor plaintiff Democratic State Central Committee nor any qualified officer, official or committee thereof nor any member of the Democratic Party primarily interested in its welfare or preservation had any connection with or knowledge of or in any way sponsored or approved the acts or conduct of defendants or any of them . . . said postcard Exhibit A, the letters Exhibits E and E1 or said poll. On the contrary plaintiffs representing said Democratic Party opposed said postcard Exhibit A, letters Exhibits E and E1, and said poll and the Committee's activities.

(b) (Statement) That the Democratic Party and its fundamental and historic policies were and are in opposition to the CDC and its policies.

(Fact) The Democratic Party and the CDC are dedicated to the same basic general objectives and principles.

The Democratic Party is the official organization and is represented by plaintiff Democratic State Central Committee, constituted as set forth below in this paragraph 9, subparagraph (f) below.

The CDC is an unofficial organization of volunteer Democratic voters.

In a relatively few instances plaintiff Democratic State Central Committee and the CDC have taken different positions on specific issues.

In those cases, plaintiff Democratic State Central Committee has not adopted or accepted the policies of the CDC. On the other hand, it has not attempted to destroy the independent character of the CDC by denying its members the right to express their opinions.

(c) (Statement and Implication) That the Democratic Party wished said voters to send money for the use and benefit of the Democratic Party and its statewide candidates to the Committee for the Preservation of the Democratic Party in California . . . Crocker Anglo National Bank, One Montgomery Street, San Francisco, California, and the defendant Committee was a bona fide committee of Democrats organized for the sole purpose of preserving the Democratic Party in California . . . and was appealing to and soliciting Democratic voters for contributions of money to be used for the use, benefit, and preservation of the Democratic Party in California.

(Fact) The defendant Committee and its postcard poll and its activities were financed by, for, and in aid of the campaign to elect Mr. Nixon Governor of California.

Defendant Marlin in a memorandum attached as Exhibit I recorded the "queries I have had from the Press and the way I am answering them" in part as follows:

"1. How are you being financed?

"A. We have appealed to Democrats throughout the State, and so far their support has been most encouraging and helpful. An appeal has been sent to some 50,000 registered Democrats—along with a Poll on their reactions to the CDC. We are hopeful that we will receive enough financial support to expand this list to some one million Democrats in California."

"2. Are you receiving any Republican money?

"A. We are not refusing any contributions—and naturally, the Republicans are interested in this campaign. We are considering extending our fund appeal to Republicans, as we believe all citizens should be concerned with the power-grabbing strategy of the CDC."

"9. Are you urging Democrats to support Nixon and other Republican candidates?

"A. We are not conducting a campaign for *any* candidates. We are campaigning for the preservation of the Democratic Party by exposing the CDC's left-wing stands and power-grabbing tactics. We are making a plea to clean up the Democratic Party."

(d) (Statement) That the defendant Committee was a bona fide committee of Democrats organized, dedicated, and operating for the sole purpose of preserving the Democratic Party, and desired and was sincerely endeavoring by the postcard Exhibit A to secure a fair and representative poll of all segments of the Democratic Party and to determine by such poll the general sentiment of the rank-and-file members of the Democratic Party toward the CDC, the policies of the CDC, and the statewide Democratic candidates . . . , and to determine whether members of the Democratic Party as a whole preferred to support the named statewide Democratic candidates, and in particular Governor Brown, or felt that in order to preserve their party from control and domination of the CDC they should vote for Republican candidates, and in particular for Richard M. Nixon for governor of California.

That the results of the poll would reflect the feelings of rank-and-file Democrats including liberal, progressive and middle of the road Democrats as well as conservative Democrats.

(Fact) The activities of defendant Committee, including its postcard poll, its letters, and its publicity releases, were instigated, financed, prepared, implemented, supervised and

272

executed by the Nixon for Governor Campaign Committee and the Nixon for Governor Finance Committee. This is evidenced by these facts:

The invoice dated September 19, 1962, from defendant Robinson & Company Inc. to Nixon for Governor Campaign Committee, attached as Exhibit G provided for a "statewide mailing to 900,000 *Conservative* Democrats, also handling and tabulating poll."

When returns were received from said postcard poll, however, they were publicized by the defendant Committee as representing the "voice of the rank-and-file Democrat."

In the publicity release attached as Exhibit H, distributed to and published substantially by various California newspapers, dated October 20, 1962, for release October 22, 1962, the defendant Committee stated in part:

"First returns of a Poll being circulated to more than one hundred thousand Democrats throughout California indicate that:
"Nine out of ten registered Democrats flatly reject the 'ultra-liberal' California Democratic Council (CDC).
"The voice of the rank-and-file Democrat is now being heard, and that voice is speaking out loud and clear against the CDC and all it represents.
"Financial support has been pouring in from all over the State, providing means of expanding our Poll, and permitting thousands of rank-and-file Democrats to express themselves on this imperative question."

Defendant Committee failed to inform the Democrats receiving the postcard poll Exhibit A and the public that said poll actually was mailed to precincts consisting predominantly of conservative Democrats.

In its publicity release attached as Exhibit H1, distributed and published substantially by various California newspapers, dated October 26, 1962, for release October 27, 1962, the defendant Committee stated in part:

"The order Kent has obtained, prevents our Committee from releasing to the Press the results of a valid poll of some half-million registered Democrats in California, on their reactions to domination of the Party by the left-wing CDC (California Democratic Council)."

273

For the reasons set forth above the questions in the postcard Exhibit A confused and misled Democrats and produced answers which served primarily the purpose of assisting Mr. Nixon in his campaign.

(e) (Statement) That "Governor Brown . . . has become their (referring to the CDC) captive." (Exhibit A.)

(Fact) This statement is false.

(f) (Statement) That the CDC in the 1962 campaign dominated and directed the Democratic Party and captured and dominated Democratic nominees, the Democratic State Convention, and leadership of the Democratic Party.

(Fact) The State Convention of the Democratic Party is made up of nominees selected by the voters in free and open primary elections. The Democratic State Central Committee is made up of such nominees and their appointees and the Chairmen of the 58 Democratic County Central Committees. Such chairmen are duly elected by the members of their respective committees who in turn are elected by the rank-and-file Democratic voters. The officers of the Democratic State Central Committee are elected by members of the Committee. The nominees of the party and its officials are therefore directly selected by the rank-and-file Democratic voter and in the case of officers of the Democratic Party by representatives of the rank-and-file voters.

10. The postcard Exhibit A, the letters Exhibits E and E1, and the publicity releases Exhibits H and H1 were advertising by the defendants Committee, Joseph Robinson, Robinson and Company, Inc., Marlin, Boyle, Healy and Fitzharris for the purpose of securing votes and money from members of the Democratic party.

They were misleading in the particulars stated in paragraph 9 and elsewhere in this Judgment.

11. The postcard Exhibit A was a pamphlet and printed matter having reference to the 1962 general election and to the statewide candidates in said election and did not bear upon its face the name or address of the printer or publisher.

12. By reason of the facts herein stated plaintiffs were obliged to spend more than $10,000 in pursuing this action and enjoining the acts and conduct of said defendants Committee, Marlin, Joseph Robinson, Robinson & Company, Inc., Boyle, Healy and Fitzharris.

13. In response to the postcard Exhibit A and letters Exhibits E and E1, various Democratic voters contributed money

to said defendant Committee. The balance of such money so collected amounts to approximately $368.50 and is now on deposit in the head office of the Wells Fargo Bank, 464 California Street, San Francisco, in an account entitled "Roger Kent and Gerald J. O'Gara, Trustees for the Democratic State Central Committee."

The parties have stipulated that plaintiffs shall be awarded damages in the sum of $100 and costs in the sum of $268.50 (or balance remaining in said Wells Fargo Bank account above described). All such damages and costs to be paid exclusively from such account.

14. The temporary restraining orders and the preliminary injunctions heretofore issued herein were properly issued by reason of the facts set forth herein and the reasons set forth in said temporary restraining order and preliminary injunction, including the following reasons:

(a) Because of the location of defendants and their agents in various widely separated parts of California, including San Francisco and Los Angeles Counties, a multiplicity of suits would have been necessary to secure damages.

(b) Any final judgment after November 6, 1962, would have been ineffectual and a preliminary injunction after November 6, 1962, would have been of virtually no value compared to the temporary restraining order issued October 22 and the preliminary injunction issued November 2, 1962.

15. Unless restrained during this action and permanently enjoined by this Court, defendants (except those defendants dismissed herein by stipulation) intended to and were and/or are likely to

(a) Publish, post, mail, circulate, and distribute the postcard and writing in the form of Exhibits A, E and E1 attached hereto or in some form substantially similar to said Exhibits.

(b) Publish, post, mail, circulate, reveal, or distribute results from the poll which they conducted or could conduct by means of Exhibit A.

(c) Solicit, collect, or accept money from Democratic voters by using directly or indirectly a postcard, pamphlet, folder, letter, or writing in the form of Exhibits A, E, and E1 or forms substantially similar to said Exhibits.

(d) Use, appropriate, spend, and disburse money received from registered Democratic voters in response to or in connection with said postcard Exhibit A and letters Exhibits E and E1.

(e) Use in some manner or through some medium said Exhibit A or the contents thereof and the matters or things growing out of or resulting from the publishing, posting, mailing, circulating, or distributing of said Exhibit A or perform acts in furtherance of or in connection with the activities set forth in said Exhibit A. In this connection all defendants represent that according to their best knowledge, information, and belief they do not have on hand, in their possession, or under their control at various United States Post Offices in California or elsewhere postcards in the form of Exhibit A addressed to various Democratic voters and not yet delivered, return postcards part of said Exhibit A, tabulations of certain return postcards which were part of said Exhibit A or alleged polls based upon such tabulations or other memoranda, correspondence or writings purporting to show the opinions and positions of Democratic voters on the candidates and issues mentioned in said postcard Exhibit A.

However, defendants agree that if any such postcards, return postcards, tabulations, polls, memoranda, correspondence, or writings are hereafter discovered by defendants and come into their possession or under their control defendants will cause all such material to be destroyed forthwith or will without disclosing or publicizing the same to any person (other than plaintiffs or to this Court) deliver the same to this Court for safekeeping or destruction as the Court may determine best.

16. Plaintiffs have filed herein undertakings of corporate surety, Peerless Insurance Company, a corporation, in due form as required by law in the sum of $10,000 as a bond given upon issuance of the temporary restraining order herein and $10,000 as a bond given upon issuance of the preliminary injunction.

17. In this action service of the complaint and other papers upon various defendants designated therein by fictitious names was made in accordance with law as follows:

Fictitious Name	True Name
First Doe	Ed Fitzharris
Third Doe	Austin Healy
Fourth Doe	Robinson and Co., Inc.
Eighth Doe	William Marlin
Ninth Doe	Crocker-Anglo National Bank of San Francisco, now Crocker-Citizens National Bank

276

| Thirteenth Doe | Recorder Printing and Publishing Company, a corporation |
| Fourteenth Doe | Bernhard A. Hansen, individually and as vice-president of Recorder Printing and Publishing Company |

18. All parties hereto have stipulated that this action shall be dismissed upon entry of judgment as to defendants, Joseph Robinson, individually, Crocker-Anglo National Bank, now Crocker Citizens National Bank of San Francisco, Recorder Printing and Publishing Company, and Bernhard A. Hansen, individually and as vice-president and general manager of Recorder Printing and Publishing Company, a corporation, and upon plaintiffs and said dismissed defendants exchanging mutual releases.

19. The postcard, Exhibit A, and the letters of October 15, 1962, and October 17, 1962, Exhibits E and El respectively, were instigated, written, financed, and published by supporters of Richard M. Nixon as a candidate for governor of California, and their agents . . . including defendants Committee, Marlin, Robinson & Company, Inc., Joseph Robinson, Boyle, Healy and Fitzharris.

20. The paramount purpose for organizing the Committee for the preservation of the Democratic Party in California and its related postcard, poll, and activities was to obtain from registered Democrats votes and money for the campaign of Richard M. Nixon.

21. Plaintiff Democratic State Central Committee, also known as the California Democratic State Central Committee, as the official Committee of the Democratic Party in California and the only official statewide Democratic organization in the State of California, was and is entitled to bring and prosecute this action.

Plaintiffs Roger Kent and Elizabeth Rudel Gatov have brought and were and are entitled to bring and prosecute this action in behalf of themselves individually and in their official capacities respectively (namely, Roger Kent as vice-chairman and member of the Executive Committee of the Democratic State Central Committee and now State Chairman of said Committee, and Elizabeth Rudel Gatov as Democratic National Committeewoman for California) in behalf of all registered California Democratic voters and members and officers of the Democratic State Central Committee and its statewide candidates at the 1962 General Election.

22. Defendants Committee and its members, agents and/or employees, namely, defendants Robinson & Company, Inc., a corporation, Marlin, Boyle, Healy and Fitzharris directly and indirectly solicited funds upon representations, express and implied, that the funds were being solicited for the use of the Democratic Party. This solicitation was in violation of Section 12301 of the Elections Code of the State of California.

None of the persons or Democratic Party officials or Democratic County Central Committees required to give such consent by said Section 12301 consented to such solicitation.

23. The acts and conduct of said defendants Committee, Marlin, Robinson & Company, Inc., Boyle, Healy and Fitzharris, and each of them in circularizing members of the Democratic Party for votes and funds through the use of the postcard, Exhibit A and the letters of October 15, 1962, and October 17, 1962, respectively, Exhibits E and E1, constitute misleading advertising in the particulars stated in paragraphs 9 and 10 and elsewhere herein.

Such acts and conduct were and are subject to restraint by temporary restraining order, preliminary injunction, and permanent injunction under the provisions of Civil Code Section 3369 of the State of California.

24. Failure of said defendants Committee, Marlin, Robinson & Company, Inc., Boyle, Healy and Fitzharris to print the name and address of the printer or publisher on the face of the postcard Exhibit A was a violation of Section 11592 of the Elections Code of the State of California.

25. Plaintiffs were damaged in a sum exceeding $10,000 which plaintiffs were obliged to spend in pursuing this action and enjoining the above recited acts of the defendants Committee, Robinson & Company, Inc., a corporation, Marlin Boyle, Healy and Fitzharris.

26. The sum of approximately $368.50 collected from Democrats in response to the postcard Exhibit A and letters Exhibits E and E1 is now on deposit at the head office of the Wells Fargo Bank, 464 California Street, San Francisco, California, in an account entitled "Roger Kent and Gerald J. O'Gara, Trustees for the Democratic State Central Committee."

By stipulation plaintiffs shall be awarded $100 as damages and $268.50 for costs. The payment of these sums shall be made exclusively from said Wells Fargo Account. Judgment for such sums is hereby awarded against defendants

278

Commitee, Robinson & Company, Inc., a corporation, Marlin, Boyle, Healy and Fitzharris.

27. For the reasons stated herein plaintiffs were entitled to the temporary restraining order issued October 20, 1962, restraining defendants Committee, Joseph Robinson, Robinson & Company, Inc., a corporation, Marlin, Fitzharris, Boyle, Healy, Crocker-Anglo National Bank of San Francisco, a corporation, Recorder Printing and Publishing Company, a corporation, and Bernhard A. Hansen, individually and as vice-president of the Recorder Printing & Publishing Company. Said temporary restraining order was regularly and properly issued and the issuance thereof is hereby approved and confirmed.

For the reasons stated herein, plaintiffs were entitled to the preliminary injunction issued November 2, 1962, restraining the same defendants. Said preliminary injunction was regularly and properly issued and the issuance thereof is hereby approved and confirmed.

28. For the reasons set forth herein, plaintiffs are entitled to and are hereby granted a permanent injunction forbidding defendants Committee, Marlin, Robinson & Company, Inc., Boyle, Healy and Fitzharris to

(a) Publish, post, mail, circulate, or distribute the postcard and writings in the form of Exhibits A, E and E1 attached hereto or in any form substantially similar to said Exhibits.

(b) Publish, post, mail, circulate, reveal or distribute results from the poll which said defendants conducted or could conduct by means of Exhibit A.

(c) Solicit, collect, or accept money from Democratic voters by using directly or indirectly a postcard, pamphlet, folder, letter, or writing in the form of Exhibits A, E, and E1 or forms substantially similar to said Exhibits.

(d) Use, appropriate, spend, or disburse money received from registered Democratic voters in response to or in connection with said postcard Exhibit A, or letters Exhibits E and E1.

(e) Use in any manner or through any medium said Exhibit A or the contents thereof and matters or things growing out of or resulting from the publishing, posting, mailing, circulating, or distributing of said Exhibit A, or perform acts in furtherance of or in connection with the activities set forth in said Exhibit A.

29. The bonds heretofore filed by plaintiffs and their corporate surety, Peerless Insurance Company, as required by the Court for issuance of the temporary restraining order and preliminary injunction are hereby exonerated and said plaintiffs and said surety are hereby discharged and exonerated from any liability to any of the defendants (including dismissed defendants) herein growing out of or connected with the filing or prosecution of this action or the issuance of said temporary restraining order or preliminary injunction.

30. Pursuant to the stipulation by all parties hereto, this action shall upon entry of judgment be dismissed as to defendants Joseph Robinson, individually, Crocker-Anglo National Bank, now Crocker Citizens National Bank of San Francisco, Recorder Printing and Publishing Company, a corporation, and Bernhard A. Hansen, individually and as vice-president and general manager of Recorder Printing and Publishing Company, a corporation, when plaintiffs and said dismissed defendants exchange mutual releases.

31. To the extent there is any conflict between earlier orders of this Court and only to that extent, this judgment and permanent injunction immediately upon filing, shall supersede the orders of this Court restraining and enjoining the above named defendants.

32. The stipulations of the parties herein and in the stipulation attached, are hereby approved, confirmed, and made a part of this judgment.

33. Except as herein specifically set forth, each party (including defendants dismissed) shall pay his or her own costs, expenses and attorneys' fees.

34. Service of a copy of this judgment shall be effective upon delivery to the attorneys for said respective defendants of a certified copy of this judgment with the same force and effect as if such copy were personally served upon such defendants.

Done in open Court October 30, 1964.

Byron Arnold
_____
Judge of the Superior Court

INDEX